To my mom, Jean Pawlucki. I pray I am able to support the psychic development of my children, students, and apprentices with the same love, gentleness, and trust she gave me.

Sarah O'Brien

ABOUT THE AUTHOR

Alexandra Chauran is a second-generation fortuneteller, a third degree elder High Priestess of British Traditional Wicca, and the Queen of a coven. As a professional psychic intuitive for over a decade, she serves thousands of clients in the Seattle area and globally through her website. She is certified in tarot and has been interviewed on National Public Radio and other major media outlets. Alexandra is currently pursuing a doctoral degree, lives in Issaquah, Washington, and can be found online at EarthShod.com.

Alexandra Chauran

365 WAYS

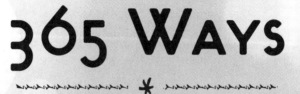

to DEVELOP *Your*

PSYCHIC
ABILITY

SIMPLE TOOLS TO INCREASE
YOUR INTUITION AND CLAIRVOYANCE

Llewellyn Publications
Woodbury, Minnesota

FIRST EDITION
Third Printing, 2018

Book design by Bob Gaul
Cover design by Ellen Lawson
Part page art © iStockphoto.com/Jelena Veskovic
Editing by Laura Graves
Tarot Spread by Llewellyn Art Department

Llewellyn Publications is a registered trademark of Llewellyn Worldwide Ltd.

Library of Congress Cataloging-in-Publication Data (Pending)
978-0-7387-3930-4

Llewellyn Publications, a Division of Llewellyn Worldwide Ltd.
2143 Wooddale Drive
Woodbury, MN 55125-2989
www.llewellyn.com
Printed in the United States of America

Contents

Introduction

Have you ever had a flash of psychic awareness that warns you of danger or blessings to come? Maybe you've had the sudden urge to call someone, who then tells you they were just thinking of you at that moment. It could be that you've had more startling interactions with your subconscious psychic ability, such as a dream that predicted the future. Or, you could be interested in the metaphysical and the limitless potential of the human mind, and want to expand your own experiences and knowledge. No matter what your level of ability or experience, here you'll find a year's worth of exercises and practices designed to develop, strengthen, and hone your psychic abilities.

What are Psychic Abilities?

The word *psychic* in the context of this book refers to a perception and an understanding derived from some source other than your ordinary five senses. You'll note that such a definition of the psychic is quite broad and would include the mundane and the supernatural. Psychic abilities could be the part of you that knows you are in love and that you are loved at the first sight of your life partner. Psychic abilities could also be the more startling ability to see the next days or years of your life play out before they happen like a television documentary.

With so many psychic abilities to cover, you're about to go on a whirlwind tour of your own psychic power, some of which may be unknown to you as of yet. We'll cover the ways psychic perceptions link into your normal senses of sight, hearing, touch, and even smell or taste. We'll also explore techniques, both ancient and modern, for amplifying and making sense of psychic abilities with various tools and rituals. Along the way, you'll pick up a bit of history and theory to build a solid base of understanding in your year of study.

My Story

I'll openly admit to being a fortuneteller with psychic abilities. By the broad definition of "psychic" in the previous section, the fact that I identify as one doesn't mean I claim to be omniscient or infallible. I have always had psychic abilities, long before I knew what to call them. I've had my entire life to develop my psychic abilities, as well as to learn the hard way what sorts of skills and abilities should come before others.

Born to a mother who had also developed her psychic abilities in a professional capacity and a father who was tolerant of my psychic exploration, I entered a life where psychic abilities were explored with curiosity; they were not shunned or feared. While in college, I opened my psychic business. My spiritual practice deepened and became serious. My psychic abilities became the means for me to communicate with my concept of deity.

I helped thousands of clients with my psychic abilities, appeared on television and radio shows, and published some books. Meanwhile, I completed a master's degree in teaching and began to take a few apprentices under my wing. It was then that I discovered how different the process of developing psychic abilities can be and how varied the outcomes. It is my pleasure to share my experience and expertise with you here.

How to Use This Book

365 Ways to Develop Your Psychic Abilities is organized to be used with the exercises in the order that they are delivered. The concepts build on preceding ones. It may not make much sense, and would certainly not be optimal, if you did the exercises out of order. That said, feel free to repeat exercises as needed; it can easily take you more than a year to complete all the exercises if you choose. If you accidentally miss a few days, try to avoid the temptation to do several new exercises in one day to catch up. Each lesson is best digested with time so it can sink in.

At first, we'll build a foundation of mundane skills, many of which you may already have. After delving into the core of techniques and tools for developing psychic abilities, we'll start working on your intuition. We'll figure out the meaning of the things you perceive with your psychic abilities. By the time you finish all 365 exercises, you should have the ability to perform psychic readings for yourself and for others. We'll finish up with some important philosophical work surrounding the ethics and effects of psychic abilities.

You need not wait for a specific time of the year to begin your study. In fact, you can begin the first exercise today. And yes, you can repeat all exercises whenever you wish. Even after you finish completely, you can start all over again and develop your psychic abilities even further. Are you ready for an exciting, challenging, or perhaps even astonishing year's journey? Of course you are. After all, you have psychic abilities!

Part One

Becoming More Observant and Keeping a Record

DAY 1

·········

Procure a Psychic's Journal

For most of the exercises that follow, you'll need a blank book or sketch-book to record the things you experience and your impressions that come to mind. The journal won't be anything you'll have to show anyone else, so don't worry if your drawing talents aren't the best or if your handwriting is sloppy. Any notebook or loose paper will do in a pinch, so grab one to get started.

The ideal psychic's journal will be more like a binder, allowing you to move pages around. That is because, naturally, you will at first want to begin working in chronological order so that you can make it through all of the lessons herein. However, as you progress past the end of this year, you may wish to arrange the pages in order of meaning, so that you can begin creating a psychic dictionary of your own personal understandings.

Another good reason for a binder is that you can have both unlined paper, for making sketches, and lined paper, for writing down your thoughts in words. At this point, just make sure that you label the date of each entry that you record. Sometimes, psychic abilities can present themselves in specific ways days before an event is about to happen in somebody's life. With dated entries, you'll be able to track any patterns in order to hone your predictions.

For your first psychic journal entry, it is best to make a goal statement. Remember to make a SMART goal. "SMART" stands for Specific, Measurable, Attainable, Realistic, and Timely. Don't make too many goals at once, but the ones you do make should be recorded in your psychic's log within a year's time.

* *Name three goals for the coming year. Make one goal physical/ material, one emotional/personal, and one psychic.*

Day 2

Observing Number Patterns

Noticing patterns is one of the psychic's most important tasks because patterns have meaning in life. Without patterns, all your senses—psychic or otherwise—would be a jumble of data without context or purpose. At first, it is hard to notice patterns. After all, we move through life disregarding things that seem meaningful as coincidences or odd occurrences. Part of developing your psychic abilities is noticing and recording coincidences and other patterns so you won't lose track of them entirely.

Your first pattern recognition exercise will be to observe and record number patterns throughout your day today. Have you ever noticed an unusual recurrence of numbers in your life? For example, you glance at a clock to see 11:11 and then later that day see a license plate and a phone number also having a series of ones. These repeating numbers are considered signals to your psychic abilities, sometimes called "angel numbers."

Angel numbers don't pop up every day, but numbers can have meaning every day. Your mission today is to carry your psychic log with you and record every time you notice a significant number. If you're a data entry person or accountant by trade, it may be too much to ask to write down every number you think might be important, but all of us could go through the day taking note of numbers that draw our attention. Pay special attention to building numbers, street numbers, and numbers of significant objects. The number itself or where you see it isn't that important; if it catches your eye, the number of minutes you set on the microwave to nuke your popcorn could warrant a journal entry!

> * What number kept showing up the most for you today?
>   Does that number have any sort of special meaning to you?

Day 3
....
Developing Memory

Memory is important for psychic abilities because everything you perceive psychically can immediately be forgotten. If you think about it, everything you experience becomes a memory a mere instant after it happens. For the psychic, this means that the accuracy of your psychic abilities is only as good as your memory and, of course, your diligence in recording your psychic experiences.

Memory can be improved, however. Actors can train their brains to remember hundreds of lines, and psychics can train themselves to notice details that may become meaningful later on. Before you delve into psychic visions of your own, it is important that you develop the ability to notice and record things in your everyday life.

This exercise is best done outside in nature. Find yourself a spot where you can see many natural objects and sit for a while. Allow yourself to soak in the scenery. Then, look down at your psychic's journal and make a sketch of all the details you can remember about the scene without looking. You won't be able to remember the number of leaves on each tree, but perhaps you'll be able to remember how many trees were closest to you, or how many dandelion puffballs or birds you saw.

At this point, this exercise in memory may just serve to show you how poor your recall may be. It certainly shows me how impatient I am when hastily making records. Improving your powers of observation and recall are important steps to developing your psychic ability. Today you have started the important practice of training your brain.

* What do you tend to notice first about your surroundings? What tends to escape your notice?

DAY 4
....

Developing Mindfulness

If you're like me, you forget to notice the beauty and meaning in the world around you when rushing everywhere, getting the necessities of life under control. Psychic abilities can be an important spiritual component in life. Rather than being a super power granted to only a few, anyone can draw upon psychic abilities to guide their life.

Do you tend to live more in the past, present, or the future? I know that sometimes I have a hard time pulling myself out of my focus when finishing a task to notice what's happening around me. The good news is that just by committing to work on your exercises once a day, you've already started developing a sense of mindfulness. You've begun looking for meaning in certain things, and this exercise will remind you to be mindful more frequently, regardless of what is going on.

Today, pick five times when you'll stop what you're doing, take a few breaths, and really be present in the moment. Observe what's happening and search for meaning. When I did this exercise, I set a timer to chime five times in the day. It was tough for me to set aside the work I was doing, the arguments I was having with others, or the things I was reading in order to be mindful. But when I did, I began to notice emotions, beauty, and motivations in my life that might have otherwise escaped my consciousness.

* *What is one beautiful thing that you noticed in a moment of your life today?*

DAY 5
....

Observing Meaning

Hopefully you were able to start getting an emotional connection with the beauty that surrounds your life. Psychic abilities often appear and strengthen in the presence of strong emotions. This exercise is designed to help you find meaning in another pattern, the human face. Our brains are trained to notice human faces and decipher emotions, even when not looking at an actual human face. That's why a yellow smiley face can convey happiness, even if it doesn't have a nose.

Today's exercise is also often best performed outdoors, in nature. Look around and see if you can find faces in your surroundings. Perhaps you'll see some eyes in the bark of a tree, or a smile made out of leaves on the grass. Maybe you can even see a face in the clouds in the sky. There are many psychic techniques you will learn later that depend on your ability to use your imagination and gather meaning out of what is inspired in your mind. Draw the faces that you see in your sketch book, and make a note of what emotions the faces are showing.

> * Look for faces in inanimate objects today. What emotions are those faces showing to you? Do the emotions of the faces you see match your own or those of people around you?

Day 6
....

Noticing How You Get Information

People have different learning styles. One friend of yours might be able to learn from what you think is a boring lecture because she is an auditory learner, learning best from hearing the lesson. Another friend may be unable to sit still in lectures, but he learns best by building things and working with models with his hands. This would be a kinaesthetic learner. These learning styles relate to how you perceive the world. A visual learner might be a natural clairvoyant, able to see psychic information, while a more kinaesthetic person could excellent at divination. An auditory person might "hear" messages in the same way we would hear a song stuck in our heads. It's best to play to your strengths and set yourself up for success.

Today, think about how you learn best. Are you a visual learner, auditory learner, or more kinaesthetic? Based on this type of learning, how do you think psychic experiences will work best for you? It makes no sense to beat yourself up for not being clairvoyant yet if that's not the best way that you sense things. Instead, focus on the skills you have as a beginner and branch off from there.

* *What is your learning style? What perceptions work best at this stage of your psychic development?*

DAY 7

Seeing the World Differently

When I was a small child, I loved to go through doorways and gateways, or even just a Hula Hoop or circle made of string. It made me feel like I was in a different world and could see everything in a new way. Sometimes, I thought I could even see the fairies and spirits who might inhabit such a land.

It so happened that my make-believe games were rooted in antiquity. Many psychics throughout history have used "seer stones" to look at the world and search for meaning. A seer stone is a rock with a naturally occurring hole. Most often they can be found where water flows and drops to erode a thin part of a stone into a hole. Even small pieces of coral with a hole can act as seer stones.

When doing this exercise, try to focus your line of sight and powers of observation by using a tool like a seer stone. You might not be able to find a stone one right away, so for today, make do by forming a small circle with your finger and thumb. Go somewhere in nature and observe the world through either your seer stone or your small field of vision. What does this limited focus allow you to see? Sketch or journal the results.

* Begin your search for a seer stone. Look for a rock that has a natural hole in it. Keep your seer stone close at hand as a tool to focus your psychic powers of observation.

DAY 8

···········

Introduction to Grounding

Today we'll turn your attention to your energy. In the context of psychic development, *energy* is not quite the same as the scientific definition, which can be electric, atomic, or otherwise; instead it refers to the life force emanating from all things as well as what living things use to effect change on the environment around them. You already naturally use energy every day. You make references to your energetic state when you say you are "low on energy," meaning that you are tired, or "full of energy," meaning you're excited.

Already you may have an intuitive sense that having too much or too little energy is not a pleasant thing. Too much energy can make you agitated, paranoid, anxious, or jittery. Too little energy can make you feel sluggish, unmotivated, and depressed. Believe it or not, you exchange energy with the earth, other people, and things in your environment. This book will help you perform these energy exchanges more purposefully in order to keep a perfect balance of energy in a process called grounding.

The first step in grounding is simply to observe your own energy. For a full day, pay attention to how you feel energetically at key points during the day, and write in your journal. For example, how do you feel when you get up in the morning? What about when you eat meals, or spend time with others? What are your feelings like when you are working on a project?

And what about bedtime? To observe your energy, close your eyes and focus on your body. Some people might "see" the energy in their mind's eye, as if in a daydream, as a light or fluid within the body. Others might feel the energy as a buzzing, tingling or fuzzy sensation. Still others feel energy emotionally. Write down your observations and notice how your energy changes depending on what you are doing, where you are, and with whom you spend your time.

> * What makes you feel full of energy? How do you know that you are full of energy? What makes you feel drained of energy, and how do you know that you feel that way?

Day 9

Visual Grounding—A Tree

Most people are visual learners, so today you can work with a very common grounding visualization, that of a tree. If you're new to visualization, don't worry, we will practice more later, but first I want to give you this practical application. When you visualize, try to see a picture as clearly as possible in your mind's eye, the same way that you might think about where a lost object is located before you go searching for it. In your mind's eye, you might "see" a very specific location, such as a shelf or a table, but it isn't actually appearing in front of you, and for some people the visualization may be fleeting and elusive. That's okay.

For the tree grounding visualization, first make yourself comfortable. Close your eyes to aid visualization. In your mind's eye, see yourself as a tree. Sink your roots deep into the earth. Even if you live in a high-rise apartment building, the roots can snake through walls and floors to dig into the earth. Imagine that excess energy is pushed out through those roots harmlessly into the earth and that fresh energy is drawn up through those very same roots. Some people like to visualize branches coming out of the head and releasing excess energy into the sky. Whichever feels best to you afterwards is the one that is right for you.

* *Try the tree grounding visualization today at least once. If possible, do the tree visualization several times so you can feel how different it feels during different parts of the day. For example, first thing in the morning might feel very different than before bedtime.*

DAY 10
....

Tactile Grounding

Not everyone is the visual sort of person. Sometimes visualization is a skill that comes slowly over time, and your first visual groundings may feel ineffective and discouraging. For this reason, I'd like to show you a few other techniques as we go along which require more tactile and kinesthetic efforts. This first tactile exercise lets you explore the sensations of energy.

For this grounding technique, you'll need to go someplace with few distractions. It helps if you choose an especially stressful time of day when your energy is likely to feel excessive, negative, or out of control. Find a place where you will not be disturbed, sit or lie down comfortably, and close your eyes. Try to perceive the energy inside your body. Some will feel energy as a prickling sensation, heat or pressure, tension, or even an ache. When I feel energy, it often feels soft and fuzzy, as if I am near a balloon with a static charge or like petting a soft animal.

It may take some time to feel energy, so don't give up. Take as much time as possible. If it doesn't work out, try again later. If you do sense the energy, the next step is to try to push that excess energy out of your body and draw up positive energy from the earth, much like you did with the tree grounding but without the visual aid. For me, it helps to remove socks and shoes and gradually relax parts of my body starting from my head and shoulders and moving down toward my feet. You might want to run your hands over your skin in a wiping motion, as if you are flicking and flinging the excess energy to the ground. To draw energy up into your body, you might feel warmth or another sensation traveling up from the earth into your body. Try breathing deeply to increase the flow.

* *Try grounding by feel, and figure out how you sense energy. Write down how you perceived the energy and what sorts of thoughts or movements helped you to move it.*

DAY 11
....

Breathing for Grounding

Breathing is a big part of meditation, a topic we'll explore later. For now, let's focus on breathing as a grounding method. This exercise will help you explore how breathing in different ways affects your energies. Again, this is a good exercise to attempt during a time of day when you usually feel at your most stressed or least relaxed.

Sit or lie down for this activity. If you are seated, make sure you are sitting upright with your spine straight so you can breathe from your diaphragm. If you are hunched over or leaning back, your tummy may be compressed slightly, which doesn't allow room for more air. Start by focusing on breathing from your diaphragm. Chest breathing makes your shoulders rise and fall, and we don't want to breathe like that for this exercise. Instead, your shoulders should stay dropped and slightly back while your belly moves in and out.

If you want to visualize, imagine pushing out excess or negative energy when you exhale and drawing in fresh energy as you inhale, as if they were clouds. If you prefer to avoid visualization, be mindful of the concept. You can even try a Sanskrit mantra *so hum,* saying *so* on the inhale and *hum* on the exhale. This mantra means simply "I am."

Next, practice breathing in different ways to see how the energy in your body reacts. Try breathing in and out very quickly and forcefully until your fingertips tingle. This practice is called "purging" and is one way to rid yourself of excess energy and carbon dioxide. Try taking slow and deep breaths and notice how it revitalizes you after purging.

* *Practice paying attention to your breathing and consciously controlling it during stressful parts of your day.*

Day 12
....

Visualizing an Object

You've already been exposed to some examples of how visualization can be a vital tool to a psychic for grounding, and you'll find that visualization becomes even more useful as your skills progress. However, since visualization is not easy for beginners, I'd like to take a step back today and practice your visualization in a way that will help you become a better psychic.

Your first step is to find an object that has meaning to you, small enough to be able to safely explore with as many of your senses as possible. It can be a piece of jewelry, your favorite mug, or even food made from a family recipe. Take a few minutes to completely explore the object from all angles. Hold it in your hands and feel the weight and texture. Smell the object. Memorize any small details. Then, set down the object and close your eyes, recreating the object in your mind's eye.

Reimagine the object's real size and details without peeking. If you forget any details, like number of ridges or an exact shade of a color, it's okay to let your mind build upon the basics with your imagination rather than stopping to peek to be correct. You're building up your mental stamina for visualization at this point; accuracy can come later. Try allowing the object to rotate in your mind's eye, so you can see all angles, including the top and the bottom. This might be a harder task if you're not naturally good with spatial perception like me. If you find all these tasks easy, try modifying the object in your mind. If it is food, visualize taking a bite. If it is a mug, visualize filling it with your favorite beverage. If it is jewelry, visualize polishing it until it shines.

* *Practice visualizing a familiar object until you can see it in your mind's eye as clearly as if you were looking at it with your physical eyes.*

Day 13
....

Visualizing a Place

If you've completed the object visualization yesterday, you'll know how daunting visualizing an entire place might seem. But remember, you can allow your mind to fill in any details that you have missed. The point of place visualization isn't to have a photographic memory. The point is to slowly build your mental visual skills and to allow your recall to grow as well. Still, it may be best to choose a location with which you are very familiar. It can be a favorite spot outdoors, your bedroom, or even your office at work. The familiarity you have with the place will help you because not only will you have already memorized plenty of details, but you'll also have a good sense of how the place "feels" to you emotionally and energetically, which goes a long way toward recreating it in your mind.

Spend a few minutes observing the location, turning around, and looking everywhere. Don't take in all the details like you're cramming for a test; rather make sure your eyes rest gently in many areas of the place and that your body and mind gets a feel for how this environment is affecting you on this particular day. Sit down and close your eyes to begin visualizing the place. Fill in as many details as possible and be aware of the size and relation of the objects in the place to your seated form. Hold the visualization, and try to visualize getting up and walking around the room while your physical body remains seated on the floor. These are the beginnings of a practice called astral travel or an out-of-body experience.

When you are more practiced with this skill, you might even be able to visualize yourself walking from this known location to a new location and see things that are actually happening. For now, work on holding the visualization strong and clear in your mind for as long as possible.

* *Choose a familiar place to visualize. Hold that visualization as long as possible.*

DAY 14
....

Noticing Your Hunches

Most people second-guess their immediate reactions all the time, and that's okay. Part of being an adult means thinking carefully about your words before you speak and pondering your choices before you act. As a result, though, it's possible to lose a little intuition when going so far as to forget that first inkling after making a valid choice.

For example, when somebody asks you a question, you might think of one answer and then change your mind before speaking. If you need to remember a phone number, you might think that you know the first three digits before giving up and looking up the number to be sure. Today's exercise will be tricky because I want you to notice those "first guess" ideas before you dismiss them entirely. I'm not asking you to act on them; write them down in your psychic journal for later, to see if you notice any patterns of when your intuition was correct.

* *Keep your psychic journal close at hand today. Any time you have a hunch, guess, inkling, or flash of intuition, write about it in your journal, even if you make a different decision an instant later.*

DAY 15

Visual Grounding—Fluid Grounding

You've already tried one visualization for grounding, of a tree. The tree is one popular visualization people use for grounding, but it is certainly not the only one. Some people may find it unappealing or too limiting. After all, what if you don't want to be a tree every day? Here's another visualization that's more mutable. I'll start with an example and then tell you how you can change it to suit yourself.

Sit down and close your eyes. Spend some time getting in touch with how your energy feels in this moment. Visualize your energy as water flowing through your body. You might notice little whirlpools in areas with more energy and some dark, stagnant water in areas with less energy. Using this visualization, flush out any of the stuck or negative energy through the bottoms of your feet into the earth, and then visualize a flow of fresh water filling you up again with energy from the earth.

You can play with this visualization using any moving fluid. For example, you can visualize smoke that is dark or light depending on the character of your energy, or you can even imagine something that is not fluid but moving in a fluid way, such as light. If you visualize light flowing in and out of you, pay attention to the light's color and intensity. Anything can be a fluid visualization, even a cloud of butterflies or an army of marching ants. Figure out a visualization personalized to who you are.

> * *Try out the fluid visualization grounding meditation. After that, personalize the visualization until it feels both interesting and meaningful to you.*

Day 16
....

Tactile Grounding—Grounding with Water

Let's take a break from all this visualization and talk about how things in the physical world can help you to ground if you ever have trouble doing it any other way. Today's exercise will require a bowl of water you can use to ground your energies. This tool is nice to use when you don't feel completely in control of your own mind. For example, if you feel too angry to sit down and use visualization to regain your calm, tactile sensations can help.

Procure your bowl of water and simply dip your hands in the bowl, willing yourself to force all the excess or negative energy into the water. No visualization is needed, although you might see something in your mind's eye anyway, and that's okay. You might also sense the energy flow through touch. The water will automatically act as a conduit for those negative energies.

You'll know that the grounding is complete when you feel more relaxed, calm, and alert. Next, simply pour the water out onto bare earth. If the energies were positive in nature, for example if you were just too jittery and excited instead of angry, you might consider pouring the water onto a plant as an experiment to see if its growth is affected positively.

* *Use a bowl of water to ground excess energy. Consider giving it to a plant and making before and after sketches for your psychic journal.*

DAY 17

....

Grounding with Food

Food is another classic way to ground yourself. As with yesterday's bowl of water, no physical tools should turn into crutches. Even if food or a bowl of water works very well for you to ground, you should not always rely on a tool. If you do, you are limited to only grounding under circumstances when such tools are available. That said, tools can be powerful additions if you need an extra boost to your grounding activity. I still use food to ground when I undertake particularly powerful psychic activities and have trouble grounding afterward.

In many cultures, celebration after a psychic day or festival involves a good, heavy feast. The commonality between most of the things served at these feasts is salt content. Salt represents the quintessential element of earth, that of grounding and stability after psychic pursuits. In fact, eating salty food can be one defense technique taken against negative magical practitioners, since their magical energy can be more easily grounded by one who has eaten salt.

To ground with food, I suggest two experiments, one with salt and one with a nice, filling meal of what you would consider to be comfort food. Try these two experiments on separate occasions, for example once in the morning and once in the evening. If you can, choose a time when you feel frazzled and ungrounded. To use the salt, just put a tiny pinch of salt on your tongue and rest with your eyes closed. To use food for grounding, consume it slowly and mindfully. Try taking small bites with a sip of water in between each bite, chewing thoroughly.

* *Attempt grounding with salt and with food. How did you feel before and after consumption? Was this particularly effective for you, or not as effective as other grounding techniques?*

DAY 18
. . . .

Grounding with Movement

Movement and dance are used around the world not only to increase psychic energy, but also to safely ground it. You don't have to be coordinated or fit to use movement as grounding. Here's an easy exercise that anybody can do in order to ground using movement. This is an excellent technique to use during times of low or high energy and can be used even if your mind gets the better of you and you can't concentrate on other more focused grounding techniques.

Begin this exercise standing. You may close your eyes if you wish, but some people find that keeping eyes closed while moving in place makes it difficult to keep their balance, so having eyes closed is not absolutely required for this technique. The general overview of this movement technique is that you are going to shake out all the negative or excess energy. Start by bouncing lightly on the balls of your feet and allowing your muscles to loosen. It helps me to start at my head and neck and work down my shoulders and arms through the rest of my body, letting the energy flick off the ends of my fingers and toes like water.

Continue this exercise for some time. You can use music if you wish. Drums work nicely for this exercise. The point isn't to tire yourself out, but rather to keep up the movement until you stop being self-conscious; when you stop thinking about it and just allow yourself to go with the flow. When you are done, sit on the floor and breathe to allow your energy to be replenished with the fresh earth energy rushing in.

* *Try grounding through movement and record how you feel afterwards. See if you can strike a balance between moving enough to ground your energy without tiring yourself out.*

Day 19
·············

Grounding with Stones

Rocks are another tool for grounding because like salt, they represent the quintessential element of earth with its associated properties of stability and calm energy. Some people find specific semiprecious gemstones to be especially powerful for grounding. Hematite is a good example. People carry a piece of the stone with them or wear it as jewelry. You don't necessarily need to run out and buy a specific type of stone to try it out. Any kind of stone will do to practice using it for grounding. If you find you like this method of grounding especially, feel free to invest in different types of stones for different purposes depending on how they make you feel.

To select a stone for grounding, you can practice by running your hands lightly over a choice of stones. You can visit a rock shop or simply go to a gravelly area or riverbed outdoors. Close your eyes when energetically examining the stones, if you wish, and wait for a sensation to tell you which stone is right. For some people, it may be a grounded sense of calmness and alertness. For others, a visual psychic flash of light or color may be your clue. Whichever rock "feels" right for you should be the first one you experiment with. Remember to trust your first instincts. You can always experiment again with a different stone later.

Keep the rock with you throughout the day and, whenever you feel particularly low or high on energy, take the rock into one hand and hold it for a bit. You need not perform any other grounding techniques along with holding the rock, although that may enhance the effects. The point for today is to just feel the help with grounding that the rock can give you.

* *Find a rock to use as a grounding tool. Keep it with you and experiment with holding it to see if it affects your energy.*

DAY 20
. . . .

Going Barefoot

There is a school of thought regarding energy flow between a person and the earth that holds that any sort of impediments, such as shoes and socks, may hinder the flow. Of course, there are many who feel that visualization and other techniques can overcome any barriers between you and the earth, even if you are on a building's twentieth story. There is a lesson to be learned, however, from all the ungrounded people who step into slippers as soon as they get up in the morning and don't unlace boots until the moment they climb into bed at night.

Today's experiment will be to go barefoot as much as possible and to have barefoot contact with natural earth outside, if possible. If you wear shoes at all today, wear slip-on shoes and no socks. Kick off your shoes whenever possible so you spend as much time as you can barefoot. If the weather and environment outdoors are appropriate, try going outside barefoot and touching the natural earth with your feet at least once today. Write in your psychic journal how you feel while barefoot, and whether you feel more grounded today overall.

* *Go barefoot as much as possible today. If appropriate, try to touch your bare feet to natural earth outside at least once. Notice how your "barefoot day" affects your overall feeling of being grounded.*

Day 21

....

Mindfulness Exercise—Connecting to People

Every day, our energies naturally interact with the energies of people around us. There is no way to avoid energetic exchange and interaction in society, so it is best to simply become more aware of it. Even if you are not in the same room as a person, you may still feel an energetic connection. It is that energetic connection between people that might have you thinking about a person right before he or she calls you on the telephone.

Today, pay attention to each person you interact with and write as many names down as you can in your psychic journal along with one word describing how you felt energetically while interacting with the person. Include people that you interact with over the phone, or even people that you thought about frequently even if you did not personally interact with them today.

To observe your energetic reaction to people, notice things like how much space you put in between the person and yourself. Notice whether you feel like talking or clamming up. Observe whether you cross your arms or legs in front of your body to block energy. Make special note if you feel drained or energized after interacting with specific people. If you have any guesses as to why the people in question affect your energy in the way they do, write about that as well. For example, some people may chronically drain energy from everyone around them, so much so that they are said to be "psychic vampires." Other people may be especially needy due to circumstance and might otherwise be energetically neutral.

* *Pay attention to your interactions with other people. How do people affect your energy when they are in the same room? What about on the phone? What about thinking about a specific person? Write down your observations in your psychic journal.*

DAY 22

....

Animal Exercise

Humans aren't the only beings who give off energy that can be sensed by a psychic. Animals do as well. In fact, this might be one of the reasons pets have such a calming effect on us. For today's exercise, you can use a pet with whom you have already forged a connection, but this exercise can be done while sitting outside watching wild birds or even while observing a spider on the wall. The point is to begin to sense animal energy, which can be more subtle than ours.

Choose your animal subject and pick a time when he or she is at rest, if possible; even better if it is sleeping. Sit as closely to your subject as possible without disturbing him or her. Try to perceive the animal's energy in any way you can. Again, this might be a visual aura (you'll learn more about those later), a pressure or warmth, or simply an emotional feeling of your own. If you can see the animal's breathing, try matching your breathing rate to intensify the connection.

Close your eyes. Try to continue to perceive the animal's energy and be aware of its proximity to you. Are you still able to perceive the energy? Does the energy seem different with your eyes closed than when your eyes are open? Spend a few minutes with the animal in this close energy connection exercise, and then check in with yourself to see how you are feeling. Do you feel more grounded and relaxed, or do you feel anxious? Ground yourself appropriately and make sure to record your feelings in your psychic journal.

* *Forge a psychic connection with an animal, either a pet or a wild animal. Make notes about your experience. What do you sense in yourself? Can you sense anything in the animal?*

Day 23

Sketching a Plant

Today's activity will actually stretch out over several days, weeks, or even months. It is an exercise in observation. One way that psychics connect with information in the universe is by becoming more observant of natural cycles such as the phases of the moon and the changing of seasons. Today's exercise will give you an opportunity to practice your sketching skills (useful for recording clairvoyant visions) and get in tune with nature.

Select a plant to sketch every day for a week. If you can, choose one that's outdoors and going through the process of blooming or producing fruit, since those growth phases are interesting. But really, you can perform this exercise with any plant, even a houseplant that shows gradual changes of growth or shifting leaves to reach for sunlight. I like to do this exercise when the cherry blossoms are blooming, as each little flower bud seems to burst so quickly into a beautiful spray of pink flowers.

As you make your daily sketches, take care to get the important parts of the image down with speed. If you love making art, you can always fill in the details later, but as a psychic your goal will be to sketch your drawings quickly; you are making records before your memory fades. In this particular exercise, the point of making multiple drawings is to observe changes in the plant. It's fine to omit the background and other unimportant details; instead, focus on the changes of the shading and outline of the plant.

* *Choose a plant (ideally outdoors) and sketch it every day for a week or a month. Limit yourself to fifteen minutes or less for your initial sketches.*

DAY 24
. . . .

Dancing in Nature

Today's exercise may feel a little silly, but bear with me. I'd like to tell you a story about how it was helpful for me to discover the beautiful and meaningful things that are meant to draw the attention of a psychic. This story starts in Hawaii, where I was privileged enough to be able to attend a spiritual dance retreat. I had been taking beginner belly dance classes for a few months and was excited to apply dance to something spiritual.

My instructor led us outside one day of the retreat to a small clearing in the tropical forest. She told us that we didn't need music to dance, that we could just become observant and dance to the "music" that nature revealed to our psychic selves. She spread us out so we wouldn't feel self-conscious about being watched and then gave us a long time to dance. When I started, I felt awkward and a little confused. I listened carefully for some sort of sound that would inspire me to dance. I heard the rushing of some faraway water and the chirping of birds, so I began moving my hips as if I was hearing a song. Then, I noticed a beautiful web with a gorgeous spider. Giving up on the sound effects of nature, I began to meditatively move to mimic the curve of the web here, or the quick movements of the spider's feet there. The best moment was when I dropped down to brush the tips of the leaf of a fern and the fern reacted, drawing its leaves quickly closed. It turned out to be a *Mimosa pudica*, a fern that reacts to touch. I would have never discovered it if it had not danced with me!

What does this have to do with being a psychic? Well, not only did dancing hone my sense of observation in a unique way, it also allowed me to let go of my inhibitions. Sometimes in order to explore psychic clues, you may say or do things that seem eccentric to others. Before my dance experience in nature, I was self-conscious whenever I danced, even when participating in a class. Now, I'm not afraid to get my groove on in public, even if it is just to the music of the cars while I am at the gas pump. I hope you will learn to follow your ears and eyes where they lead you, even if society might think it strange.

* *Go out and do some meditative movement in nature. Find a sound or sight that moves you to dance.*

Day 25
....

Notice How Your Energy Affects Others

You've started observing how the natural energy of other people affects you. Some people have infectious energy when you are around them, while others seem to drain others of energy whenever they come around. Today, your duty is to start observing what sort of energy *you* have on others. You'll find that the way your energy affects others has to do with your own energy level and with your mood. You already know that it feels a lot more draining to be around a sad or angry person than a happy one.

You may need to make a few journal entries to keep track of how your energy affects others. For example, before you leave the house you may want to first document your moods and energy levels. Then, write about the people you interact with throughout the day, and how they react to you. Make note of body language and tone of voice. For example, a person crossing his or her arms in front of you may subconsciously be doing that to block your energy if it feels overwhelming or uncomfortable. If you talk with people on the telephone, make note of who ends the conversation first.

If you feel like experimenting, you can even see if people react differently to your energy if you ground yourself before interacting with them. Tomorrow, you'll learn a bit about shielding, and in part 5, you will find out more about expanding your energy, which are some more tactics you can use to affect how people interact with your energy. Some people feel uncomfortable at first with energy working because they don't want to affect other people against their wills. That's a noble opinion, however, you can choose how to present yourself to the world energetically and then leave the choice of how to deal with it to others.

* *How do people interact with your energy? What can you do to change the way that people interact with your energy? Include your thoughts on this in today's notes.*

Day 26
·············

Shielding

Shielding means to protect oneself with a bubble, shell, or other metaphorical protective layer of energy. This skill is vitally important for a psychic, because psychics have to be able to read the energy of others without being affected by it. A psychic who cannot shield may feel drained or burned out after performing a psychic reading because they've either taken energy from another person or given up some of their own.

Everyone psychically shields themselves naturally. Some people are more effective at shielding than others, which is why some people seem like rocks in the face of energetically draining people while others may seem more sensitive. If you are naturally a sensitive and empathetic person, you'll find that shielding is a skill that will be especially helpful and important to develop.

To shield yourself, visualize any sort of barrier between yourself and the interactions around you. Some people imagine a bubble, some picture a ring of fire. Others might visualize a wild animal protecting them by standing guard. Your shield can change from day to day or from situation to situation.

Practice with one shield visualization until you can picture it clearly in your mind, even when you are feeling stressed.

* *Invent a shielding visualization that is easy and effective for you. Draw a sketch of your shield in your psychic journal so you can look at it later and see how you may have changed.*

DAY 27
....

Centering

Centering is a practice that goes hand in hand with grounding, so before you do this exercise, be sure you feel comfortable with at least one of the grounding exercises provided so far. The idea behind centering is to feel like you know where you are in the universe and are stable. I know that sounds very vague, so it might be more helpful to describe how you feel when you are uncentered and how that can affect your psychic practice.

When you feel uncentered, you are easily distracted and not very confident. You might make mistakes more easily, or second-guess yourself. Think of the way you feel when you make a wrong turn and get lost, and you'll start to understand what being uncentered is like. When you are uncentered, the world seems like it's in flux. You may feel unwilling to start an activity because you feel like there is not enough time before you have to do something else. Conversely, a centered person makes time for psychic development and feels ready to take whatever time is needed in the space that is given.

To center yourself, first make sure you are thoroughly grounded. I like to face east, because having a sense of direction is one external way for me to feel centered. Try to think only about the here and now. A visualization that helps me to feel centered is to close my eyes and imagine a column of light going through me from the top of my head down to my feet. It extends infinitely out into the universe in both directions. Spreading my arms, I imagine a lateral shaft of light going through my shoulders and out both hands north and south. Now, in my mind's eye, I am a little "You Are Here" plus sign in the universe, and I feel centered and ready to begin psychic work.

* *Work on centering yourself immediately after grounding. Try grounding more often, at least once a day, and build centering into the routine so that it's automatic.*

DAY 28
....

Mindfulness Chime

Learning to live in the here and now and be observant for psychic signals is something you'll have to start working on before you dive into many psychic activities. However, living in the here and now is harder than it sounds. This is especially true for people interested in psychic activities, as they have a natural proclivity to think about the future. They can become too busy and unobservant. When that happens, it won't matter how amazingly their psychic powers have developed, because they simply won't listen to and act upon them.

When I work as a hospital chaplain, I gain wonderful perspective. After helping people in the hospital, I realize what sort of daily details of my life are unimportant, and I start to notice the beauty surrounding me and significant events that mean something to my psychic mind. Unfortunately, if I take a break for even a few days, I immediately fall into the natural trap of getting aggravated with everyday life and forget what is important, sacred, or psychic. Not everyone can volunteer to work with dying people to gain perspective, so I recommend using a mindfulness chime.

Today's experiment is a mindfulness chime. Set a watch, phone, or computer timer to chime throughout the day. I recommend at least five times in the day. Every time that the chime sounds, come to a safe pause in your activities as soon as you can and take time out to tune into yourself and your environment. Really listen to your body and your feelings, and open up your eyes to the happenings around you. What did you notice today that you would have otherwise missed if you had not taken the time to be mindful?

> * Just for today, set up a mindfulness chime. It can be five times in the day or, if you are very ambitious, it can be every waking hour. Take a few minutes to observe and record what you notice within and around you.

Day 29
....

Daily Metaphor Poem

Today's exercise is a creative one that helps you understand symbolism. Symbolism is when a picture represents deeper and more abstract truths. As a psychic, you may sometimes see pictures in dreams or visions that are symbolic. Therefore, it is helpful to start understanding metaphors now. Your psychic development will start to speak a new language to you, and the faster and more fluently you learn that language, the better you will become at interpreting your own psychic experiences.

We will start with metaphors for yourself, since your first psychic readings will be upon yourself. Today, write yourself a metaphorical poem based on an object that you see, either around you in your real life or in your mind as in a dream or vision. Here is the poem format and an example:

I am as a _Plaid (red)_. → *Stable, Scottish, pattered.*

Red, _Square_, _Patterned_. (Some words/phrases that describe the object)

My greatest fear is _People / hard_. *too = fear people hurting me. vol enough really*

My deepest hope is _Pink. → clothes. Family_. *as I've seen I also*

For example: I am as a house. Strong, warm, stable. My greatest fear is that the love of a family will not fill me up. My deepest hope is that I will endure.

Another example: I am as a dog. Loyal, adventurous, joyful. My greatest fear is that I will become lost. My deepest hope is to be a companion.

You'll discover a lot about yourself by writing these quick poems.

* *Write a brief poem that is filled with metaphor. Ideally, you can try writing these poems once a day for a month. Look around you or in your dreams for subjects of the poem that represent you.*

DAY 30
....

Beginning a Dream Journal

The advice I give most frequently to people who want to develop psychic abilities is to start a dream journal. Why? Our dreams are entirely composed of the subconscious, the source of all psychic abilities. By starting psychic work with your dreams, you begin with a practice that is already comfortable and stretch yourself further. With a greater understanding of dreams, you can expand your psychic experiences to your waking life more easily later on.

This is not to say that dream journaling is easy. If you do not start writing in your journal within a few seconds of waking, you are likely to forget the vast majority of your dreams, even very meaningful and psychic ones. In fact, this is one of the more difficult things you can do. It is too easy to roll over and go back to sleep. If you don't think that you have very many dreams, you'll be surprised at how many more dreams you seem to have, simply because you pause to observe them upon waking. However, I must suggest that if you have an absence of dreams and also are troubled with a lack of restful sleep, you might have sleep problems that require a trip to the doctor.

To start a dream journal, set yourself up for success. Place a hard-backed journal, a writing implement, and a small light within arm's reach of your bed. Warn anyone else who sleeps in the room with you that you might be waking in the night or in the morning and switching on the small, unobtrusive light in order to record dreams. Force yourself to record any snippets of dreams that you remember. Over time, you'll find that you remember more, if you dedicate yourself to this psychic development discipline.

* *Begin a dream journal. Make sure you set up a dream journal station with a source of light, your journal, and a writing implement within arm's reach of your bed.*

Reviewing Your Journal

You've completed thirty days of psychic development, so it's time to review your journal. Reviewing your psychic journal is important for several reasons. Not only will you see the progress that you have made, but you might also notice predictions that have come true that you did not notice previously. Also, reviewing your journal will help you learn the more subtle art of interpreting symbols that form repeating patterns in your journal. For example, if you repeatedly have dreams about flowers and you notice in your journal that the word "flowers" appears over and over again, you'd probably start investigating why flowers keep appearing. They're more than just pretty plants to your subconscious, and they might symbolically represent something spiritual or more meaningful to you, such as femininity, beauty, or something else you associate with flowers.

When reviewing my journal, I like to read through all the entries carefully with a highlighter and a colored pen. I like to highlight anything I wrote that seems to be very psychic. For example, I do this if I had a dream or a vision of seeing a friend I hadn't seen in a long time and then the next day I saw him or her. Any sort of déjà vu should be highlighted for its predictive qualities. Notice if there's a pattern in the length of time between your psychic experience and when the event comes to pass in real life. After that, I like to circle all the nouns that might be symbols, like in the above example of flowers. If I notice one repeating, I tally up the number of times it repeats on a separate page. Later, I can meditate on the symbols that reappear most frequently.

> * *Review your psychic journal. Highlight any precognitive sections and circle any nouns that may be symbols, tallying their number on a separate page.*

DAY 32
....

Psychic Vampires

You've already carefully observed and written in your journal about how different people around you affect you in different ways. Some people in your life may leave you feeling energized and inspired, while other people can leave you feeling tired and crabby. Colloquially, those people who deplete energy (usually for their own gain) are called psychic vampires. They might not be doing so intentionally; they might actually need to behave in that way. Strange as it might sound, infants are the worst psychic vampires around! In some cases, psychic vampires who are acquaintances can be avoided. However, if you live with or work with a psychic vampire, you'll need to learn how to deal with the energetic behavior so you can continue your psychic development unhindered.

The best way to deal with psychic vampires is a combination of two of the skills you've practiced already. When you observe that a psychic vampire is affecting you, shield yourself. After you have shielded yourself, assess your energy and ground yourself. It is possible that the psychic vampire exchanged negative energy with you, which can be harmlessly grounded into the earth. You can then replenish any depleted energy with fresh energy.

Keep in mind that negative energy will be transformed by mother earth back into energy that can be used for positive ends.

* *Practice dealing with a psychic vampire quickly and smoothly by shielding and then grounding. You don't need to have a psychic vampire actually present to practice!*

DAY 33
. . . .

Fasting

So far, we've worked with grounding in many different ways. However, there is such a thing as being too grounded for psychic work. When you are too grounded, you are connected very closely with the earth and with the here and now. As such, it may be difficult for you to enter a trance state and let your mind take flight to explore the past and the future during psychic work. Signs that you are too grounded are that you feel unable to experience psychic phenomena or you intellectualize whatever you're doing and talk yourself out of psychic practice. Luckily, there is a straightforward way to enhance your psychic abilities even when you feel totally grounded in the ordinary and the mundane. Throughout human history, people have used fasting to be able to let go of the mind and body and to focus on spiritual and psychic matters.

Though fasting is not appropriate for children or for women who are pregnant or nursing, for healthy people a short fast may be just the trick to help with psychic development. Fasting might be just as simple as not eating a heavy meal before psychic work. Or, you can deliberately refrain from food for several hours. When doing heavy-duty psychic work, I like to drink juice instead of eating for the day and then perform my psychic work in the evening. Always have some food handy, even if it is just a granola bar, to help you ground directly after your psychic work.

> * *If fasting is right for you, consider trying to fast for a few hours today before meditation. If fasting is not appropriate for you today, refrain from eating a heavy meal until after your meditation.*

DAY 34
....

The Astral Plane

The astral plane is a theoretical construct psychics use that refers to a dimension of existence that is fully spiritual or intangible. The astral plane can be visited through dreams, meditation, and trance states. If you visualize something on the astral plane, it will appear. After it appears on the astral plane, you can choose to manifest it in your ordinary life, which we'll call the terrestrial plane for the sake of differentiation. On the astral plane, you can also choose to meet spirit guides, spirits of the dead, or other entities. Chances are, you've already visited the astral plane through dreaming and daydreaming.

The trick is to visit the astral plane without thinking about the terrestrial plane and becoming distracted. One way to make this easy is to sit down to meditate and build yourself a homebase on the astral plane. You can make this homebase be anything you like, outdoors or indoors, but it helps if you make it feel very homey when you go there. You might want to place a lot of paths or doors in your astral home base for easy travel to other locations in the astral plane. What sorts of things will make it feel inviting and comforting? Pleasant weather? A tea kettle on a stove? Beautiful art? Fresh flowers? Use your imagination to create imagery satisfying to you. Try meditating and visiting your astral homebase once a day to make it a familiar space you can return to at a moment's notice.

* *Create a personalized home base on the astral plane through meditation and visualization.*

DAY 35
. . . .

Grounding with Incense

Here's another grounding technique that may work for people who feel more connected to air and sky than earth, and is also helpful for developing your visualization skills. Incense smoke moves through the air like a fluid, making it one way to easily understand the fluidity of energy. You can choose any incense for this particular exercise as long as you find the scent pleasant and relaxing. You may find that floral scents, such as rose, might be especially helpful. If you don't have any incense at all, you'll have to use your imagination.

Light the incense and relax in a seated position, watching the rising smoke. Take note of how your body feels and how you perceive your energy to be flowing in the moment. Next, attempt to visualize the energy flow in your body as incense smoke. It may help some people keep their eyes closed during this visualization, but for others it may help to continue to keep eyes open and watch the incense smoke for inspiration. Notice where in your body the incense seems to collect, stagnate, swirl, or dissipate. Visualize your entire body filled with incense that moves smoothly and quickly, just like the incense you burn. You can ground in the usual way if you feel that there is too much or too little energy represented by your incense visualization, since this technique focuses on the flow more than anything else.

> * *Practice an incense visualization while grounding today to focus on the flow of your energy. Practice while burning real incense, although imaginary incense can be used if necessary.*

Day 36
....

Psychometry

Psychometry is the practice of gaining psychic knowledge from an object. For example, a psychic investigator might handle a murder weapon and use psychometry to identify the murderer or the victim. A more mundane and common example is using psychometry to connect with past events and people, like old pieces of jewelry to remember a grandmother or a wedding day.

You can practice psychometry by holding your hands over a bag of your own things, but I find that the practice is more effective and exciting if you can get a friend to collect some meaningful objects without telling you why they are special. Hold the object in your hands and explore all its qualities: weight, texture, the view from all angles, and even the scent. Close your eyes and recreate that object in your mind's eye as clearly as possible, as if you were having a daydream about it. Meditate for a moment and see if you can allow the space around the object in your mind's eye to be filled with a vision. It's okay if you perceive information about the object in other ways instead, such as a strong emotion. Make note of what you experience, and see if you can gain knowledge from objects you would not have otherwise known.

> * *Practice psychometry, preferably with a friend's help.*

Day 37
....

Feeling Auras

An aura is a field of life energy said to surround all living things. This energy is not electric or magnetic, but rather a spiritual metaphor for the force that individuals can exert on their environments. Every person has an aura, and some people can see the auras of animals, plants, or even inanimate objects such as sacred stones. Later in the year, we'll work on seeing auras, but right now I'd like to focus on how you can observe psychic things with your sense of touch, since not everyone is the sort of person to see psychic things automatically happen right before their eyes.

This exercise is best performed with a friend, although it is possible to perform it on a pet, a plant, or yourself. If you do this exercise with a friend, tell your friend to close their eyes and imagine a scenario in which he or she is trying to gain respect and attention, such as when giving a speech. While your friend concentrates, extend your hand toward their shoulders and slowly move to touch them while paying attention to any sensations you experience. Some people feel auras as heat, pressure, or a prickling sensation. I tend to experience them as a fuzzy feeling, like static electricity. Again, some people might not have a physical sensation, but might instead feel an emotion or a sense of knowing where the edge of the aura lies. Write down your experiences.

* *Try feeling someone else's aura.*

Part Two

Dreams, Meditation, and Trances

Day 38
·············

Lucid Dreaming

Every healthy person dreams, but remembering them is another matter. Most people dream while not realizing they are dreaming. However, there is a special class of dreams called lucid dreams where you realize that you are dreaming and can even control how the dream plays out. Lucid dreams are useful to psychic development because dreams are one way to access your subconscious and intuitive self. The more you control your dreams, the more you can choose which direction your psychic development will take.

The first step to lucid dreaming is remembering your dreams. You've already taken the first step by keeping a dream journal. If you force yourself to fully awaken and write down your dreams as soon as you begin to gain consciousness, your dream memory will improve. If you feel like you never have dreams, it might help to take vitamin B and make sure you are getting proper amounts of sleep. If you don't have dreams you remember and you can't seem to get restful sleep, it may be time to talk to your doctor about visiting a sleep specialist. Begin the process of going to bed slowly. Don't eat right before bed, and don't exercise for at least three hours prior to bedtime. Take a relaxing hot bath if possible.

The easiest way to attempt lucid dreaming is to focus on the topic you'd like to dream about while lying in bed. For example, play out an issue with a relationship or visualize the face of the person to whom you'd like to speak. Your mind will naturally wander, and you can gently remind yourself of your topic again whenever you wish. It may take a few tries before your brain gets the idea that you want to dream about a particular topic, so don't quit right away. Make sure to record the dreams in your journal and think carefully about what meaning they might hold for you.

* *Allow enough time for a long bedtime routine tonight so that you can attempt lucid dreaming and record your dreams upon waking.*

Day 39

Silent Receptive Meditation

The simplest yet arguably most challenging form of meditation is silent, receptive meditation. And yet this is precisely the sort of meditation with which you should begin your psychic practice. With silent, receptive meditation, you clear your mind. As a blank slate in the gap between thoughts, psychic messages can be more easily received, discerned, and understood. This type of meditation should be the foundation upon which you can build other meditation techniques such as visualization and trance.

It is hard to clear your mind. Don't beat yourself up if you can't do it right away. There are some things you can do to make it easier. For example, make sure that you are in a place where you will not be disturbed and turn off or put away all distractions. Make sure that you are comfortable, your body is at the right temperature and that you are neither too hungry nor too full. Ground and center yourself fully. If you find meditation a challenge, set a timer for a very short time. When I got started, I literally could not meditate longer than thirty seconds! Now I can meditate for hours if needed.

Keep paper and a writing implement nearby, but don't write anything down during your meditation. Wait until after your timer has gone off before writing down any impressions that you receive, even if it's just an ache in your backside. Meditation, like persistent physical exercise, can take time and practice to notice a payoff. However, over time it can lower your blood pressure, reduce your daily stress and develop your psychic abilities.

* *Block out time in your schedule every day for meditation practice. It can be five minutes or less to start. Record any impressions you receive during your meditation.*

DAY 40
....

Trance Breathing

Breath control is one tried and true method of trance induction. By focusing on your breathing, you can hypnotize yourself. On top of this effect, by controlling the amount of oxygen you are taking in with each breath, you can affect your consciousness. Think about it. When you yawn do you feel more awake and energized afterwards, or do you feel sleepy? How does your breathing depth and rate change after a yawn? Trance breathing is like a spiritual yawn, allowing you to transition to a different level of alertness for psychic development and work.

Start by focusing on your breathing and trying to push out all thoughts except those about your breaths. This might be enough to induce a trance for some people. The next step is to control your breathing. Begin by breathing from your diaphragm by straightening your spine and allowing your belly to move in and out as you breathe. Keep your shoulders down, and focus on the breath low in your lungs rather than up high in your chest. You may notice that your breathing naturally slows this way. Allow your body to relax with each exhale.

Square breathing is a common practice of breath control: breathe in for four counts, hold for four counts, breathe out for four counts, hold for four counts. How long should the four counts be? Some people use heartbeats; others choose whatever feels sustainable. At first, square breathing may feel very uncomfortable or distracting. The distraction is a good thing. Allow it to busy your mind to erase all other external thoughts. The discomfort will last until you fall into a groove, which may take a few moments for your heart rate and oxygen needs to stabilize. After this happens, you may be surprised to find the effort associated with square breathing disappears. It may take several sessions of practice before you can stop thinking so hard about square breathing and allow your brain to enter a trance state.

* *Try square breathing during your meditation today to see if you can induce a trance state. Record your results.*

Day 41

Walking Meditation

Meditation doesn't require sitting absolutely still, although that is the best method for beginning silent, receptive meditation. It's okay to try using a walking meditation to see if that method works better for you. If you've ever experienced some form of "highway hypnosis," where you forget the miles that you've just driven, using walking meditation may be a safer method for trance induction. When attempting a walking meditation, however, it is a good idea to not have safety concerns. Travel on a well known path far away from any automobile traffic, free of tripping obstacles so you can let your mind go.

Begin your walking meditation by grounding and centering. Don't skip this part, which can be easy to do if you're excited to be outside for a walk in the park. As you begin walking, choose a focus such as your breathing or your footfalls or a spot in the distance that can be your destination. Don't let your attention waver from your focus during your meditation. Since a walking meditation isn't usually isolated from all possible sources of external distraction, you may find things catching your attention, like a bird singing on a branch or a beautifully colored leaf. Take note of these and then allow your mind to return to your focus. When you are done, record anything significant that you noticed, as these could also be considered signs or omens.

If you are lucky enough to have a labyrinth near you, perhaps at a church or a park, trying walking the labyrinth while meditating. If you are industrious, you can look up photographs of labyrinths online or at your library and then create your own out of string in a field of grass. The point of a labyrinth is to represent a journey inward and then an equivalent journey outward, and it's a perfect way to descend into a meditation through walking and then ascend back out of the meditation to rejoin your everyday waking life.

* Try a walking meditation while focusing on your breathing
  or footfalls.

DAY 42

Heartbeat Meditation

Listening to your heartbeat is another way to focus during meditation. By listening to your heart rate, you can allow your heart rate to slow naturally, which can be a healthy way to calm down and achieve a meditative state.

Blood flow control has been used spiritually throughout history to induce trance, and meditating on your heartbeat is a safe way to use this ancient practice.

I like to listen to my heartbeat by feeling it. While seated, I hold a hand over my heart and feel the beating that way. Sometimes I will feel my pulse at my neck with two fingers instead, if my heartbeat is too faint underneath my clothes. My resting pulse has always been very slow, like a metronome, and since beginning meditation and exercise it has dropped to an even lower healthy rate.

You can begin by simply observing your heart rate. You can measure your resting heart rate before and after meditation by counting how many beats you feel within ten seconds and then multiplying it by six to figure out the beats per minute. Next, try to focus on your heart rate until it is the only thing in your attention. You may find that your heart rate slows. Pay attention to any sensations in your body or psychic perceptions you feel. If you like, you can also experiment with square breathing, using your heart beat to count the beats. Using square breathing, your breaths will slow at the same rate as your heart rate slows.

After heartbeat meditation, open your eyes and stretch a little bit. Stay seated and alert for a moment and get up slowly. The slowing of your heart rate might make you feel light headed or see stars. Take your time so you don't fall. This meditation can also be used in order to relax before sleep.

* *Try meditating to the sound and feel of your heartbeat in a simple and safe method of blood control trance.*

Day 43
. . . .

Dream Question

When I was a kid, I thought that whatever it was I concentrated upon when I went to sleep would be remembered when I woke up. I would use that to try to remember chores, but it didn't seem to work. Later, as a young adult, I tried it as a study technique at college to try to remember what I learned. That was more effective, but mostly because I began to puzzle over questions and dream about them. By doing so, I learned the material more effectively. It was as if I was giving myself more homework in my sleep.

Now that you have begun the process of recording your dreams, you are ready to ask your subconscious a question to try to see the answer. The trick is to concentrate on your question enough that it is burned into your brain without preventing yourself from going to sleep. Hopefully, your practice of clearing your mind during meditation will help. You might also try writing a question over and over again on a piece of paper before you lie down to sleep. After you turn out the lights, turn your mind to your question and draw your mind gently back on track whenever it wanders. You might even find that the question or its answer pops into your head as soon as you regain consciousness. When you wake up, don't forget to write down whatever dreams you remember, even if they seem to not be related to your question at all.

What question should you ask? Since your future is up to you, the best questions to ask are how to achieve your goals. So, instead of asking "Who will I marry?" you could ask, "What are the traits of a good marriage partner for me?" Or better still, "How can I procure a happy marriage life as soon as possible?" Select your question carefully so that you feel prepared to deal with any answer you receive, even if the answer might not be the one that you hope for the most.

* *Try asking your subconscious a question before you go to sleep.*
  Record any dreams, even if they seem to have nothing to do with
  your question.

DAY 44

Shamanic Journey

If you're ready for an advanced technique today, you can start your own shamanic journey. Shamanism has been practiced in many cultures and is aided by a few tools. Ideally, you will have a drum beat (either a friend to drum for you or a recording) and a stone you choose from the outdoors to help ground you and bring you back from your trance. I first practiced this outdoors near a campfire, and the experience was very powerful. During this trance, you may enter the astral plane and encounter animals that may speak to you. It's tradition that a beginner should not speak to insects or reptiles while on these shamanic journeys, so you may follow this advice too if you wish.

Shamanic drumming is usually at a rate that sounds very fast and not musical at all, in the range of around 200–400 beats per minute. That's a pretty fast drum beat to maintain, and I find it impossible to get into a trance if I'm beating the drum myself. I like to record the beat or to get a friend to beat the drum for me. You can also download or purchase previously recorded drum beats.

Before getting started, choose a stone to hold in your hand. No matter where you go on your shamanic journey, you can always turn your attention to the stone in your hand to come out of your trance and back to your own body, safe wherever you started in the real world.

Start the drumming and close your eyes. In your mind's eye, visualize getting up and finding a hole, tunnel, or door in the ground to journey through. When you get to whatever is on the other side, you will be on your shamanic journey. Pay attention to any guides you meet and what they have to say. When you feel you're done, you can travel back through the portal or turn your attention to the stone in your hand. I often find that I stay in the journey as long as the drum is playing, so choose an amount of time for the drum to play before you journey.

* *Try going on a shamanic journey and record what happens.*

DAY 45

Swing Meditation

Another way to induce trace states traditionally in many cultures is suspension and binding with cords, which often involve some pretty extreme and advanced techniques. You can achieve a beginner's version of such a trance state using a hammock or a simple swing on a playground. There is something about the gentle back-and-forth motion of a swing that induces trance states. That may be one reason why rocking works so well to put babies to sleep. One of my small children often goes into a waking swing trance on the playground or in the tree swing in my backyard. Even waving my hand in front of her face doesn't snap her out of it until the swing has come to rest!

Ideally, you'll have a partner to gently push your swing or rock the hammock, but this is one trance that you can induce yourself and keep the rocking motion going with your own body. Close your eyes if you can, but keep your eyes open if the motion makes you dizzy or sick with your eyes closed. Before you climb aboard the swing, ground and center yourself thoroughly. Set a meditation timer, especially if you're alone, just in case you fall asleep or lose yourself in a trance. Then climb aboard and swing as slowly as you possibly can while still maintaining a very predictable rate.

As you swing, focus entirely on the sensations that you feel from the swinging motion and from the swing or hammock pressing upward upon you against the force of gravity and the centrifugal force of your movement. Try not to think about anything else, but pay attention to any special psychic perceptions you may receive. You may find that this lulls you into a deep trance or even near sleep. Be careful not to fall off the swing, and it is okay to end your meditation early if you are worried about falling. Exit the swing slowly and carefully and then ground and center yourself again. Record anything interesting about your experience.

* *Try trance meditation in a swing or hammock.*

Day 46

Dreaming of Spirit

Another interesting way to use your psychic dreams is to connect with the spirit of somebody who has died. This is a wonderful way to be able to hug and talk to somebody again that you have lost. I find that dreaming of a spirit, like the spirit of my dad, is a very fulfilling practice that leaves me feeling loved and happy when I wake up. It can also be a great way to receive messages from spirits, so you can ask spirits questions if you would like advice or even just to find a lost object.

Dreaming about a spirit is a practice that is very much like approaching your dreams with a question. You will need to think about the spirit you wish to contact a lot before you go to sleep. The only difference is that you'll need to politely ask for the spirit to visit you, rather than simply demanding an answer from your own subconscious. You can write the request on paper over and over again, using the full name the person used in life. It may help to meditate on a picture of the person before you go to bed, studying their facial details thoroughly.

As you lie in bed, make a special appeal to the spirit that you'd like to draw into your dreams. I find that it helps to assure the spirit that you won't be frightened by a mere dream, as you extend your invitation. Some spirits may be concerned that an appearance would harm your grief process, make you afraid, or make you think that you're crazy. As long as you feel that you are truly ready, you can help reassure those spirits as well. Do take such thoughts to heart, though, and choose a spirit that you will be comfortable contacting no matter what that spirit may have to say. If you have a recently deceased spouse or child, for instance, it might be best to choose somebody like a grandmother that died long ago, if you need some space and distance immediately after death. Again, make sure to record your dreams, even if they seem to have nothing to do with the spirit, as they might be highly symbolic.

* *Invite the spirit of a deceased person into your dreams, ideally a relative or a person you knew well in life (rather than a celebrity) for your first attempt.*

Day 47
....

Running Trance

Running combines several trance techniques that you've practiced so far. Running gets the heart pumping and the blood moving quickly, for a blood control trance. Running creates particular breathing patterns, for a breath control induced trance. And, running produces endorphins from exercise, which acts as a natural drug that promotes trance induction. Running also has the same effects as the walking meditation, which allows your footfalls to hypnotize you. I find that running in a trance state can be incredibly powerful.

For your running meditation, choose a well-known path away from traffic and tripping hazards. A treadmill would work. Hold on to the hand rail, though, to avoid falling off when deep in meditation. An outdoor track such as that found at a school would be ideal as well. Ground and center yourself, then walk for about five minutes to warm up and stretch out your muscles. Jog as slowly as you possibly can. With my short legs, I can run as slowly as 3.5 miles per hour, but it may be a bit more brisk for you if you have long legs or are a trained runner.

Choose one of the trance foci with which you've worked already: Heartbeat, breathing or footfalls. Try not to rotate through them too fast, or else you'll distract yourself out of a trance. In fact, for your first time, you'd do best to pick only one for your entire running session, which if you're new to running may only be half a minute. It's okay to take walking breaks if you need to do so to accommodate your fitness level, but try to keep your heart rate and breathing up to whatever is a safe and healthy exercise level for you so you can release those endorphins. After your attempt, walk for another five minutes to cool down, then ground and center yourself again. You may find it helps to eat a heavy meal afterwards.

* *Try trance running. If it is enjoyable, try trance running three days a week for twenty minutes or more.*

DAY 48
....

Mantra Meditation

A mantra is a statement made over and over again during meditation. A mantra can be a message of devotion to a deity or guru, or it can be an affirmation for yourself. For today's exercise, I'd like you to choose a mantra that is a personal affirmation. You can study books about mantras in Sanskrit or other languages if you wish, but for this exercise I'd like you to use English or another language you are fluent in (a language that you can think with, not just speak with).

When I write my own mantras, I like to invent one that is rhythmic, not too long or complicated, and that I can say as I breathe in as well as when I breathe out. This circular breathing helps me to not interrupt my meditation. Here's a simple mantra: "Life is good." When I use this mantra, I can whisper it so that I'm saying "life is" while sucking breath in and "good" as I'm breathing air out. Your mantra can be "I am lovable," "There is abundance in the universe," or anything else you would like to affirm or draw into your life. Pay attention to any psychic perceptions you may feel that are related to your affirmations.

You can choose to repeat your mantra throughout a timed meditation. Say it slowly enough that your breathing rate can be slowed down to a meditative rate, similar to what you can achieve through square breathing. You can also choose to do a counted mantra meditation. Sometimes this is done with prayer beads, a traditional Hindu number being 108. You can buy prayer beads, create your own, or just tie knots in a string or length of yarn in a pinch. Using a mantra and prayer beads is a great way to practice daily meditation if you are loathe to use a timer.

* Create your own mantra and meditate with it. Optionally, you
   can create your own prayer beads or a length of knotted string.

Day 49

Chanting Trance

I am having you do a chanting trance right after a mantra meditation so that you can see the subtle differences between these two practices. During a mantra meditation, you use a gently breathed mantra as a focus and allow that energy to flow through you while you observe the flow. During a chanting trance, you forcefully project energy by chanting, in order to induce a trance. For that reason, I'd like you to choose a chant that is a little more than a whispered affirmation.

You can perform a devotional chant by chanting divine names, or by intoning the word "om," the sound of the universe. Or, you can make up your own chant. For a chant, you don't have to pick one that you can say while breathing in, because you'll be taking breaths in between repetitions of the chant. I suggest that you choose something that you would like to be true in the future, and then chant it as if it has already happened. In this way, you create the future as you predict it, which increases your psychic ability. So, if your affirmation was "I am lovable," your chant might be "I am loved."

For a chanting trance, you'll want to choose a time and a place where you can chant fairly loudly without disturbing anyone so you can chant without feeling self-conscious. Remember to ground and center yourself before you begin. You can sing your chant, or say it in a monotone voice if you like. Imagine that you are projecting your voice outward and that the vibrations are dispersing as positive energy into the universe. When you are done, take time to ground and center yourself, making sure that you feel fully grounded before you get up. Trance chanting can be a highly energetic practice, so if you don't ground properly afterwards you might feel jittery or exhausted.

* *Try trance chanting with a chant of your choice.*

DAY 50
....

Dreaming with Someone

For today's exercise, you'll need to grab a partner and try to connect with one another in a dream. This is an exciting way to develop your psychic abilities because it is fun and offers confirmation and validation. You can pick somebody close to you, even somebody in the same bed, or you can pick somebody distant from you, although it may help if you can both agree to go to sleep around the same time.

I like to attempt this by agreeing ahead of time on the dreamscape. You can choose a setting based on a real place that both of you have visited before, such as underneath a tree in a particular park. Before going to sleep, talk with the person and make sure you're on the same page. You can look at photos of the person if you wish, and write his or her name down using the same techniques for contacting a spirit.

As you lie down in bed and turn off the light, you'll need to do some active visualization. You can picture your dream partner's face and think about his or her name, and you can begin to construct in your mind the meeting place where you will be waiting for him or her. It is okay to switch back and forth between these visuals, but try to draw your mind back on task if you start thinking of something else entirely. When you wake up, record any remembered dreams even if they have nothing to do with the meeting place or the person in question. Call your dream partner as soon as possible, even if you don't remember much, and compare notes. Even if you didn't dream of each other, your dreams might turn out to be very similar. Ideally, try again for several attempts.

* Pick a dream partner and agree to try to dream with one another when you go to sleep tonight.

Day 51

Incense, Tea, and Bath Trance

Here's another simple trance you can do that plays on the old trance induction technique of using drugs to influence your body minus using drugs that might be dangerous. Instead, you'll use incense, herbal tea, and a bath to alter your mental state. The result of this combination can be just as intoxicating as some mild trance-state drugs. If you undertake this task mindfully, you can increase the effect of these mental tools, so approach this practice with a degree of reverence and by removing any distractions from the experience.

Choose a time for your bath when you can be left completely alone and hopefully not have too many distracting sounds from family members or roommates in the house. Turn off your phone and put away the reading materials, because you'll need to be alone with your mind for this practice. Brew a calming herbal tea such as chamomile, and draw a hot bath. You can add relaxing herbs such as lavender to your bath as well. Choose an incense that relaxes you and puts you in the mood for psychic work. For me, that incense is usually frankincense because it allows me to feel that I am blessing the area with positive energy for my work. Sage is another good incense to use, as it cleanses an area of any negativity that might affect your psychic senses.

If you like, you can light candles for mood lighting, or simply dim the lights to allow for a more relaxed atmosphere for trance meditation. You may set a meditation timer if you wish to avoid falling asleep in the tub. Pour yourself a cup of tea, light the incense and climb into the bath tub. Sip the tea and focus on the physical sensations in your body from the scents and the warmth of the water of the bath and the tea. Sip the tea rhythmically and continue to focus on the sensations you feel and nothing else.

* *Try to induce a trance by lighting some incense and taking a bath with a cup of tea.*

DAY 52
....

Dream Travel

You've already had a brief introduction to the astral plane during meditation. Most dreams take place on the astral plane so you don't purposely have to try to travel there when you perform astral travel while dreaming.

An exciting experiment is to try to travel in the real world during your dreams in a practice that is sometimes called ethereal travel.

I very much enjoy traveling during dreams, as it gives me a chance to fly. Since I am Wiccan and practice with a coven, I like to imagine that I am flying off to join my other witch friends at the Sabbat if I am ever forced to stay away from the real circle due to illness or travel. Traveling during dreams is also a fun way to test your psychic ability by looking for confirmation afterwards. Was the weather what you saw in your dreams? Did the theater marquee really say what you saw in your dream? You can also use it as a method for visiting a dream partner. Always get permission from somebody before you visit them in your dreams. I can say from experience that it feels really creepy to have somebody else's "dream self" creep into your bedroom at night.

To practice dream travel, as you lie down in bed you can visualize a double of yourself floating lightly out of your body into your bedroom. If you like, you can also visualize a silver umbilical cord connecting your dream self to your body. You can follow that dream cord home whenever you wish, and it cannot be severed or tampered with in any way by anyone without your permission. Your dream self can fly through walls, so you can float through the ceiling and fly around unhindered. Follow roads like a map if you wish. Dip low to see freeway signs to see if you can read them in your dreams. Note that some people can't read in dreams, so don't feel too frustrated if that happens to you. When you awaken, write down as many details that you might be able to verify as you go about your day.

* Try traveling during your dream. Notice and record any details that might be verifiable.

Day 53

······

Exercise Trance

This trance draws from a similar principle as the running trance that you have tried earlier. This time, I'd like to focus on the druglike trance effects of endorphins. Choose a simple and familiar exercise that can elevate your heart rate and breathing to a moderate degree. Try to choose an exercise simple enough that you won't be adding additional trance techniques; the idea is to only focus on the endorphins produced by sweating it out. For example, jumping jacks or squats might be ideal, but this will really depend entirely on your fitness level. What works up a sweat and a brain full of endorphins for a normal desk jockey might feel like nothing to a Navy Seal.

Set a timer for your exercise trance, which will again be based on your fitness level. In general, it's a healthy idea to try to get at least twenty minutes of cardiovascular activity, but if you're not ready for that you can just do a few minutes for your first attempt. Ground and center yourself before the exercise. Stretch and warm up slowly until you build up to rigorous exercises, and then gradually cool back down and stretch. Ground, center, and then take a few minutes for seated meditation, taking special care to note the sensations in your body. Do you feel any soreness? Buzzing sensations? A feeling like you are floating? Are there any other psychic sensations that come to you?

Continue to sit until your heart rate has slowed back to your resting heart rate. Record anything you noticed during the trance meditation. Get up slowly and carefully, and consider having a heavy meal to continue the grounding process. Were you able to achieve a trance state? If not, is there any way you can simplify or focus your exercise next time? Write down your initial impressions. This can be a challenging technique to master, but one that can be very effective and much safer than taking drugs for inducing trance.

* *Try inducing a trance state through simple exercise.*

DAY 54

Dream Interpretation

Interpreting dreams is tricky business because the things that you see in dreams are highly symbolic. If you see an ex-friend, your dream may not be about your ex at all, but about the time in your life or the personal characteristics that ex represents. Likewise, a terrible car wreck or teeth falling out might represent a loss of control in your life, and not those terrible circumstances actually coming to pass. By now, you've hopefully collected a number of dreams in your journal. I've also asked you to highlight any dreams that did turn out to be precognitive and literally came to pass so that you can note any patterns regarding when they occur. You should also have been circling nouns that might be symbols, and tallying them up on a page.

Take a look at the symbols that appear most often in your dreams. They may be people such as a spouse or a parent, or they may be common everyday objects like cars or telephones. You might even notice particular building structures as themes, such as narrow hallways, doorways, or bridges. You might notice particular weather or certain times of day in which your dreams appear to take place. Choose just one of those symbols and turn to a page in your psychic journal. Write the word across the top and start brainstorming meanings.

The meanings for the word can be well known cultural meanings or meanings that are personal to you due to an experience you've had in life. Try to draw any parallels between why this symbol was in your dream and what's going on in your life right now. If you can't find the connection, choose another word that appeared in a dream and analyze it in the same way. Now analyze those two words together. Does a new meaning pop into your head when the two terms are juxtaposed? Leave plenty of blank space on the page in your notebook. Chances are that some of your symbolic meanings will change over time as you have more life experiences with those things or as you start to notice patterns in your dreams that make the meanings more clear to you.

* Go through your dream journal and try to interpret a few
  recurring symbols.

DAY 55
....

Scourge Trance

Time for another ancient practice toned down for the modern beginner. Scourging is a practice that has been done throughout history to induce trance. Ancient Christian penitents would flog their own backs during prayer. More recently, sauna and steam bath users have gently whipped their backs and shoulders with palm fronds to stimulate blood flow and relaxation. If you have access to palm fronds and a steam room, this would be an excellent trance meditation for you to try. However, a similar effect can be experienced using an exfoliating loofah and a sugar scrub in the bathtub. In a pinch try mixing a half cup of coconut oil with one cup of sugar to make your own.

When performing a scourge trance, the trick will be to focus on the sensations on your skin and nothing else. As a result, you'll probably want to perform this trance alone so you won't feel self-conscious. However, if you do have a partner who is understanding about your goals, by all means invite the person to deliver the scourge and talk through the first few minutes so the sensation is light enough to your taste. Make sure to ground and center before you start. Draw a bath or enter your steam room. Apply the sensations to your skin lightly. You don't want to injure yourself, only create a predictable sensation firm enough that you can feel it every time. You shouldn't even leave a mark. If you're using a scrub, make the scrubbing motions be rhythmic, just as they would be if you were scourging yourself with palm fronds. It will be the physical sensations as well as the rhythm that lulls you into the trance.

The psychic energy gained from scourging may feel very intense if you are a sensitive person. You may feel like you are floating or get light headed. It is okay to end the session early and ground yourself if you feel like you need to do so. Write down any feelings that you had about the experience. How do your emotions feel? Do you feel more level-headed and relaxed, or were emotions brought to the surface? Were you able to achieve a trance during your first attempt? Throughout the day after scourging, you may also feel more psychic or "thin skinned," so keep recording in your journal any other experiences with empathy or other psychic impressions that you get throughout your day.

* *Try inducing a trance through scourging or by applying gentle but intense rhythmic sensation to your skin.*

Day 56
. . . .

Transmission Meditation

Transmission meditation is a technique discovered by author Benjamin Crème of the esoteric tradition. Crème believed that meditation could be used not only as a way to bring in psychic news from your surroundings, but also to improve your interactions with people around you and the fate of the planet at large. The idea is that you open yourself to the universe and the divine, receive energies, and act as a battery for those people and forces in the world that are moving our communities toward a positive destiny. This method of meditation is unique for the psychic because it is not designed to induce psychic senses. That is, you won't receive any messages of any kind during transmission meditation. Instead, you develop yourself as a conduit for creating your own destiny, and in doing so are more able to achieve your goals as a psychic.

The practice of transmission meditation is simple. Set a meditation timer for a short period of time for your first meditation. Some people choose to practice in a group, and they say a short opening invocation asking for energy to descend from the universe or the divine through the body of the meditator in order to manifest love and power on earth. Today, I'll have you practice a technique borrowed from transmission meditation without needing to gather a meditation group or say the great invocation.

A good amount of time is whatever you're able to achieve with silent, receptive meditation at this point in your development. Seat yourself comfortably, close your eyes, and focus all of your attention at the point on your forehead just between your eyebrows. This point, called the ajna center, is believed to be a vortex of psychic energy within your body, sometimes called a chakra. Whenever your attention naturally wanders from this point on your body, silently think of the sound "om" as if you are chanting the word "om" without saying it aloud. In doing so, allow your attention to direct itself back to the ajna center. As a beginner, you may have to think "om" with every breath, but as you practice, you will be able to experience gaps of pure meditation.

> * Try practicing the transmission meditation technique of focusing on the ajna center and thinking of the word "om" to hold your attention.

DAY 57
. . . .
Trance Dancing

Trance dancing has been used by many cultures for psychic development. The practice of trance dancing has been used to talk with spirits of the dead and even to banish psychic illness. Trance dancing can combine breathing techniques, rigorous blood flow and endorphins from exercise, but for today's practice I'd like you to use a more relaxed and slow form of trance dancing. By focusing on your body's movements, you can let go of external distractions and allow your energy to flow freely. As such, trance dancing is a good to do before a psychic session in order to get those psychic juices flowing.

Start by grounding yourself. You might want to use the movement grounding that you've already learned. By getting your body loosened up, you'll avoid feeling stiff or strained and you'll also get rid of any self-consciousness that you might feel about looking silly. Psychic trance dancing is not the sort of thing that you'll be taking to the floor of the Goth club. Trance dancing will be movements that arise prompted by your own energies rather than by anyone else's observations.

Choose music that starts out slow but ends fast. It helps me when trance dancing to only focus on one movement aspect at a time. So, for example, rather than moving through space or changing levels, I might focus on just making circles in all the ways that I can. Make circles by turning, circles with the shoulders, hands, or hips. Focus on a single shape or form of movement over and over again in different ways, stretching your mind to the point of exhaustion by finding new ways to execute that movement. If you find yourself drawing a blank, slow down your movement.

When you feel finished or when your music ends, stop and seat yourself. Allow some time for quiet, receptive meditation, and then ground yourself. Make sure to record anything you sense during this time. How do you feel? Do you feel that your general energy levels are decreased or increased by this activity? If you were not able to achieve a trance this time, you can try again when your energy is at a different level, or with different music.

* Try dancing to induce a trance. Observe what it does to your energy levels.

DAY 58
....
Lengthening Your Meditation

If you've been dutifully practicing meditation, now is the time for you to begin extending the length of your meditation sessions if you haven't already. This might cause some of you to groan at the thought. However, the point of lengthening your meditation is that it will actually help your psychic development. Meditating for a longer period of time allows you to get past the more distractible first few minutes to sink into the brain state in which you are open to receiving psychic messages. Meditating longer will also allow you to more quickly reach a meditative state so that you can enter that headspace at the drop of a hat when wanting to perform a psychic reading. Beginners meditating for short periods of time only get to experience the tip of the iceberg when it comes to reaching that sweet spot in meditation where psychic abilities reach their peak. It's time for you to dig deeper.

Unless you've really fallen in love with another meditation technique, I suggest going back to quiet, receptive meditation when expanding your time meditating. The key to success is gradual improvement. If you're not meditating daily, start with frequency before length, even if you can only meditate for thirty seconds in one sitting. If you find meditation very challenging, only increase your meditation time by up to a minute, and only add a minute to your meditation time about once a week. You can see how gradual your improvement will be, but it is better than quitting your practice entirely out of frustration.

Make sure that you log your minutes spent in meditation so you can see how your concentration improves over time. Include some notes about how you feel afterward and whether you felt the meditation session was productive or just too distracting to get off the ground.

* *Increase the duration of your meditation sessions.*

DAY 59

....

Increasing the Frequency of Dreams

You've already started some good work on increasing the frequency of your remembered dreams just by making a commitment to log your dreams. The more you force yourself to write things down as soon as you regain consciousness, the more skill you will gain at being successful with the process. That said, there are a few other things you can do to aid your dream interpretation and psychic development. Most of these things are lifestyle changes, so it's a good time to take a look at how your dreaming plays a role in your life right now.

Are you getting enough sleep? It only takes about ninety minutes to complete a sleep cycle, but if you are chronically sleep deprived, getting under seven hours of sleep, you might drop into a deeper sleep stage that omits dreams. Athletes and nursing mothers need extra sleep as well. Some things that aid sleep are avoiding screens like computers and television sets a few hours before bedtime, and gradually allowing lights in your home to dim as you prepare for rest. Avoid using your bedroom for waking activities like hobbies and work. Your bed itself should only be used for sleeping or sex, not watching television, eating, or anything else. Condition your brain to know when bedtime is coming and it's time for you to enter the world of dreams.

Check in with your nutrition. It could be that vitamin deficiencies make it more difficult to remember dreams, so make sure you're eating your fruits and vegetables and taking a vitamin supplement if necessary. Finally, add exercise to your morning routine. Vigorous exercise can help aid sleep and dreams, as long as the exercise is not done too close to bedtime.

* *Take an inventory of your sleep habits and your lifestyle surrounding sleep and dreams to see if minor improvements could be made to increase your dreaming.*

DAY 60
. . . .

Deepening Your Meditation

Now that you've started to lengthen your meditation time and have a few more foundational skills, it is okay to deepen your meditation so you can access more of your psychic senses. By going into a deeper meditation that's closer to a sleep state, you will be able to dream while awake and thus able to see visions or to experience other psychic senses. Before you get started with deep meditation, it's a good idea to observe some simple safety practices. For example, don't go into a deep meditation when you're in charge of watching small children or if you have to hop in a car and drive afterwards. Treat your deep meditation sessions like you would enjoying an alcoholic beverage—responsibly.

The basic procedure you will follow to deepen your meditation combines a trance induction technique followed immediately by a long, quiet, receptive meditation session. So choose your favorite trance technique and set a meditation timer to help you return from your meditation. You might even wish to hold a rock like you did during your shamanic journey to aid in your return to a normal state of consciousness. If you want to meditate more deeply, you can add additional techniques such as fasting. My big tip for you is to spend extra time grounding yourself after a deep meditation session. Take care to record your initial results. If you fell asleep, you're going too deep and may need to ease up on the length of your meditation or your trance technique. If you don't sense a difference in your meditation, it's time to practice trance induction more.

* Increase the depth or intensity of your meditation sessions.

Day 61

....

A Spiritual Retreat

Just drawing from the fact you are still engaged in your lessons here, I would gather that you're someone who makes spiritual and psychic goals every day. However, there's really no replacement for setting aside a time and a place for solitude and exclusive psychic work. In many cultures, psychics retreat from society, enter their own worlds, and return bearing messages and blessings from the outer realms. Today, see if you can carve out some time in your life for a spiritual retreat.

The characteristics of a psychic spiritual retreat should be: solitude, psychic development, and a change in scenery. The experience of a new place is like the shamanic experience of leaving your ordinary everyday life. The solitude allows you to listen to your own psychic promptings without having to think about the thoughts and needs of others. Psychic development can be your overall goal, so you can plan out a few exercises from the past to practice again and leave behind any distractions that might otherwise steal your time and attention.

Take time today to consider a spiritual retreat during which you focus only on your psychic practice. Mark time on your calendar. It might be a long weekend camping trip, overnight in a hotel, or a trip to a beach cottage.

If you're a busy mom of young children, as I am, you might have to make do with a rare long soak in a bathtub for now, and make plans for next year.

* Plan a solitary spiritual retreat during which you will only work on your psychic development.

Day 62
. . . .

Meditating with Music

Until now, I have been sparing when recommending meditation music except when it complements a specific purpose such as for shamanic journeying or trance dancing. This is because even the most relaxing, dreamy, and abstract meditation music can be distracting to your brain. Without your active participation, your brain attempts to anticipate the music or follow a melody, and it can make true meditation difficult to achieve even if it staves off boredom. I still believe that beginners should be able to practice quiet, receptive meditation without music. Eventually, though, it can be consciously used as a focus and can produce a trance effect.

You can pick music of choice for a music meditation, but I suggest using something familiar to enhance its predictability. It should be slow so you can relax and focus on the music without the feeling like it's rushing past you too quickly. Pick a long song for practice so you can meditate without having to change gears when the music switches tracks. It also may help to meditate in a dark room so you can focus only on your auditory senses.

Ground yourself, sit or lie down, and close your eyes. As you listen to the music, focus all your attention on the sounds you hear and nothing else. You may choose to visualize or conceptualize the music as a way to help your focus. Here are two exercises to try. If you're a kinesthetic learner, you can move your hand with the music. As the high notes play, move your hand higher and as the low notes play move your hand lower. If you're a visual learner, picture the music as a bright and colorful ribbon moving through space. When the song ends, you can end your meditation, ground, and make some notes about how you feel.

* *Try meditation while listening to music as your focus. See if you can achieve a trance state.*

DAY 63

Guided Meditation

I tend to shy away from extensive guided meditation when training a novice. I believe guided meditations can be used to impress one person's inner landscape upon another. It's useful for teaching purposes, but in some cases it can be limiting or even coercive. That said, guided meditation can be a simple stepping stone for a beginner because you can relax and let your imagination take the driver's seat. So, I'd like to teach you how to write your own guided meditation based on the classic Hero's Journey tale that repeats itself in many stories and myths throughout history. Read the questions below and write your answers down.

You are meditating in the ordinary world, but something calls you to take a journey to the astral plane. What is it?

You meet a guide who will take you on this journey. What does your guide look like?

You are crossing the threshold to a new world on the astral plane. What is this transition like?

You are given a gift. What is it?

You are returning back through the threshold to the ordinary world. How do you feel?

* Record yourself speaking a guided meditation aloud slowly. Try meditating while playing the recording back for yourself.

DAY 64
....

Creating Music

Creating music can also be a meditative act, entirely different from sitting and listening to music. In fact, some of your psychic impressions may come to you in the form of music or lyrics. When you create music, the sound can follow your mental state, speeding up when you feel energetic or in a trance and slowing down if you feel like you are relaxing into a deep but gentle meditation. If you play an instrument already, you can use your instrument of choice, but I don't suggest trying to practice a song you've already invented in case you get distracted trying to perfect it. Instead, during this meditation you will let your creative juices flow.

If you aren't a musician, using a drum or even a makeshift drum out of a box or a coffee can will work. Clapping hands and singing works very well, and both are used in shamanic practices the world over. Start soft and slow. If you choose to sing, I like to start just by humming. As you feel more comfortable and relaxed, you can get louder if you like and change the tempo or keep things the same as you feel appropriate. Allow yourself to be open to your intuition to direct the music.

When you are finished, ground yourself and be sure to write down any words that came to you as you were creating music. There may be psychic messages hidden in the words, or you might just be expressing your feelings at the time, another excellent use of your senses. If you know musical notation, you can jot down some notes or record it to help duplicate and study the song later. But remember that creativity is the meditative tool here.

* Create music during meditation and see how that affects your consciousness and your receptiveness to psychic sensations.

DAY 65
....

Creating Visual Art

For many people, psychic abilities are strongly tied to visions, and as you move forward into scrying divination, you'll be asking your mind to create psychic visions that you can see. Creating visual art during meditation is a good aid for your brain to start making representations of what you're sensing. For this meditation, you'll be creating freeform art in much the same way as you did during the music creation exercise, except that you will have a visual art representation afterwards to keep as a record.

Choose your art weapon. I like using watercolor paints when meditating because they're affordable and the flow is smooth onto paper, giving me a mellow meditation feel. I have also used colored pencils or a simple pen or pencil. If I feel compelled, I can move my hand without lifting it from the paper for continuous art creation. If you can get the same experience from a different art medium, you are welcome to do that as well.

As you ground yourself, close your eyes and allow yourself a couple of moments of quiet, receptive meditation before you begin. Then you can open your eyes and begin to create your art. If mental pictures come to you, depict them on the paper. If not, allow yourself to create art without an end picture in mind. You might be surprised at a hidden symbolic meaning that pops forth when your art is complete. When you are finished and grounded, jot down some words about your impressions. Don't forget to write the date on your work of art so that you have the option to compare it to later attempts.

* *Create a piece of visual art during meditation.*

DAY 66
....

Paying Attention to the Moon

The moon is tied to your psychic development. The full moon is often used by psychics as a time of heightened psychic activity. The waxing moon, too, can be used as a time to contemplate increasing psychic development or simply contemplating phases of growth in your life such as career and love potential. The waning moon is a good time to meditate about things that you'd like to decrease in your life, such as negativity or unhealthy habits. Some psychics use the dark moon as a resting time to focus on grounding. As you develop your psychic abilities, you might start to notice that your results depend upon the phases of the moon to some extent. For example, you may remember more dreams during the full moon.

Find out what the moon phase is right now. It might be as simple as looking outside, or you might wish to look at a lunar calendar or research the information online. You can even download an app for that. Find out when the next full moon will be and mark that on your calendar to remind yourself to work extra hard on your psychic development that day. I like to mark out the full moons for the entire year on my calendar along with the time the moon reaches its peak for optimum use in my psychic practice.

Finally, I'd just like you to remind yourself to notice the moon phases as you work with your psychic development. It may make the difference between being pleased or puzzled by seemingly random bursts in your psychic ability. In your psychic journal, write at the top of each page a blank like this: "Moon: _____." You can add the moon phase when jotting down observations or recording a dream.

* *Take time to record the moon phases in your psychic journal from now on.*

DAY 67

Meditating on Tarot Cards

We'll begin exploring divination tools in part 4, but tarot cards are one divination tool that can also be used for meditation and psychic development. The more that you contemplate some of the big and universal symbols that frequently appear in psychic visions and divination tools, the more easily you'll be able to make sense of the messages that come to you. Tarot cards are a deck of seventy-eight cards that are each full of rich symbolism. Getting a deck of tarot cards and meditating with them is sort of like using flash cards for your psychic skills. Today I'd like to teach you how to begin using them as a meditative aid.

When laid out in order, starting from the Fool card and ending with the World in the twenty-two major arcana and progressing through each of the suits in order, the tarot cards tell a story with the classic Hero's Journey themes. I suggest you progress through them in order. You can flip open your psychic log and write down one tarot card per day. Meditate upon the card and pick out all the visual symbols. Write down the associated meanings for you go, in much the same way that you did for individual dream symbols, but this time for the card as a whole.

If you don't yet have your own tarot deck, you can start today by looking up the images of some of the tarot's major arcana symbols like the Sun, Moon, Empress, Emperor, Death, Devil, or Lovers. You could also choose one of the four suits: pentacles, swords, cups, or wands. Make a note on your shopping list to get a deck of tarot cards of your own choosing as soon as you can. Tarot cards are a wonderful tool for psychic development.

* *Procure a deck of tarot cards and meditate on one card, recording the meanings that seem readily apparent to you.*

Day 68
. . . .

Automatic Writing

Automatic writing is a practice by which a psychic writes without thinking, allowing the psychic messages to come through. It is an excellent tool for spirit communication, in particular, because it allows for messages to come through unhindered, sometimes even in the handwriting of a deceased loved one. When used for spirit communication, automatic writing can be considered channelling, because the psychic acts directly as a conduit for the messages from the dead. The practice of automatic writing feels remarkably similar to the visual art exercise that you were given before.

You don't have to choose to try spirit communication for your first automatic writing session, but if you do, you should choose to invite a spirit of someone that you knew and trusted in life, and you should practice shielding before getting started, focusing on the intention that only the harmless spirit you want should make it through your shield, and any other mischievous spirits should be rebuffed. Don't forget to ground yourself before and after this, since the psychic activity can be intense for some people.

Keep your eyes open during automatic writing if you like. Just let the pen scribble on paper and don't censor as you write. You might have to make out some mighty sloppy handwriting when you're done, or you might be surprised with doodles or symbols. Take your time with automatic writing, because it can be a trance activity, and hopefully by now you've learned that achieving a trance state can take some time.

* *Try automatic writing.*

DAY 69
. . . .

Worry Dolls

Worry dolls are a fun dream tool you can purchase or make yourself. Originating in Guatemala, these dolls are supposed to aid sleep and happy dreams. They're usually only about as big as the tip of a thumb, and are made of mostly string. Worry dolls are usually used as charms. Tell them your worries and place them underneath your pillow. The dolls do the worrying for you as you sleep. Of course, in your psychic development, you learn that your dreams can also empower you with advice about your worries while you sleep, so your worry dolls can have an extra special purpose.

You can buy pre-made worry dolls, or make your own. I've made my own worry dolls from miniature wooden craft clothespins, cloth, and markers. You can even make some from fabric or paper in a pinch. Make several of them, because ideally you'll give each doll only one worry to mull over while you sleep. Prepare yourself to use the dolls in the same way that you prepared to ask yourself a dream question. Only this time, you don't have to keep obsessing over the question as you fall asleep. The dolls will do that for you.

When you wake up, write down any dreams you remember, even if they have nothing to do with your worries. Thank your dolls for the work they did as well. Write down your impressions about the process. You can store your dolls near your bed for quick access in the future. If your dolls begin to wear out, you can dispose of them through burial and make new ones as needed.

* *Create worry dolls and use them as a dream aid.*

Day 70

. . . .

Channelling

Your work with automatic writing can be your first foray into channelling, or being a conduit for spirit communication. Now you can layer some of the techniques that you've already practiced, using them to enhance your ability to channel spirit messages. Channelling is traditionally done in a trance state, and you can speak the words from the spirit instead of writing them down, if you wish, although that might make things harder to record. In my experience, the trance state make things harder to remember, or perhaps easier to forget, just as in a dream. So, if you'd like to try channelling messages verbally, I suggest grabbing a recording device or a partner who can watch you and take notes.

Before you get started, ground and shield yourself thoroughly. Call upon the spirit that you want to channel in your mind, and use the same focusing techniques that you used in order to call a spirit to you in your dreams. Engage in the trance inducing technique of your choice and then sit in quiet, receptive meditation. You can begin automatic writing, or you might begin channelling aloud.

After you are done, thank the spirit no matter what happened or did not happen. Ground yourself and check in with how you're feeling. Write down any impressions that you received, even if you didn't end up speaking them aloud or doing any automatic writing. Next time, you can try a different trance induction technique or a different spirit to see if you get better results.

* Try channelling a spirit by combining trance techniques with automatic writing or verbal channelling.

Day 71
....
Earth Meditation

Sometimes a meditative experience can be grounding rather than a head-in-the-clouds or trancelike experience. You've already practiced some forms of grounding, so here's another guided grounding meditation you can use to recharge. Don't worry if you fall asleep during this meditation. You can read it aloud to yourself in a recording or have somebody read it to you for best results.

Close your eyes and imagine you are at the mouth of a large cave that leads deep into the earth. As you enter the cave, it is dimly lit but comfortably warm. Walk down, deep into the cave. As you progress, you feel closer to the earth, like a small creature. Continue walking down, deep into the cave. The tunnel gets gradually smaller, allowing you to feel your way through the darkness. The walls and floor of the cave are quite smooth. Walk down, going deeper. Soon, the cavern becomes so small that you have to make yourself small and creep forward to continue. You can go no further, but curl up on a warm ledge that hugs your body. Feel the contact with the earth all around your body as you curl up in a fetal position. You might hear the humming of the earth or feel the buzzing energy. When you feel rejuvenated and rested, arise and walk back out of the dark cave toward the light. Open your eyes.

* *Try a grounding, relaxing, earth meditation.*

DAY 72
....

Dream Sachet

Creating a small charm to help enhance your psychic dreams is simple. Procure a small sachet or sew one out of cloth. The colors yellow or purple invite your intuition to take flight, so if you have a choice, they would make excellent colors for the small fabric bag. I've even used a paper envelope in the past to stand in for a bag. Fill the bag with good smelling herbs to enhance your dreams. Lavender is my favorite, chamomile is another good dream herb, and rosemary aids psychic visions and is one you might have lying around the kitchen. You can even throw in one of your worry dolls for good measure. Close the sachet.

You can charge your dream sachet with your intention by making it during the full moon and taking it into your meditation session with you. Focus on your hopes to increase your dreams and hold the sachet as you meditate. Use quiet, receptive meditation and pay attention to any messages you receive that might indicate a positive sign.

As you go to sleep, if you put a worry doll in your sachet, you can ask it your question and then place the sachet under your pillow or inside your pillowcase. Allow yourself to smell the herbs as you fall asleep. Lavender always gives me a peaceful and relaxed feeling and helps me fall asleep more quickly. Keep in mind that eventually the herbs will lose their freshness and you can burn or bury your sachet and create another one. Pleasant dreams!

* *Create an herbal sachet to help enhance your dreams.*

DAY 73
....

Dumb Feast

You've already learned the basic techniques for trance and channelling, so it's time to take things one step farther with your psychic development. Channelling is one form of possession, when a spirit is allowed to enjoy the use of a psychic's body in order to impart a message. Today, I'd like to share with you another simple technique for spirit communication that is suitable for beginners. A dumb feast is when a psychic shares a meal with ancestral spirits. During the dumb feast, a psychic might experience the presence of the spirits through psychic senses, or may even experience possession similar to channelling in which the living psychic eats food on behalf of the spirits. Traditionally, dumb feasts are performed near Halloween, but they can be done any time.

Choose the spirits you would like to invite to your dumb feast. I suggest that they be blood ancestors. Decide what meal you will serve. It should be one that they would have liked in life. If you know what your deceased Grandma's favorite dish is, for example, you can serve that. If you don't know, make a good guess based on the culture in which they lived. At the meal, portion out a small plate for yourself and an offering plate with a tiny sample of each food for the ancestors. Ground yourself, ask the spirits for their presence and then silently eat. As you slowly eat, if a trance state comes to you, allow yourself to sink into it. When you are done with the feast, sit in quiet and receptive meditation for a time. Record any messages that come through. Leave your offering outdoors. It's okay if wildlife eats the food, as they can be representatives for your ancestors.

* *Prepare and serve a dumb feast for your ancestral spirits.*

DAY 74

Dream Catcher

A dream catcher is an excellent charm to make to increase your positive dreams and decrease the negative ones. I've been making them since childhood, and I'll give you some simple instructions here. You'll need a few crafty supplies, but you can get as basic or interesting as you like. At the very least you'll need a very bendy stick or vine for the frame (a circular frame from a craft store works even better) and some string. You can embellish your dream catcher with beads, feathers, or other baubles. The idea is that any bad dreams will be distracted by beads and caught in the net, while good dreams will be filtered through and allowed to drip down into your mind.

Tie the stick or vine into a circular frame. You can soak it in hot water to make it more pliable. Next, take your string and loop it in loose loops all the way around the circle. Then, make another circle, this time looping through the loops you've already made instead of the frame. It should sort of look like you're building a spider web from the outside in. When you get to the center, secure it with a knot and add beads (representing bad dreams) if you like. You can add a hanging loop to the top and dangly decorations below. I like to include feathers I find outside. Meditate on your intention for the dream catcher as you make it. Hang it directly over your bed.

* *Create your own dream catcher.*

Part Three

*

Omens
and Signs

DAY 75
....

What Do You Want?

The first (often overlooked) step to receiving a psychic reading is to decide what it is that you want to hear. It's fun to practice psychic skills anytime, but when we have a true need for our psychic abilities, chances are there will be a specific outcome we have in mind. It's okay to want a specific answer from your psychic senses. In fact, it's bad to deny that you have a bias and then look for the answer you want. Instead, you can turn your desires into helpful energy by phrasing your inquiry properly.

For example, if you're out of work and struggling for money, chances are that in your frustration you'll be asking yourself, "When will I get a job?" Your overdue bills and ignored job applications are going to naturally prompt you to focus on a timeline. Rationally, though, you probably know that your job hunt success depends on choices that you make every day, or even every moment of every day. Therefore, it is more helpful for you to ask the question, "What can I do in order to get a suitable job most quickly?" You've gotten at what you truly want, which is an action you can perform so you won't feel so helpless. After all, even if you'd gotten the answer to your first question, there would be nothing more to do except to tentatively mark your calendar.

Likewise, if you are yearning for marriage and children, the question might pop into your head, "Will I get married?" Think about whether that answer is truly what you seek. An affirmative answer might make you smile, but nothing more. A negative answer would be devastating. Neither answer is empowering. Instead, you can decide carefully on your goal, whether it is marriage in the next year, marriage to a good match, or even marriage to a rich and stable spouse, and seek information that will be auspicious for your goal.

* *Write down a few life goals. Figure out good questions to ask your psychic self about those goals, ones that can give you answers that empower you to act.*

DAY 76

....

Best Times for Readings

You've already learned a bit about timing readings around the full moon for best results. Near Halloween and the first of May are also excellent times for psychic activity. We'll explore some other timing aspects later, but you might be wondering about reading frequency and when to apply your psychic senses to your life when facing a real problem. It is the old problem of crossing your fingers while waiting for the results of a contest to be announced. The winner may have already been picked, so does it help anything to use psychic abilities or to try to influence the outcome with your mind? Again, think carefully about how your psychic abilities empower the rest of your life, and save your effort for times when you can make a difference.

Frequency is another issue entirely. As a professional psychic, I have many repeat clients. Some come for readings only on their birthday and around the New Year. Some come in almost daily for specific issues. Pay attention to when you make a decision regarding your question. For example, I often have people ask when they can have a follow-up reading on a relationship issue. I tell them they can come back when one of them has made a choice that can significantly change the course of the relationship. Otherwise, the reading may be too similar to be productive or interesting.

A special case is the reading where grief issues may be apparent. If somebody has just died, you may want to wait until you are emotionally ready before performing psychic readings on that person's spirit. Remember that you are sensitive during this time, and any negative information, even if it is regarding some mistake you've made, might be emotionally devastating. It is better to give yourself some time and distance before addressing grief problems.

* *Think about a specific life topic such as love or money that you would probably want to ask about in your life more than once. Make a plan to address that issue a few times this year, on days that are especially good for psychic readings.*

DAY 77

Changing Your Destiny

Until now, we've explored some questions you might ask yourself while things are up in the air. Psychic ability is fun to use when you've got a fifty-fifty chance of success. However, your psychic skills can really shine in your life if you're looking at a situation you know is not turning out well. The process starts out by using common sense rather than psychic ability. The basic principles are the same that you have applied so far; you will need to find a way to ask empowering questions. This time, however, there may not be any easy answers. Those questions are still worth asking.

Choose an area of your life that isn't exactly shining at the moment. For example, as a new mom, my physical fitness was not doing so well, and as a young college student, I felt my love life was not heading in the right direction. Your life focus right now might be obvious to you and those around you, or it might be a focus to which your dreams and meditations have led you. Logically examine the situation from all angles. You might even want to brainstorm solutions on a piece of paper or by calling a friend for some outside perspective.

Next, take a look at the options before you to change your destiny. Think about the pros and cons of each, perhaps jotting them down in your journal as well. Choose one option to try for a specific amount of time, hopefully one that you can quit and try something new if you change your mind after that specified period of time. Ask your psychic self through one of the methods you've tried already how to best implement your choice to achieve your desired outcome while minimizing the negative effects you anticipate.

* *Choose an area of your life that isn't going well to work on. Find a*
  way to ask an empowering question of your psychic self in order to
  change that aspect of your life.

DAY 78

When the Universe Says No

We've all probably heard stories about a person cancelling a flight at the last minute because of a bad feeling and then later learning the plane was in a bad accident. I have plenty of stories about listening to my intuition. I knew somebody who decided to cancel a move to a different state based entirely off of a psychic reading. These leaps of faith are perhaps more startling than stories about trusting your instincts and going for something you want, like love at first sight. As you move forward in your psychic development, especially in the next part of the book where you will learn more about divination, you'll receive some definite negative answers. Now is a good time to start thinking about what to do.

You probably already know some bad omens. A bad feeling, butterflies in the stomach, or sickness might be an extension of your psychic senses. Popular lore says that breaking a mirror or having a black cat cross your path might portend bad luck. These might certainly be omens to some people to whom those symbols have negative meaning, and those omens can be heeded to good effect. Start thinking now about how much you trust your psychic senses and what consequences you are willing to endure in order to trust them. Next time you see a bad omen, it will be you who decides whether or not to draw the line.

* *Think about the last time you saw what you thought was a bad sign or had a negative feeling about something that seemed to come more from your psychic senses than your rational mind. What did you do about it? What was the result?*

DAY 79
. . . .

Looking for Opportunities

One of the best and most exciting uses for psychic abilities is to explore your options for the future. You've probably been drawn to psychic work because of the compelling way that psychic abilities tell your story. Through a dream, a sign, or a system of understanding, you begin to see how your destiny can play out. As you progress through the exercises, you will be guided away from the trap of thinking there is always only one possible outcome. I've shown you that the first thing you should do to create your own destiny is decide on your goals. The second thing you must do is discover the paths that lead to those goals.

Today, use your psychic intuition as a source of creativity and imagination. The depths of your psychic abilities for this purpose are far greater than a mere intellectual exercise. This is because your psychic abilities access your subconscious as well as possibly the collective subconscious of the human race. Choose an issue or situation in your life for which you would like to do a little problem solving. Instead of leaping immediately into brainstorming or writing a list of pros and cons for different options, decide on a psychic technique you'd like to use to discover your options. You can choose dreaming, meditation, automatic writing, or whatever you like. Just make sure that your query focuses on discovering options rather than choosing between them or making them happen. After you've performed the psychic technique you've chosen, write in your journal and do some intellectual brainstorming with the insights you received when you accomplished that state of mind.

* *Use your psychic abilities to discover opportunities that lie ahead.*

Day 80
....

Choosing Between Two People or Paths

It is common for people to consult psychic sources when choosing between several options. For example, I often have clients who need to choose between two different lovers, job offers, or possible homes to which they could move. In the next part, on divination, you will encounter tools that can help you with these questions. However, it just so happens that they can already be addressed by applying the basic skills you've learned already.

There are two different ways to confirm a choice between two different potentials. The first way is to use intuition to choose a path on its intrinsic worth; for example, asking any deities you worship or your dreams to indicate to you which one is the best for you. An omen or sign would point out one or the other, as clearly as if you were flipping a coin, but without much additional fanfare. Another option for psychic exploration is to pick one path and perform a psychic reading on just that option, taking a look at what life would be like if you made that choice. After exploring one or both options in this way with your psychic abilities, you would make a choice based on your intellectual analysis of your psychic experience.

Both methods have their merits. The first method is obviously quicker, while the second might require more than one intense session of dreaming, trance, or whatever specific psychic technique you wish to apply. However, the second method can feel more empowering, as you are allowing yourself the best opportunity for research and trusting your own judgement based upon your psychic abilities, rather than trusting the psychic impressions alone.

* *Think of a choice you must make between two options, and use your psychic abilities to come to a decision.*

An Identity

Another common question to ask of your psychic abilities is for the identity of a person—for example, a potential soul mate. The techniques in today's exercise can also be used to hone in on the identity of a place of employment or even a city or town. A mistake beginner psychics often make is to ask their divination tools, dreams, or subconscious in meditation simply to reveal the identity of a specific person. The psychic's abilities then respond by sending a hodgepodge of riddle-like symbols. A guitar? Does that mean he plays the guitar? What on earth does the number 3 mean? Is that his age? A date when I will meet him? The psychic messages provide more questions than answers.

This can be solved by getting more specific with your line of questioning, and later on you'll find out how to get more specific with your tools as well. For now, I suggest using your psychic abilities to discover the identity of a person you would like to meet. It could be the identity of a person who can help you network for a job opportunity, or just the identity of your next new friend. Next, decide on a specific sign you would like to experience to identify the person. Some suggestions: letters in the person's name, the first and last initials, hearing their name, the name in full, or see the person's face.

Then, choose the psychic technique of your choice and employ your question. Hopefully, you will experience a clear identifying symbol instead of other identifying factors that might be more confusing or difficult to interpret. In my experience, letters can sometimes get mixed up (especially in dreams) so if you have trouble reading a name, try asking for initials or to hear the name.

> * *Try to learn the identity of somebody that you have met or will meet, using your psychic abilities.*

Day 82
....

Timelines

Another popular question to want answered is the question of "when?" It's time to start looking at some theory behind determining timelines and especially for determining when to seek a timeline. Again, this is something that will be aided by several divination tools, but as a beginner you can get started already with some of the basics you'll need to use later on with divination.

First, let's recap some timeline questions that are not ideal for use with your psychic abilities. Refrain from asking questions like "When will I get married?" or "When will I get a new job?" You would do better to alter your question. After all, your choices every minute determine whether that day will be sooner or later, and the most important way psychics can move toward their goals is by creating their own destiny. Ask instead how you can achieve your goal as quickly as possible.

Appropriate timeline questions, on the other hand, are about lucky dates or times that can help you achieve goals you are working on anyway. For example: "What is the most auspicious wedding date for us to choose during June of next year?" Or, "Should I go back to school in the fall semester or in the spring to make academic success more likely?" As with the identity of a person, get specific by asking for seasons or specific numbers.

Since numbers can be easily mixed up, ask for one number at a time if you find yourself getting confused.

* *Use your psychic abilities to discover a lucky date for doing*
  something in your life.

DAY 83

Fixing Broken Questions

In Douglas Adams' *Hitchhikers Guide to the Galaxy*, a supercomputer called Deep Thought was asked the question, "What is the answer to life, the universe, and everything?" After churning and thinking for seven and a half million years, it came up with the answer "42." It turned out that the phrasing of the question was important when seeking an answer to the ultimate question! They discovered that they needed a question that would give the answer meaning.

So far in this part of the book, you've learned a lot about crafting questions. However, you will still make mistakes. It's important to know when your question is the problem and to be able to fix it. Here are some clues that your question is not working and some quick remedies.

Are you frightened by the answer you might get to your question? That's the biggest sign that your question is broken. You might need to wait until you are more emotionally ready to ask about that topic at all. It's also possible you have to rework your question so it isn't a final answer, but instead is a question about how you can improve the situation at hand or be happy with the situation as it is. Are the answers too vague? Try asking for specifics like letters, numbers, colors, or sounds. Do you keep getting an answer you don't like? That's not a problem with your question, but it does indicate that you should work on changing the outcome rather than applying more psychic readings right now.

* *Think about a time when you were not quite satisfied with an answer you received using your psychic abilities. Change the way you would ask that question.*

Day 84
....

Sign of the Day

Looking for omens is fun and can change the way you pay attention to the world around you. Try going for a walk in the morning and looking for a sign of the day. Ask your psychic self to help bring your awareness to something that will be a sign for you to signify the way your day is likely to proceed. After doing so, go for a walk. I enjoy doing this out in nature, but it could just as easily be performed on a busy city sidewalk. Allow your eye to be caught by something that will be your sign of the day. Perhaps it will be a particularly pretty autumn leaf, the fallen feather of a bird, or something else.

If you can take that sign with you, do so. Alternatively, you can sketch your sign of the day in your psychic journal. Use your symbolic interpretation skills to brainstorm a few potential symbolic meanings for the sign, as well as writing down your initial impressions of what it means and how you felt upon viewing the sign. At the end of the day, write again about the sign and how well you think it fit the outcome of your day. Looking for a sign of the day is a good way to flesh out your own personal symbol dictionary. Go for walks in diverse locations and chances are you will notice new things every day. Your guess as to what the symbol means can be crosschecked with how your day turned out before bedtime.

* *Go for a walk and look for a sign of the day.*

DAY 85
....

Asking for a Specific Sign

In Italian witchcraft, spells were often cast that included a closing asking for a sign such as the barking of a dog, or the croaking of a frog. If the designated sound was heard after the spell, it was confirmation that the spell was going to work effectively. Without asking for a sign, those sounds might have been interpreted differently or ignored.

You too can ask for a specific sign. This is a great alternative to time-frame readings. For example, don't ask, "When will I meet my next good love match?" Try asking instead, "Show me the following sign when I meet a good love match: _____." Fill in the blank with something you'll recognize. It could be the croak of a frog, the sound of your favorite love song, or the appearance of your favorite song bird. Whatever sign you choose, make sure that it is clear and concrete.

Today, you can try asking for a sign as the confirmation of a decision. "If I should _____, please show me the following sign: _____." Later, take a walk to look for the sign. Or you could engage in silent receptive meditation and wait. Choose the psychic technique that makes sense at the time. Make sure to record the results, whether positive or negative.

* *Ask for a specific sign to confirm a decision.*

DAY 86

....

Watching Candles for Signs

Candles are used by psychics as tools in many ways. Fire scrying, for example, is the practice of gazing into the flame in a state of trance or meditation to look for symbolic shapes in the dancing light. Allowing wax to drip into a bowl of water is another form of divination, one that yields wax droplets that form shapes which can then be interpreted as symbols. A more direct omen is to simply observe the way a candle burns. A flame that jumps high can be a good omen, while one that goes out before the wax has melted down may be a negative omen. A flame pointing in a specific direction may be meaningful if it points toward a person or place of significance.

Try watching a candle for omens. Light your candle while asking a question. For this first try, choose a question with a yes/no answer so you can watch for the most simple of omens. Allow the candle to burn down while you meditate, and record your observations in your psychic log. Later, find out whether your candle omen confirmed the answer to your question correctly. You can also branch out into the other forms of candle divination mentioned above if you'd like to experiment. Use your symbol journaling to add new symbols to your personal dictionary if needed.

* *Observe a candle for omens.*

DAY 87

....

Your Household Omens

If a broom falls over, company is coming. There are countless old wives' tales that have turned into household omens. However, it is more important at this point in your psychic development to start fleshing out your personal symbol dictionary than it is to fill up your head with folklore. Today's exercise will be a challenge, because it is easier to look for omens when out on a walk in nature than it is to see them in your own familiar environment. Every day, we acclimatize ourselves to our homes and the happenings within them. A psychic, however, should be able to notice a sign even if it occurs in a mundane context.

Some signs you may have already noticed subconsciously. You might be able to tell what sort of day you're going to have just by looking out the window in the morning. Or you might notice a certain way your pets behave before you get a visitor. If you're drawing blanks, try asking your psychic self for a sign of the day and then take a walk around your home and then sit in silent, receptive meditation. This exercise will hone your observation skills, since you may have learned to filter out noises and movement in your home that could be signs.

Write down some of your household omens in your journal as you discover them. This particular exercise is difficult, so you may need to repeat it over several days, but it will hone your observation skills. If you live with other people, you might ask them what sorts of signs they've noticed around your home as well.

* *Discover and document some omens within your own home.*

DAY 88

....

The Trouble with Numbers

You've learned a bit about asking for symbols like numbers to appear in your life observations, dreams, or visions. By now you may have run into the problem of numbers appearing scrambled up. This can happen a lot when asking for a date or for an amount of money. (Obviously, you're not going to be guessing the winning lottery numbers any time soon!) There are limits to psychic abilities. However, your problems with numbers might be fixed by conceptualizing them in a different way. Divination techniques in the next part of the book will also make things seem a lot clearer.

For now, it's time to start thinking of other ways that you can visualize the numbers, other than simply the numbers that you see on the printed page. For example, when asking your psychic self for an amount of money, you could visualize it as a stack of dollar bills instead of a number behind a dollar sign. Dates can be visualized on calendars. Age can be shown by the physical characteristics of a person or a building. A time in history can be surrounded with symbols of what surrounded you at that time. Think of how fundraising is often represented using a poster with a thermometer. You can do the same when asking your psychic self about numbers that indicate time or money. Experiment with asking for numbers in a new way, and see if your answers become more clear or relevant.

* *Find new ways that numbers and amounts can be represented as a psychic symbol.*

DAY 89

....

Déjà Vu

Déjà vu is the experience of feeling like you have lived something before. It can be a purely neurological phenomenon based off of your memories. If you have ever felt like you've lived the exact same few seconds before, that's true déjà vu. For the purposes of psychic ability, however, déjà vu can be expanded to cover more experiences. A psychic sense of déjà vu might occur when you feel like you have met somebody before, even though you are meeting for the first time. It can also happen when you witness a very rare circumstance happen twice, for example, seeing two different red boats during the same day, once in a painting and once being pulled behind a truck on the freeway.

So, what does déjà vu mean to the psychic? I believe déjà vu is the subconscious—the source of psychic information—saying, "Hey, pay attention!" It produces the same feeling as when angel numbers crop up repeatedly in one day. When you experience déjà vu, it's time to stop and use your observational skills. Are there any signs about? Is the déjà vu centered on a symbol, as in the red boat example above, or is it just a strange feeling that you've experienced things before? Are your psychic abilities trying to tell you that a person or a place is significant to you? You can use the psychic techniques you have learned so far to ask yourself what the meaning of your déjà vu experience might be.

* *Have you experienced déjà vu? If so, write down the circumstances surrounding that feeling. If not, ask for a déjà vu sign and wait for it to occur.*

Day 90
....

The Flight of Birds

Ornithomancy is the practice of watching for omens in the flight of birds. This is a practice that skirts the line between watching for omens and divination. You will find that the more you learn about how birds can be understood as signs, the more you will build a system of psychic understanding. This is one way that you can develop your psychic abilities through frequent practice. Traditionally, ornithomancy is practiced by listening for specific bird calls, which may become meaningful when you ask for a sign and when you begin to associate your local birds with seasons and emotions.

Today, I'd like you to perform a simple version of ornithomancy, using the flight of birds. You'll need to find a place where birds congregate. The easiest way is to ask a yes/no question, relax your gaze, and wait for a bird to cross your field of vision either from right to left or from left to right. The former is a positive omen, while the latter is an answer to the negative. You can add in the mannerisms of the birds to add emphasis to your interpretation. For example, a quickly flying bird might symbolize quick success at your goal, while one that has many stops and starts in its path of travel could represent a similar journey metaphorically.

* *Try practicing simple ornithomancy.*

Holey Stones

By now, as a psychic, you might be feeling a little bit overloaded with omens. If anything can be an omen, how do you tell the difference between what is an omen and what is not? For some people with natural psychic ability, your observations and visions might be actually scary. You can tone down your psychic senses through grounding as needed, but what if you want to turn them back on without feeling that sense of being surrounded by a cacophony of meaningful signs? One tool that you can use is a holey stone. It is very similar to the seer stone we used for practice viewing on Day 7, but instead of expanding our psychic reception, the holey stone is used to confine the sighting of omens to only those seen within it.

A holey stone is traditionally a stone with a natural hole in it. This can happen around rivers, or but it can also be a piece of coral rather than a stone. The use of holey stones has plenty of tradition behind it, but others have used knot holes in wood or other things as peepholes. The idea is to tell the psychic part of your mind to limit your psychic visions to a very small frame of reference. That way, you can focus only on omens that you see through the hole and not on anything external.

Find or make a peephole to be your holey stone. Take it for a test drive by looking for a sign of the day through it. Try out some ornithomancy by using your holy stone as your field of vision so that the birds can cross it more quickly and thus give you the divinatory messages faster. Make a sketch of something meaningful that you see through your holey stone.

* Find and use a holey stone to focus and train your psychic observation.

DAY 92

....

Dealing with Bad Omens

We've already explored how you should approach a situation in which the answer to your psychic inquiry is no. But, sometimes omens that seem negative come forth unbidden. You might not even be asking a question when you accidentally drop and break a hand mirror or spill a shaker of salt, and yet those are commonly seen as bad omens. You can't call in sick to work every day you see a black cat cross your path, so you'll have to learn how to deal with bad omens as they arise. Remember, you are in charge of your own destiny.

Start by exploring the omen's significance further; it could be that you are misinterpreting it. After all, black cats aren't bad luck to everybody, especially those who love them as pets. Set aside some meditation time to receive psychic insight about the omen. Start by asking how to prevent any negativity foretold by the omen. You can choose a psychic technique to gain answers. You might find that the solution is as simple as avoiding something or someone for a time. Once you receive your answer, proceed cautiously with your day, paying attention to how other people and environments affect you. Make sure to journal your results, especially if you did notice any misfortune, so you can better respond to such an omen in the future.

* *Think about a bad omen you have seen in the past. What specific misfortune, if any, befell you after seeing that omen? What would you do in the future to heed the warning of the omen?*

DAY 93

Flower Petal Picking

This simple form of divination is one that we may all have tried at some point during childhood. Even though I was never a boy-crazy girl, I still remember picking flowers and pulling petals one by one, offering "he loves me" and "he loves me not" with each petal until I reached the last one. Though this game can be predictable if you know whether the number of petals is odd or even, you can push yourself to use it as a divinatory tool, even if you allow for the idea that your subconscious self is the one calling the shots.

Your inquiry of the flower doesn't have to be about love. You can answer any yes/no questions by picking petals and alternating the words. You can even use flower petal picking to choose between two paths or people. For those who find divination intimidating or complicated, going back to this childhood game can be a pleasant and clever trick for evaluating how your psychic ability has grown with you over time. Best of all, you can use the time plucking petals as a meditative time, especially if you choose a blossom with many petals.

Pay attention to the emotions you feel while you undertake this activity. You might sense impressions about your answer before you see the visible evidence from your flower divination tool. When you are done, write down the results in your psychic journal. Ideally, you'll be able to do this practice with a fresh flower from outside that is in season, but do what you can with the weather conditions you have.

* *Try picking flower petals and tap into some childhood memories as you practice simple divination.*

DAY 94
....

Wishbones

Here's another childhood divination technique that can be embellished for psychic use. Typically, the wishbone of a turkey, chicken, or other bird is broken by two people, one person holding each end wishbone. However, it can also be done by one person, especially if done on behalf of a spirit that can no longer participate in the family ritual. The term *bonfire* comes from "bone fire," and the broken wishbones can be burned in a fire while watching for omens, just as you did with a candle. Wishbone breaking is a childhood tradition worth rekindling.

Collect and dry wishbones before breaking them. I'm vegetarian, but my husband is not, so I have him save the bones from the roast chicken lunches he sometimes has at work. I save them for a special occasion. If I have a wish, I set my intention and break the wishbone by myself or with another person. Then, I burn it in a fire and watch for any omens. You can try this yourself or just start making arrangements to collect the wishbones. Wishbones can be an excellent offering to ancestral spirits if you want to contact them with your psychic abilities.

* *Begin collecting wishbones to do some psychic divination about your own wishes, or to use as an offering to spirits.*

DAY 95
....

Skipping Stones

A well-known verse in the Rede of the Wiccae written by Lady Gwen Thompson reads, "Where the rippling waters go, cast a stone and truth you'll know." Likewise, in Charles Leland's *Aradia: Gospel of the Witches*, a witch is compelled to go to the middle of a stream at noon to conjure truth about the future. There's something special about the practice of skipping stones, and the practice can be both meditative and full of omens.

Skipping stones is a skill, but one that's fun to develop. Skipping stones can be done at a creek, river, lake, retaining pond, or any available body of water. Choose stones that are flat and smooth, though it may take some practice to find out what size and weight work best for you. Toss them askance at the surface of the water to try to skip them, adding speed and spin so that the rock bounces across the thick surface tension. You can ask a question to which you'd like a truthful answer before skipping rocks. As you skip a rock and ask away, notice whether you are more or less successful at your skipping when you ask about a particular topic. Take note about how large or small a splash it makes, and think about how the sign applies to your question. A big splash might be a good sign if you're trying to "make waves" in the office with an important speech, but it might not be a great sign when trying to blend in with friends.

If you skip stones long enough, you might receive messages as if you are in a trance state, so be aware of any feelings or other psychic sensations you get. Write down your impressions before you end your session. You might find that meditating by a body of water is a peaceful activity that becomes addictive.

* *Skip stones to seek a psychic answer to a question.*

Day 96
. . . .
Cloud Gazing

This skill is definitely one you will use later on with other forms of divination. In scrying, a tool such as a fluid, tea leaves, or fire is usually used to look for shapes that can be symbols. The way you see these shapes is exactly the same way you see shapes when looking at clouds in the sky. And the more you hone your ability to quickly pick out shapes in the clouds as they move across the sky, the better you will perform as a psychic when you pick up different scrying tools. Start now.

Grab a sketch book and go outside to find some clouds. This can even be done while looking at an overcast sky by looking at the lumpy bottoms of the merged clouds, but of course the ideal clouds would be the white and fluffy cumulous clouds. To open up your psychic potential, ground yourself first, and consider starting with a session of meditation or trance induction. Then, take a look at the clouds and write down or sketch the first thing that comes to mind. Depending on the weather, the clouds may change quickly, so don't delay your recording of data. It's okay if one symbol changes into another symbol. The transition of one thing to another might have meaning as well, for example a heart breaking or a cloud shaped like an arrow hitting another cloud.

* *Scry using clouds in the sky.*

Day 97
....

Easy Haruspicy for the Squeamish

Delving into the history of psychic development, an ancient form of searching for omens was haruspicy—searching for omens in the entrails of dead animals. I'm not going to ask you to become your own butcher, unless that's your thing. However, you can perform haruspicy with a raw egg. If you're vegan and don't want to use an egg, you can even perform haruspicy with the bugs on the windshield of a bus or car that have already accidentally sacrificed themselves to the cause.

Haruspicy differs from scrying because it has specific traditional signs to observe. Bloodiness is a negative sign, while clear shapes and edges to what you see are good signs. Colors that are uniform and bright are considered a good sign, as are clear bits. Anything that is very unusual or unnatural is a very bad sign, so haruspicy becomes advanced when practitioners become very familiar with their subject.

More complicated haruspicy can be done, but this simpler practice will introduce you to this unique way of seeking omens, and also to the concept of giving a sacrifice in order to gain psychic power. To a lesser extent, you must give a part of yourself—be it time or effort in study—to develop your psychic abilities.

* *Try out some simplified haruspicy.*

DAY 98

. . . .

The First Star You See

Have you ever wondered why legend says that the first star seen in an evening can grant a wish? I have two theories. Firstly, the act of wishing is very strongly tied to psychic ability. It is your intention, when applied to your developing psychic talent that sees opportunities and likelihoods. It is what attracts you to the future that you seek. Secondly, the powers of observation that exist in the moment, such as when seeing the first star in the sky and feel the accompanying hope, stimulate your psychic senses.

So tonight I would like you to renew this tradition by combining some of the skills that you've developed so far. Think ahead of time of a wish you'd like to make. Decide upon your goal and choose the best path toward that goal, and wish for that path to be made more likely. Then, wait up as dusk falls and allow yourself to sink into a quiet, receptive meditation as you wait for the first star to appear. When it does, focus your intent above all else. Practice driving other thoughts from your mind. It's not enough to speak your wish in the classic rhyme, "I wish I may, I wish I might, have this wish I wish tonight." Then, record your perceptions about your wish. Later, pay special attention to your dreams for omens about how your future regarding this wish will play out.

* *Wish upon a star.*

DAY 99

············

Appearance of the Moon

The dark phase of the moon is traditionally a period of rest and renewal for psychics. It's not that it is bad to perform psychic readings during the dark moon, however it is not known for its psychic properties. Thus, some psychics choose to avoid reading during the dark moon. The appearance of the waxing crescent, therefore, is a special time for psychics. The first sight of the waxing crescent moon is associated with psychic development and the slow but steady growth of abilities. Living where I do, in the Pacific Northwest, the appearance of the waxing crescent moon isn't as predictable as the calendar claims. After all, I often have to wait a few extra calendar days for the cloud cover to clear before I actually see the moon phase affecting my psychic abilities. Seeing that moon is therefore worth celebrating.

Cuing your subconscious that there's psychic work to be done can enhance your psychic abilities and your motivation. Here's an activity you can do with a candle, bowl of water, and a small dark cloth. Fill the bowl with water, set the candle in the middle, and cover the whole apparatus with the dark cloth during the dark moon to signify the time of rest. Every night, check outside for visible confirmation of the waxing moon. When you see it, uncover your bowl and light the candle. Look for candle omens and, if you choose, drip a bit of the wax in the water to look for a sign forming a shape. In the next part of the book, you will learn about water scrying as well, which can be performed when you repeat this exercise at another dark moon.

* *Mark the date of the dark moon on your calendar, and prepare to welcome the waxing crescent moon with a small celebration afterwards.*

Day 100

·············

Shooting Stars

Shooting stars are another event that allows you to combine psychic observation of omens with your skills of asking the right questions. Therefore, there are two ways you can use shooting stars. You can wait until you see a shooting star, make a careful wish of intention for the future and then wait for an omen. Alternatively, you can meditate on a question while looking at the night sky and wait for a shooting star as your omen. There are other omens to view as well, such as the flight of owls or bats. Or they can be the sounds of the night, like the croak of a frog or the barking of a dog.

The ideal time to use shooting stars to confirm the answers to questions, of course, is to wait for a meteor shower. During a meteor shower, you might see several shooting stars in a minute. Your psychic questions can be just as rapid fire, and you can watch the character of the shooting star to analyze your omen. Does it seem to fizzle out quickly as it drops like a stone across your field of vision, or is it a magnificent arc from one side of the sky to the other? You can apply this metaphorically to answer your question. If your question goes unanswered for several minutes during a meteor shower, that too is an omen. The lack of an answer can be just as meaningful as a negative sign.

* Look up when meteor showers will occur in the coming year, and mark those dates on your calendar so you can sit and observe them.

DAY 101
·············

Good Luck Charm

Just as making smart wishes is one way that a psychic can create his or her own destiny, a psychic can also work hard to obtain good luck. What is good luck? There are so many different ways you can go in life, but all your choices must be contained within the framework of your destiny. Good luck is living a life that goes with the current of your destiny and helps you follow your bliss. One reason we ask our psychic senses to tell us which path to choose is so that the "lucky" path will become more apparent. Finding a good luck charm is one way to enhance your psychic senses when it comes to picking the luckiest outcome.

Traditionally, a four-leaf clover is lucky because it is associated with faeries and other elementals. In many cultures, such beings are tricksters, and to find a four-leaf clover is an indication that you are in their favor. It is lucky, indeed, if the fairies aren't targeting you for their mischief. If you are in the right location and season, spend some time in meditation outside where clovers grow, fingering through the leaves to find the fourth one on a stem. If this is impractical where you live, try finding a lucky penny, another charm of good fortune. I carry a lucky charm with me when I go to do readings for others, slipped into the velvet bag that holds my tarot cards or pendulum.

    * *Find a lucky charm to keep with you when you do psychic work.*

DAY 102
....

Weather Watching

The sky is a capricious thing, perhaps controlled by those same tricky elementals that play games with our fates. Before we had computer models to help predict the weather, people had to use their intuition and observations to figure out what the weather was going to do. Weather was tied to the success or failure of raising crops and livestock and by extension, connected to the well-being of the people. For example, think about the common adage, "Red sky at night, sailors' delight. Red sky at morning, sailors take warning." The observation was meant to predict storms. A ring around the moon was said to predict snow. Today we can appreciate the joy or dismay they must have experienced when viewing the omen.

    View a sunrise, sunset, or both and make notes about your impressions. What does the weather seem to be saying to you? Dig deep to pay attention to your intuitive ideas about the weather as well. Predicting the weather in the atmosphere or the weather in your life energies is more than a science. It requires experience seeing the systems at work and observing how they play out. You probably have more experience doing so than you know and must merely learn to trust.

* Observe the weather and intuitively predict how it will turn out for the day. How does this metaphorically compare with predicting the outcome of a given day in your life?

Day 103
....

Birthday Lore

In some ancient cultures, an astrologer was an important person to have on hand in the event of a birth, especially for the wealthy and powerful. Even now, plenty of lore surrounds birthdays. On birthdays, you can make a wish for your destiny. A birth date is considered to be a lucky number, which is why so many people use birth dates when they play the lottery. A common poem gives insight as to how the day of the week might affect personality, just as the day of the month affects personality in Western astrology and the year affects personality in Chinese astrology. The poem goes something like this:

Monday's child is fair of face
Tuesday's child is full of grace
Wednesday's child is full of woe
Thursday's child has far to go
Friday's child is loving and giving
Saturday's child works hard for a living
But the child born on the sabbath day
Is bonnie and blithe and good and gay.

* *Figure out the day of the week that you were born. Does your personality fit the lore? How well does your personality suit your star sign or your Chinese astrology animal?*

DAY 104
. . . .

13

As I write this, it is Friday the thirteenth in the year 2013. The number thirteen is often thought to be unlucky and associated with the occult. Witches' covens number thirteen at a maximum and ideal number. As a result, some people fear the number thirteen. When visiting casinos in Nevada, I was surprised when I found out that some of the hotels there don't even label the thirteenth floor, instead jumping straight to fourteen where the thirteenth floor should be. Some of the fear of unlucky thirteen somehow bleeds over to the number three, which is why that floor is chosen as the restaurant or lobby in many casino hotels for guests who don't want to try their luck by staying on such a floor.

The number thirteen can't be entirely avoided, and it simply isn't true that it is bad luck. However, it can be a good way for your subconscious to get your attention, especially if you do have some curiosity or a little fear about the number thirteen. Today, hone your observational skills and look for things that contain or involve the number thirteen. Banish any fear from your mind, and instead use the appearance of the number thirteen as an excuse to be mindful.

* *How often does the number thirteen sneak into your day with no ill effects?*

DAY 105

....

Self-fulfilling Prophecies

I've focused a lot in this chapter on making wishes to create your own destiny. However, the other side of the coin is that you can inadvertently create a negative destiny for yourself. Of course, nobody wishes for things to turn out poorly. Nevertheless, there are ways people can set their course for destruction. Firstly, one can misinterpret omens as negative. Secondly, one can see a valid negative omen but refuse to take evasive action.

This can happen in mundane ways. For example, have you ever found a skill you thought you could never master? Perhaps it involved a struggle with math or sports or creative arts. If you were to set your mind to that thought, every instance of failure while working on that skill would seem like an omen of confirmation. Even though you can improve on any one of those skills with hard work, you will provide your own limitation until you choose to overcome it. Likewise, some of your most illuminating psychic work will involve overcoming your own psychological barriers to your true destiny. Your confidence will lead to the satisfaction of helping yourself, and others, with your psychic readings. Today's meditation should be on your own self-fulfilling prophecies, and whether you wish to continue those limitations.

* *Choose one self-fulfilling prophecy in your life you will resolve to overcome.*

DAY 106
. . . .

Wishing Well

Today's meditative act will be to cast a coin into a wishing well. Notice how three symbolic psychic acts are combined in the lore of a wishing well. First, you must find the coin to be cast, which is the good luck charm. Second, you must make a wish using your positive intention that you use when asking questions. Third, you must cast the coin into the water, much in the same way as you did with skipping stones, while remaining alert for omens.

Take care not to toss pennies or other coins into natural bodies of water like lakes and streams, as they can affect the wildlife in that ecosystem. Instead, go to an indoor or premade wishing well structure where coin tossing is encouraged. I have seen some fountains in malls, amusement parks, and zoos where the coins tossed in are regularly collected and donated to charitable causes. Who knows, you might end up granting somebody else's wish as well. In a pinch, you can toss your own lucky charm into a bowl of water and meditate over that.

* *Make a wish by tossing a lucky coin into a wishing well and meditating on the outcome.*

DAY 107
. . . .

The Evil Eye

Have you ever been so angry at someone that you glared at him or her very hard? So hard that perhaps you gave yourself a headache? At that moment, you were giving that person the evil eye. If your victim noticed you, it could have been seen as a bad omen. It is possible to ward off some bad omens, and this is especially true when the omen represents external malice from other people who might wish you harm. Crossing fingers is thought to ward off the evil eye, for example. Today you can make a charm to dispel this bad omen. This charm would be a great tool for a developing psychic to carry around.

Several semi-precious gemstones, notably tiger's eye, are used for warding off the evil eye, but you can make a charm against the evil eye with a found stone and some paint. In the Middle East, you can find glass charms against the evil eye called nazars, which look like a white and blue eyeball on a blue background. You can replicate that by painting a rock blue and adding a white eyeball with a black pupil. This paper weight can be used to ward against the evil eye. I've also made a makeshift version of this by choosing a white rock and coloring the back of it with blue permanent ink, adding a black ink pupil.

* Ready yourself with simple defenses against the evil eye. A charm, crossing fingers, and your shielding practice are all effective.

DAY 108
....

Lucky Bugs, Insects, or Arachnids

We don't even notice how many tiny critters are around us every day. Some of this is probably deliberate on our part. As it happens, though, these creatures can be omens, many of them portending good luck. Crickets are good luck omens, so the sound of a cricket can be asked for as a sign. In China, crickets were kept in cages for their beautiful and lucky singing. If you live in an area where crickets are abundant this season, consider asking them to chirp for you as an omen to the answer of a question.

Another excellent sign of good luck is the ladybug. Ladybugs are beneficial consumers of plant-destroying aphids, and you can even purchase the bugs as a natural means of pest control. Seeing a ladybug is an excellent omen.

I know a lot more people who fear spiders than ladybugs, but did you know that they too are good omens in the home? While cobwebs should be swept up, an active web maintained by a spider is a sign of psychic protection in your house. Whenever possible, these creatures that are good omens should only be gently excluded from a home and not killed.

* Keep your eyes out today for bugs that are good omens. Record your sightings.

DAY 109

Try Again Later:
The Right Time for a Reading

I remember playing with a Magic 8 Ball as a child. The toy gave several affirmative and negative answers, but the most infuriating message you could get was "Try again later." What was a frustrated child to do? I never knew whether to wait five minutes, an hour, or a day! As a more careful adult, I now wish that every divination tool had a built in measure to verify whether or not it was a good time for a reading. Ideally, you'll be able to do some of the determination. Are you feeling cranky, drained of energy, and unable to ground? Are you grief-stricken or too devastated from a recent breakup to be able to perform an *unbiased* psychic reading? Simply using your intuition can work as well to determine whether the timing is right.

Today, before you try your meditative practice, begin by meditating about whether the time is good for psychic trance work or something more, or whether it's best to only do the amount of meditation that keeps up your stamina for concentration and nothing more. It may seem like overkill to meditate about meditation, but take it as a sign that you're beginning to get into the realm of advanced practice.

* *Choose a practice to do before a reading in order to determine whether or not the reading should be performed at this time.*

DAY 110
....

Astrological Observations

Hopefully, you've been continuing to note the moon's phases in your psychic journal to see how they affect your psychic practice. Consulting an astrological calendar is also a good idea, as you can see how other astrological events affect your life and your psychic practice. Astrology calendars come in all forms: wall calendars, spiral bound datebooks, pocket calendars, and even smartphone apps. Choose one you can integrate with your lifestyle in a way that your eyes will come across it each day.

At first the symbols and degree numbers may seem confusing, so for now I'd like you to just be mindful of patterns. Don't get too tangled in the planetary aspects or asteroid movements. Instead, notice how the sun signs change month to month as the sun moves into a new astrological sign. You can make a note in your psychic journal saying "Sun in: _____" to make sure you remember what sign to record. As the sun transitions through the signs, you may notice different issues in your life taking the forefront over time.

* *Begin observing how astrology affects your life by noticing in what sign the sun is traveling during your psychic journaling.*

DAY 111
....

Reading Body Language

We all know that body language is a huge part of communication. Body language has a deeper symbolic meaning as well. As a psychic, you can observe your own body language, the body language of people you're reading, and even the body language of people you only meet in visions and dreams to receive meaningful messages. For today's exercise, you may want to make a sketch of your own body position or the body position of a person you saw that caught your attention, especially if it was a spirit or person in a dream.

Notice any overt body language first. Is the person standing like Superman, or is the body more closed and passive? Are there signs of aggression or desire in the body language? Next, consider the body as symbolically divided into three components. The legs and hips represent a message about the physical realm, the torso and arms represent the emotional realm, and the head and face represent a spiritual message. Are there any further messages you can divine from the motion of the feet, hands, and eyes when the body is interpreted in this way?

* *Use the human form for simple divination.*

Part Four

Part Four

Divination

Day 112

....

Yes/No Stones

Remember when I told you about how the Magic 8 Ball sometimes tells you when *not* to do divination? Remember how I had wished that every divination tool had that feature? Well, guess what? Today you'll discover a way to add this feature to any other divination tool or method. Get a small bag and two stones. On one stone write the word "yes" with permanent ink and on the other write "no." Now, instead of meditating for a while on whether or not you should perform divination, you can simply reach into the bag and draw a stone. In addition, your bag with two stones can be used to answer simple questions that only need an affirmative or negative answer.

Why did I ask you to meditate on divination first, and offer this tool later? I think meditating about divination is a good idea; there's value in contemplation that involves actively processing a question and your readiness for the answer.

I hope that the simplicity of this tool will impress upon you the importance of using your developing psychic skills such as grounding and concentration when performing divination no matter what. A tool does not excuse you from using your psychic skills.

* *Create a simple "yes/no" divination system using two stones and a bag.*

Day 113

. . . .

Fire Scrying

Let's start working on scrying by using a tool you've already used when looking for candle omens—fire. Fire scrying, however, is usually best done over a proper fire, using wood. The reason for this is because you get an extra tool when the coals become red hot. Pull back the burning logs to reveal brightly glowing embers. The streams of light flickering across those coals are called salamanders, and they can be watched as intently as the flames. Look for shapes that have meaning.

If you can't build a large fire, a candle will do, but try to focus on the flame rather than the specific candle omens described on Day 86. Meditating on the candle flame following a trance induction can allow you to see shapes and perhaps pictures near the base and the tip of the flame of your candle. Make sure your candle is in a very safe container, since trance states can often inadvertently transition to sleep.

* *Practice some fire scrying.*

Day 114

. . . .

Water Scrying

As you might imagine, water scrying feels very different from fire scrying. The element of water is a calming influence, and you may find that you have to induce a trance using a rigorous method before you're able to see any visions while water scrying. Also, since you will be gazing at the surface of water as a focal point, there will be no easily shifting light to form a shape for your imagination. Instead, you'll have to rely on your trance state a little more so you can almost dream what you see.

Fill a dark bowl with water to the brim. You may have to experiment with lighting and with your angle of seating as you sit in meditation. I prefer dim lighting in the room and I like to sit myself looking almost directly down into the bowl, however some people have more success if they gaze across the top of the water. Give yourself time for water scrying. It requires simple tools, but you'll have to combine those basic psychic skills well to achieve success. If you have a tough time today, try again during the next full moon. Some people also try scrying in a bowl of milk during the full moon with greater success.

* *Attempt water scrying.*

DAY 115

Smoke Scrying

Smoke scrying combines two elements, those symbolic building blocks of the universe, air and fire, and thus it can be just as invigorating as fire scrying with the added symbolic bonus to your intuition from the element of air. I recommend creating smoke by burning incense. Since you'll be getting up close and personal with this incense for a while, choosing one you enjoy and that doesn't irritate your lungs or eyes will be more important than anything else. However, I recommend sage for cleansing and banishing, and Frankincense for inviting blessings. Any sort of incense burner will work, though I prefer a charcoal burner for maximum smoke. Also be sure to have your psychic journal nearby; shapes seen in smoke are usually very fleeting, so recording them right away is a good habit to get into.

Light the incense before doing your normal preparations such as grounding and any initial meditation or trance induction you feel you need at this stage. The burning incense will help get you into the right headspace and relax you while you prepare. Then, open your eyes and look to the swirling smoke. Notice how the smoke looks different closer to the source of the burning than it does as it wafts up toward the ceiling or the night's sky.

* *Attempt smoke scrying with incense.*

DAY 116
....

Tea Leaf Reading

Tea leaf reading is one of my most favorite methods of divination because the whole process is a ritual. Ideally, you will need the following: a round-bottomed cup (as close to round as possible on the inside), a saucer or plate, and a loose-leaf tea with fairly small leaves. Heat the water and steep the leaves free-floating in your cup without restricting their movement. Contemplate your question as the tea steeps. Then, sip your tea carefully, trying not to ingest the leaves. Meditate on your question and nothing else.

When you are done, leave a tiny amount of water in the bottom of your cup with the leaves. Swirl the cup around clockwise three times and then overturn it onto the saucer or plate. This maneuver will take some practice, but should result in some leaves spread across the bottom and sides of the cup. The shapes you see in the leaves at the bottom represent the past, the present, and personality characteristics. Those on the sides represent the future, and nearest the rim are outcome and destiny. Consider taking a picture of your tea leaves as they are in the cup. The best part about tea leaf reading is that this form of scrying can be shown to others to compare and ask questions. What shapes do your friends and family see in your cup?

* *Try a tea leaf reading.*

DAY 117

Crystal Ball Reading

I love crystal ball reading so much that I've included it here even though I know not everyone has access to a real quartz crystal sphere. For what it's worth, I've been able to take free "test drives" with many crystal balls in gem shops and metaphysical bookstores without having to buying them. I've done this a lot and have never been kicked out once. When and if you do purchase one, you don't have to spend a lot of money. It doesn't matter whether your crystal ball is large or a tiny crystal in a pendant. What matters is that the ball is mostly clear and not too cloudy, but with many small inclusions. Inclusions are the small, iridescent defects naturally present in the crystal. Watch those little shapes that glisten and shift as you turn the ball. Decide what they are shaped like, just as you would if you were watching clouds in the sky. In fact, the process will feel a lot like tea leaf reading.

As a focal point for meditation purposes, you can use any sphere (even one of glass) or an unusual gemstone. Other materials are not quite the same as crystal ball reading, but you may have some psychic insight that comes to you gently through such focused meditation. Your method will be different, however, and the process will feel more akin to water scrying than to tea leaf reading.

* *Try crystal ball reading.*

Day 118
....

Bibliomancy

Here's a divination method that doesn't require you to run out and gather or purchase materials. All you need is a book, and you can use this one if you want; all your materials are right here. In bibliomancy, a randomly selected page and passage is analyzed for deeper metaphorical meaning on a topic selected beforehand. The best books for this are randomly selected off shelves or those that have highly meaningful scripture or other symbolic spiritual content.

Since this is another simple technique, remember to focus on the process rather than the technique itself. Take care to ground yourself, induce a trance for the page selection process, and point your finger to the line you feel most drawn to. Read the phrase aloud and write it down in your psychic journal. Sometimes the verbal associations or intuitive thoughts that occur to you when you are writing will be deeper and different than your first impressions when your eyes scan the page. At any rate, record first impressions as well as any other analysis that comes later. Both interpretations may be meaningful for this intellectual and spiritual practice.

* *Try out bibliomancy.*

Day 119
. . . .

Pendulum Dowsing

Though pendulum dowsing is simple, it is still my go-to method for certain questions. Today, I'll lead you through the initial process of making and calibrating a pendulum for yes and no answers, but a pendulum can also be used over a map, book, or chart, for more detailed answers. Pendulums are plumb-bobs that hang from a string or a chain. You can purchase them or make your own. A simple pendulum can be assembled from a necklace chain and a ring.

To use your pendulum, pinch the chain or string between your thumb and forefinger. Then, loop the string or chain over your pinkie finger so that the pendulum dangles freely off of it. This should allow it to swing back and forth or to move in a circle. Now, calibrate it by telling it, "Show me *yes*." Wait and watch the movement or lack of movement as a response. If it moves in a circle, take note as to whether the circle is clockwise or counterclockwise. Tell it, "Show me *no*" and wait again. Be aware that as long as the *yes* is different than the *no*, a still pendulum is just as clear a sign as a moving one

* *Procure a pendulum for dowsing and calibrate it.*

Day 120
. . . .

Book Test of a Spirit

A book test is another version of bibliomancy, but here it is combined with another psychic element so the spirit gives the psychic a name of a book and a page number. The psychic then opens to that page and reads for significant words from the spirit. This is an opportunity to hone your psychic medium skills through one technique that can give you the name of a book and a page number.

So far, you may have experienced receiving information through trance meditation or dreams. Choose a method and ask for a spirit to give you the information through that method. Remember, the messages you receive may be highly symbolic, so it may be a bit of a riddle to figure out the title of the book, or the spirit may just simply show you a picture of the book's cover art and make things easy for you. When you find the given page, read it all the way through and then meditate on the content. Write down any specific words or phrases that jump out at you as messages from the spirit.

* *Try spirit communication through bibliomancy.*

Day 121
....

Your Body as a Pendulum

I love this technique for times when you don't have any tools at all. Your body becomes the pendulum as you stand, and you allow yourself to wobble on your feet to divine the answers. This is also a good technique for psychic development because it helps you notice the small body movements that are indicators of your own intuition. When you use a physical pendulum, those movements are so hard to notice that it often seems like the pendulum is moving itself. This exercise will help you see that your divination is under your own power.

You can begin with a calibration exercise. Stand up and ask to be shown what a *yes* answer looks like. If you can close your eyes and maintain your balance, do so. Pay attention to all the tiny movements and wobbles of your body. Do you feel a slight tilt, lean, or an urge to move in a certain way? Then, ask to be shown what a *no* answer looks like. After this, you can ask yes or no questions of your psychic self and pay attention to the movements of your own body as they reveal the answers to you.

* *Try divination using your own body as a pendulum of sorts.*

Day 122

....

Aleuromancy

Aleuromancy is written divination by baked goods. If you've ever had a fortune cookie at a Chinese restaurant, you've already practiced some simple aleuromancy. You can have a fortune cookie today, or step it up a notch by trying your own form of aleuromancy. Here are some other practices that count as aleuromancy, and which are fun to practice with friends. Perhaps you can surprise your friends with a fun psychic treat today.

If you're a baker, bake a lucky treat. Bake a set of muffins, cupcakes, or other treats and include a surprise in only one of them. I suggest baking an edible nut or other filling inside one so that you won't end up choking anybody. The person who gets the treat with the surprise inside can be considered lucky and the king or queen for a day. You can also write fortunes directly on the top of cookies that can be selected at random. If you're not a baker, you can do some simple aleuromancy by writing out fortunes of the type that are in fortune cookies, making slits in the side of donuts, and hiding the fortunes inside each one.

* *Try a delicious form of divination by baked goods.*

Day 123

Make a Scrying Mirror

A scrying mirror can be used very similarly to the practice of water scrying. The mirror is traditionally dark in color, unlike a bathroom mirror, and can sometimes be concave or convex to produce optical illusions on the curve of the glass that help aid your eyes and your imagination to see visions. Either the glass itself is dark in color, or the back of the glass is painted black. My favorites are convex scrying mirrors, one of which you can make using a piece of glass intended to cover the face of a clock. You can find glass like this at any watch and clock repair shop.

A simpler scrying mirror can be made from any old glass-fronted picture frame and some black paint. If you have a choice, pick a picture frame that is dark and dull so it won't be distracting while you are gazing at your scrying mirror. Paint the back of the glass black and allow it to dry before putting it back into the frame. You can keep your scrying mirror wrapped in black velvet and take it out when you want to use it, especially on auspicious occasions such as the full moon.

* *Make a simple version of a scrying mirror.*

Day 124

Rhabdomancy

Rhabdomancy is divination using a stick. Though we'll cover the classic water dowsing using a Y-shaped stick in a few days, today I'd like to tell you about some divination you can do with a straight wooden stick. Procure a stick that is about as long as a pen. In fact, a wooden pen or pencil will do. If you like, you can choose a magical wood such as witch hazel to enhance the psychic properties of your experiment. You can also get a piece of paper to be a diagram for your stick to point out answers. The paper can have numbers, letters, or answers such as "boy" and "girl" or the classic yes and no. For your first experiment, you might want to just try yes and no. We'll explore dowsing charts a little later.

You can divine using your chart in two different ways. One is to lay the stick on its side and spin it quickly. When it stops, the end of the stick will point to your answer. When your chart becomes more detailed, you may have to designate only one end of the stick to be a pointer. Another means of divination is to stand the stick up on its end and try to balance it as carefully as possible between your answers on the chart. You'll have your answer when the stick falls down on one answer.

* *Practice divination with a short, straight stick and a simple chart or diagram.*

Day 125

Graphology

What does your handwriting say about your personality? How about your friends, family, and celebrities whose handwriting you've seen? Graphology, or handwriting analysis, is an impressive art, and there's much to learn if you want to study it in depth. For today, however, I'd like to introduce you to a few basics. As a handwriting sample, you can write "The quick brown fox jumps over the lazy dog." This sentence includes every letter of the alphabet. Then sign your name so you can analyze your signature.

Are your pen strokes bold and high pressure, or light and gentle? This represents your emotional energy. Small or left-slanting lettering is the work of an introverted person, while larger or right-slanting handwriting is ascribed to extroverts. Do your letters slant neither right nor left? If so, you're pretty reliable. If the first letter of your last name is much larger than the rest, it indicates a deep connection with family.

* *Try some handwriting analysis on yourself.*

DAY 126
. . . .

Magical Ink

Magic inks can be made and used for psychic work. I've made several inks from a resin called dragon's blood. A simple ink can be made by holding a candle against some glass and then scraping the soot or lamp black off with a razor to mix with water. If you have a wood stove, you've got plenty of lamp black on the glass door of the stove, though you should scrape it off with a credit card so you won't permanently damage your door. Use the ink with a quill to journal your psychic thoughts.

Even with regular ink, you can enhance your divination practices in several ways. You can add the ink to your water when water scrying to make the surface look extra dark. In a few days, you will be learning a bit about palmistry. Splashing ink on your palm and looking for symbols in the ink splashes can be an exercise you can try today before we add on the layers of meaning with palmistry. Make sure to photograph or sketch your palm if you try this today so you can do more analysis later.

* *Make or use some ink to enhance your psychic practice.*

Day 127

Water Dowsing

Dowsing for water is a classic psychic skill; one my mother practiced in the desert when she was a child. For this exercise, you'll need a Y-shaped stick. Hold the stick by the two short branches, and try to sense with your body where the longer branch feels like it wants to point. Walk with the stick and try to use your psychic senses to feel when you should turn or stop. This is a tactile sort of psychic ability, so your hands may feel a heaviness or a wobbliness in the stick.

Why dowse for water today, when it's readily available in most places? Water dowsing has a lot of practical history behind it, so it is a good skill for the developing psychic to study. I know some friends who used water dowsing in a home to find the exact location of water pipes in the wall. Plus, this skill might save your life—you never know when you might get stuck in the desert! Try water dowsing in a building or when hiking in an area where you could stumble upon freshwater streams.

* *Try the art of water dowsing.*

Numerology

Numbers have meanings we will explore in-depth in part 7, when we examine some common symbols. For now, let's use numerology to find a few of your lucky numbers, which you can analyze further later on. First, let's find your life path number, which is found using your birth date. Add the single digits in your birth date together. For example, since I was born on June 4, 1981, I would add 6+4+1+9+8+1. If you get a double-digit answer, add those two digits together until you get a single digit answer. Your life path number represents the opportunities and challenges you'll discover during this life.

Next, find your expression number using your name. Assign each letter in the alphabet a number starting with the letter A as 1 and going through 9 and then repeating 1 through 9 until the alphabet is complete. Add up the numbers that make your name and then reduce them by adding them together in the same way you did with your life path number. You should end up with another single-digit number. Your expression number represents your personality. Both your expression number and your life path number should be lucky numbers for you.

* *Calculate your life path number and your expression number.*

Day 129

. . . .

Casting Bones or Stones

Another ancient art is the art of casting bones or stones. The basic practice will feel like a harder version of tea leaf reading. As you cast a jumble of bones or stones onto the ground or a table, they'll fall into place to form symbols, but the symbols will be harder to read or see since they are discrete objects and not clumps. Shapes you might see are arrows, circles, squares, triangles, hearts, or faces. You'll have to use your imagination, and the technique may feel limiting at first.

Gather your chosen stones or bones. You can use pretty rocks, little trinkets, or even dried chicken bones, which makes the practice feel very ancient and spooky even in a modern living room. Whatever you use, keep everything in a small bag so you can shake them up and cast them onto a surface. If you like, you can use a placemat or a circle drawn on paper to limit which ones are read or to represent the past versus the future depending on where they land. You may wish to stand back a few feet to pick out larger shapes. Make sketches of the basic shapes formed and write down your initial impressions from those symbols.

* *Try casting bones or stones.*

Day 130

Runes and Ogham

Runes and ogham are two tools that add on to the technique of casting bones or stones, this time by writing letters of ancient alphabets on the tools. Runic alphabets are characters traditionally drawn on stones, and ogham is an ancient alphabet that is traditionally drawn on small sticks that are cast like bones. Each letter is not just a sound, but may also have an additional meaning. Thus, some runic systems are not alphabets at all, but pure symbols. Witches' runes, for example, have crossed spears representing conflict.

You can create your own set of runes or ogham by drawing on some sticks or stones with permanent marker. You can use one of the traditional alphabets by looking up their symbols and meaning, or you can make up your own symbols based on any you've seen during your psychic development. These personal runes can be especially helpful at this stage of your psychic abilities to strengthen and grow them. Combine the meanings you see on your tools with the shapes you see when casting them.

* Make or use a set of rune stones or ogham sticks.

Day 131

Metal Dowsing Rods

Today, you can make a set of metal dowsing rods to practice your dowsing skills further. I like to make them out of a length of thick copper wire. If you don't have copper wire, they can be made with metal clothes hangers and some wire cutters. Cut two lengths of wire about the length of your entire arm. Bend both wires so they each are shaped sort of like the letter L with the short part of the L being about as long as your hand is wide.

I find the use of these to be much easier than using a classical dowsing stick. To use them, hold one in each hand by the short part of the L so that the long parts hang over your hand and out in front of you. Hold them loosely enough that they can swing freely. If they point in a direction, that means to walk in that direction. If they cross, that means to stop. You can ask your metal dowsing rods to find water or even to find a missing lost object.

* Create your own metal dowsing rods out of a clothes hanger
  or a length of copper wire, and then take them for a test drive.

Day 132

Dowsing Chart

You've made a very simple dowsing chart for a small stick. Today, I'd like you to create a chart or diagram that can be used for a plumb-bob style pendulum. You can make various charts for whatever answers you'd like to find. For example, if you want to discover somebody's sun sign, you can draw a wheel of sun signs and then hold the pendulum over your drawing. If you want your pendulum to spell out words, you can write out the alphabet in the same way that it is laid out on a spirit board. We will learn more about spirit boards tomorrow.

One of my favorite charts for pendulum dowsing is to discover an auspicious date. Draw a fan shape on a piece of paper. The fan will be made up of rows of numbers. Start at the bottom of the fan and make a row of numbers that represent years. The next row up should represent months in a year. The final row should represent days in a month. Now, you can move your pendulum up from the bottom of the fan to the top, pausing at each level to divine first the year, then the month, then the day. The years can be limited to just a few years, or you can add levels to your fan to divine the decade, century and even millennia.

* Create a diagram or chart for a plumb-bob style pendulum.

Day 133

Spirit Boards

A spirit board (sometimes called a talking board) is a chart used for communicating with spirits along with an indicator, sometimes called a planchette. You can buy commercial spirit boards like the Ouija Board, or you can make your own. All you need to make your own is a pen, paper, and a small drinking glass. Write on the paper the entire alphabet, in large letters and spaced out enough so they can be indicated by the mouth of your overturned drinking glass. You may also wish to include the numbers 1 through 9, adding a zero after the nine. Write YES, NO, and GOODBYE for when you want to end the session.

An induced trance state is best for spirit board use, and be sure to ground and shield yourself properly before calling a spirit that you would like to consult. You can use the spirit board with a partner or alone. Place one or two fingers on the overturned cup and allow it to slide gently across the paper under your hands. It should feel much like the process of automatic writing. You may close your eyes if you wish, especially if you have a partner who can record the results of your session. When you are done, thank the spirit and say goodbye.

* *Make your own spirit board and try it out.*

Day 134

Palmistry

Palmistry is another broad subject about which an entire book can be written. And wouldn't you know, I have written an entire book on the subject! That said, it's good to know some of the basics of palmistry. You can start looking at the hands of your friends and family so you can tell the difference between different hands and notice when someone has a unique feature. Those unique features are what developing psychics must learn to recognize, as it must be with all of your omen observations.

Start with your dominant hand. The line curving around your thumb is your life line. The line dividing your palm that branches from it is your head line. The third main line, above your head line is your heart line. Deep lines represent strong energy. Some people "run cool" on less energy than others. If your lines have branches that touch one another, those lines may be meaningful as well, showing how those aspects of you are connected. At this stage in your development, the most helpful thing to do would be to compare your palm with that of someone else. Are some lines shorter or longer than others? Does one person have more lines, and are they different depths? Does it make sense to you given the complexity, energy, head, and heart of the other person?

* *Identify the main palmistry lines in your hand and in the hand of another.*

Day 135
....

Tarot for Storytelling

We're about to spend several days studying the tarot, and several more will come later when learning about symbols. The reason I think tarot cards are so important to psychic development is not only because they help with divination, but because they act as flash cards for important symbols common to all people. They also help you with the basic psychic skill of storytelling. First, get your hands on a tarot deck. You may already own one, or you can buy one at a bookstore. Practice telling a story using the pictures on the cards. If a card is upside down, go ahead and turn it right side up, at least for now. Later, we will talk about the meaning of reversals.

Consider the stages of Joseph Campbell's Hero's Journey, which I introduced when you were designing your own guided meditation. The three basic elements of the story that describes the journey of us all are: separation, initiation, and return. Those themes are broken down further into more components, some of which include: a call to adventure, refusal of the call, supernatural aid, crossing a threshold, a road of trials, meeting the divine, receiving boons, and crossing again. I've simplified this significantly so that you can practice building these simple story elements into a story in your mind as you flip through the tarot cards.

* *Practice telling a story with tarot cards.*

DAY 136
....

Major Arcana

A tarot deck has seventy-eight cards in it, many of which seem similar to a regular playing card deck. The major arcana are the twenty-two cards that stand out as cards you wouldn't see in a regular deck. These numbered and named cards—starting with the Fool and ending with the World—are the most powerful cards in the deck energetically, and they often show up copiously in readings for people who are at a crossroads in their lives. You can perform readings with the major arcana alone.

For today's exercise, start by removing all the major arcana from your deck; we'll be looking at them alone. Line them up in order from the Fool to the World right side up, and try flipping through them and telling a story. Hint: they follow the Hero's Journey, so use some of those cues if you feel stuck. When you are done, shuffle the major arcana cards and draw one for yourself. Does the card's role in your story make sense for this stage in your life's story right now?

* *Try telling a story and doing a reading with major arcana cards.*

DAY 137
....

Court Cards

Beyond the major arcana cards are cards numbered ace through ten for each of the four suits. After those are the court cards, which are all the "people cards," usually pages, knights, queens, and kings for each suit. Pull out these cards (sixteen in total) and see how they are all characters or roles in stories. In many tarot decks, the pages and knights look younger than the kings and queens. And in some decks, the pages are female characters, and sometimes are renamed. Sometimes the Cups and Wands feature people with lighter hair colors, while the Swords and Pentacles show people with darker hair colors.

Organize your court cards into their four suits, and see if any of the characters look like younger or older versions of other characters within the same suit. What do you think? Do they look like father and son, mother and daughter, or do they look like a young person growing up into an older person with greater power? Shuffle the court cards and draw one at random. Does this represent you or perhaps some other important character in your life?

* *Examine the tarot's court cards.*

DAY 138
....

Swords

Let's go through each of the suits of the tarot cards now, starting with the suit of Swords. Separate out all the Sword cards in your deck including the Sword court cards and excluding the major arcana. Line them all up starting with the ace and ending with the king. Flip through the cards in order and tell a story. Try following the basic form of the Hero's Journey. Now, shuffle your Sword cards and draw one at random for yourself. Does it suit you?

Swords are the suit of communication and of conflict. They represent all that is intellectual and of the mind. Often Sword cards represent paths of education, long-distance communications over the telephone or Internet, signing contracts, writing, working with computers, and miscommunications that lead to breakups or aloofness. Some Sword cards may not seem pleasant at all. Think about the advice that the cards hold for how to avoid the fate depicted in them.

* *Explore the tarot's suit of Swords.*

DAY 139
. . . .
Cups

Today, we'll examine all the cards in the suit of Cups. As you did with the Sword cards, separate all the Cups from your deck and line them up in order. Go through them one by one, telling a story with those familiar Hero's Journey themes. As you do so, notice the similarity between the stories as they were told as well as the differences. It may feel like the same story told but with different characters or in a different season. Shuffle and draw a card of the day from this suit. Record your impressions.

Cups have to do with emotions, especially love and your loving relationships with people. These cards may speak strongly to your intuition and your dreams. They may also relate to health, especially the emotional health of the mind. Think of the cups as full of energy, and when that energy is low or spilling from the cups, there are problems in the mind and heart. As a suit, Cups also have a lot to do with artistic creativity and the physical creation of new life in a womb.

* *Explore and experiment with the tarot's suit of Cups.*

DAY 140

. . . .

Pentacles

Let's explore the suit of Pentacles today. In some decks, this suit may be called something else, like Coins or Disks. Separate out those Pentacle cards and line them up in order to tell their story. Compare and contrast with the stories as told by the other suits. As the Pentacle props are brought into play, you may notice that the focus shifts from the characters and their actions or interactions to the objects and their environments. Draw a card from the suit of Pentacles for yourself today.

The Pentacles are the suit of financial concerns, as you might have guessed from the optional renaming to Coins in some decks. More symbolically, Pentacles have to do with everything physical and material, such as the body, nutrition, house and home, careers, and obligations. The suit of Pentacles also speaks to the friendships and platonic relationships in your life. When you are dealing with Pentacle cards, always lean toward a practical explanation rather than one that is airy and spiritual or emotional in nature.

* *Explore the tarot's suit of Pentacles.*

DAY 141

. . . .

Wands

Cards of the suit of Wands can sometimes be tricky in a reading because they span across a lot of topics that aren't really related to each other, at least superficially. Pull your Wand cards, organize them, and tell their story by looking through them one by one. Draw your card of the day from this suit and write down your initial impressions. Notice how the Wand cards differ from the other suits in how they tell the classic Hero's Journey story.

Wand cards are related to passion and dynamic energy. They bring in a little more creative energy than Cups, but they can also bring destructive energy. Wands cards are also related to relationships and the communication that happens in relationships. When subtle chemistry is at work and people have to read between the lines, a Wand can bring powerful energy with just a wave. People and situations in the story of Wands may tend to get carried away with themselves.

* *Explore the tarot's suit of Wands.*

DAY 142

....

Tarot Spreads

So far, I've been asking you to tell stories with tarot cards by lining them up in order and going through them from beginning to end. But when we do readings on peoples' lives, we often want to look at only a small part of the story and examine the details happening in that moment. For this reason, it's valuable to add another layer of interpretation called a tarot spread. A tarot spread is a special arrangement for the laying of cards that gives each card a specific role or scene in the story it is telling.

Today, try out the simplest tarot spread, the three-card spread. Shuffle all your cards together and draw three of them, flipping them over one by one, making sure each is right side up. The first one represents the past, the second one is the present, and the third is about the future. Adding those features to your understanding of each card, tell the story as it appears to be happening. You might notice that the hero goes backwards in the story, or might even go in circles. That's okay, such is life!

* *Try a simple tarot card spread.*

DAY 143
....

Tarot Reversals

Until now, I've encouraged you to ignore upside-down cards and turn them upright. Now you are ready to add the special meaning of upside-down cards called reversals to your readings. Be aware that different psychic readers interpret reversals in different ways. I've noticed that some tarot decks make sense with one mode of interpretation while other decks work better with another method. Here I'll introduce a couple simple methods for your experimentation.

The Negative Aspect Method: Every virtue can be a vice. For example, excessively strong leadership can sometimes be bossiness. Experiment with reading reversals as a negative aspect of the upright card. This experiment may work best for beginners if reading major arcana cards only.

The Needs Method: This simple method just means that all reversed cards represent things that are needed but not yet fulfilled. This method is helpful because it gives advice sprinkled throughout your reading.

* *Incorporate inverted cards into a reading.*

DAY 144

Playing Cards

Did you know that you can do tarot-like readings with an ordinary deck of playing cards? This form of cartomancy is fun and a great tool to use with people who might be a little scared of tarot decks. Many tarot decks feature pictures with sexuality and/or nudity, violence, or themes that could be considered inappropriate for children, so a regular playing card deck is a good fallback.

When using a regular playing card deck, you can still do spreads and read reversals. Swords become Spades, Cups are Hearts, Wands are Clubs, and Pentacles become Diamonds. The meanings of the knights and pages combine in the jacks. As you draw the cards, think about their stages along the Hero's Journey and about the character of the suit to guide your interpretation. Later on, you'll learn more about interpreting numbers, which can add another layer to your interpretation.

* With your tarot card skills, perform a reading using a deck of regular playing cards.

DAY 145

Choosing Your Weapon

Now that you've had a whirlwind tour through some basic forms of divination, you might have found some favorites. It's all right to narrow your choices to a select few, but be mindful as to what sort of answers your preferred methods of divination may give you. If some of them are limiting, you'll want to keep practicing others just to keep them in your tool belt, even if they're not your best or favorite.

So how will you choose a method of divination? First, find out what answer you seek. If you want a general reading, for instance, tarot is an excellent tool, because the cards can help you narrow down your focus to specific life messages with the suits. But what if you want to see a face or a name? The tarot cards aren't really useful for that, but scrying such as with tea leaves or a crystal ball reading would be ideal. What if you want to pick a specific number? In that case, your pendulum on a diagram or a spirit board might be the quickest and easiest tools for the job.

 * *Think up some questions that are best answered with different divination tools. Try out the appropriate tools on each question.*

Day 146
....

Recording Divination

At this point in your psychic development, you might be slacking off a bit on writing in your psychic journal. Has the initial excitement of recording dreams and symbols worn off? Maybe your attention has been entirely devoted to the rapid-fire introduction of new divination tools and methods. Even if you are using your journal religiously, it may be hard to decide what to write down, so now is a good time to refine your approach.

I like to use a camera to take pictures of everything from tarot spreads to runes. Sometimes sketching is actually best, because it helps capture what I saw in the moment. For example, I might sketch my palm rather than photocopy or photograph it, because it shows what lines or features caught my interest in the moment. Likewise, drawing a sketch of what you see in your tea cup can help you remember what you saw if later you forget and can no longer interpret a blurry blob in a picture. Written words in your journal should be your first impressions, and you should include them even if a photograph is present. A picture is worth a thousand words, but your words still matter when it comes to interpreting something that could have many meanings.

* Decide on a system for recording your divination attempts.

DAY 147
. . . .

Improving Divination through Practice

At this stage in the psychic game, practice makes perfect. It might get boring to do readings for yourself by yourself every day, but treat it as a discipline for your practice. Make sure you do a reading in some form daily, although you can allow yourself a rest during the dark moon, if you wish. Now is the time that you might start thinking more about performing readings for others. You'll read more of the ins and outs of reading for others in part 9, but for now you should know that it is okay to branch out. Your family and friends may be eager test subjects.

One of the best decisions I made when I first started reading for strangers was to offer my services online. As long as the people for whom you are performing readings know you are a beginner and that you're still practicing, it can be very fulfilling to help others over the Internet. There are plenty of opportunities out there for honing your skills. You'll never run out of people who want to try out one of your excellent readings.

* *Create a plan for practicing your psychic readings frequently.*

DAY 148
....

Combining Forms of Divination

Sometimes when you choose your method for divination, one tool doesn't quite cut it. You might start out with a tarot reading, for example, and then branch out into a pendulum dowsing when a timing question comes up, or into a crystal ball reading when you want to try to see a spirit. That's perfectly okay. The many different tools are just there to aid your psychic practice, and you don't have to feel like you're failing at any one tool if it can't do the job by itself.

In fact, you might purposely combine tools to see how it enhances your psychic practice and adds another layer onto the interpretation of the results. For example:

Try picking out a tarot card using your pendulum.

In a dream, ask a spirit to show you what method of divination to use the following day.

While your tea is steeping for a tea leaf reading, perform bibliomancy to come up with a question.

Ask your spirit board to show you the expression number of a spirit.

* *Perform a reading using a combo of several different forms of divination.*

Part Five

*

Clairvoyance

Day 149

Clairsentience

Clairvoyance means "clear seeing," and it speaks to the visions that you might see, whether they be in dreams or through holy stones. In general, though, in this part of the book we will be exploring clairvoyance without tools, to develop a more hands-free psychic ability in you. Clairvoyance is often paired with other "clairs" that speak to your other senses. I'd like to lead you through an exploration of all your other senses first, since they will add to, and enhance, your clairvoyant experience.

This first sense, clairsentience, means "clear knowing," and I introduce it first because it is often the first form of intuition to develop in a psychic beginner. Clairsentience is when you just know that something is true, even if it is not yet revealed to you through logic or experience. You can encourage clairsentience through meditation and trance induction. Clairsentience can be experienced as an idea popping into your head, or you might experience it as an emotional sense of peace and well-being.

* *When have you experienced clairsentience? Meditate and ask your psychic self for a clairsentient experience.*

Day 150

Clairtangence

Clairtangence ("clear touch") is a psychic sense of feeling. You may have already experienced this when you practiced psychometry (touching an object) or when you tried to feel somebody's aura. Clairtangence can also most frequently be felt by psychics through a temperature change. Most people I know get warm when they are "running energy"—that is, pulling energy from the earth, grounding it back into the earth, or exchanging energy with another person on purpose, like during a psychic reading. Not me, though. I tend to get very cold every I run energy. If I'm going to be doing a lot of psychic readings, I like to have a blanket nearby!

Using temperature clairtangence can also be an excellent way to sense the presence of spirits. You may have heard ghost stories in which the characters experienced a chill when a ghost entered the room or passed through them. You can experience that same chill when you invite the spirits of your ancestors and loved ones to meet with you in meditation.

* Practice clairtangence today by going back to psychometry, aura sensing, raising energy, or by inviting a spirit to send you a chill.

Day 151

Clairaudience

Clairaudience means "clear hearing," but different psychics experience this form of hearing in different ways. You don't necessarily have to hear the psychic messages with your physical ears, as if the spirits were whispering to you. Clairaudience can border on clairsentience; you can "hear" the messages the same way that you "hear" a song stuck in your head. However, if you have heard a message with your physical ears, you'll be relieved to know that this is normal. Perfectly healthy people can hear voices that way.

Hearing voices happens when the brain relaxes into an alpha wave state. That is why many people can hear voices when they are just falling asleep at night and when they are waking up and showering in the morning. Another way to induce this alpha wave state is through meditation. If you'd like to have a clairaudient experience, therefore, you have another good reason to practice lengthening and deepening your meditation. Ask your psychic senses to speak to you with a voice you can hear.

* *Attempt practicing clairaudience.*

Day 152
....

Clairalience

Clairalience means "clear smelling," and at the first glance might seem like a pretty weird psychic sense. However, when you think about how scent is the sense tied most closely to memory, you can see how scent associations might be useful for the developing psychic. For example, if I smell a certain sort of cigarette smoke, I associate it with my late father more quickly than any omen I might see. Scents can also be a big clue about the seasons. If you ask a timing question and get a fleeting whiff of spring flowers or holiday cookies, for example, you'll get an idea of what your psychic self is trying to tell you.

Try meditating while asking for a scent as a clue. You can even ask for a spirit to come visit you and bring a scent to mark its arrival. Close your eyes in seated meditation, and make sure that you choose a place that does not have other distracting scents. When you are done, write down any impressions in your psychic journal, even if you didn't smell anything. Note that it is okay to write down smells that are explained by natural circumstances. The coincidence of your roommate baking cookies that smell like an old family recipe is still meaningful.

* *Try to sense psychic messages with your sense of smell.*

DAY 153

. . . .

Clairgustance

By now, you've spotted the pattern and know that if we're covering the five senses, there's got to be a psychic sense of taste. Clairgustance is just that psychic sense, and it is almost inextricable from your psychic sense of smell. In fact, you might experience the combined psychic sense as an overwhelming taste and smell at the same time. Sometimes, clairgustance can override your normal sense of taste while you are eating, for example during the practice of a dumb supper.

You can plan a dumb supper and invite your ancestors to experience clairgustance. While it is a good idea to prepare foods your ancestors would have liked, blander dishes encourage your clairgustance more effectively. You may also wish to have some salt nearby to put on your tongue four grounding yourself afterwards or if you feel overwhelmed by this psychic sense. Ask your psychic self to experience clairgustance before you begin, and make sure you record your experience.

* *Try to experience a psychic sense of taste.*

DAY 154

....

See Your Own Aura

During an earlier exercise, you were asked to try to sense someone else's aura by feel. An intermediate psychic skill is the ability to actually see an aura. Seeing an aura can be tricky at first, and many beginners must work hard to induce trance states and achieve meditation to see their first auras. However, once you get used to your own psychic skills and abilities, you'll need less effort to see auras, and you might even wonder how you ever missed seeing them before.

Start with your own aura. You can look at yourself in the mirror or just focus on your hand in front of your face. Ground yourself and then induce a trance through a method that raises your energy. Project your aura by imagining that you're trying to get somebody's attention, like your crush just entered a crowded room, or as though you were about to give a speech about something important to you. Then, concentrate on the outline of your body, relax your gaze, and give yourself time. Be careful not to stare too hard at your skin or bright clothing in front of a light background, or you might experience the optical illusion that looks like an aura but is not a true aura. Let your eyes move lazily around the outline of your body, not lingering too long in one spot.

* *Try to see your own aura. Record your impressions about its color, shape and intensity.*

DAY 155

Auras of Animals

After you've practiced on your own aura, try to see an animal's aura. Animal auras may appear more subtle, but they will also be less influenced socially by the act of you viewing their auras, unlike human partners. You can view the aura of any animal; not necessarily a pet. Wild birds are a possibility, but I do find that a sleeping cat or dog is the best subject, since they hold still.

Depending on how easily you saw your own aura, you may be able to drop, shorten, or change your trance and meditation techniques when trying to view the auras of animals. It's okay to experiment with different combinations of psychic techniques. Now is a good opportunity reduce the amount of mental preparations you have to do before you can see auras. If you don't find success in an instant, try harder and try again. It's better to have your dog or cat look at you funny rather than a friend or family member when you're trying to work up a trance.

* *Try to see an animal's aura.*

DAY 156

Auras of Plants

Some psychics can see the auras of plants and even rocks. Let's step up our psychic development and try to see plant auras. Plant auras may look subtle or very different to you than your own aura or the auras of animals, so prepare for another challenge. Choose several different plants if you'd like to see if any are easier to view than others. You can take your time to work up a trance with this one; you don't have to worry about your subject getting bored and wandering away.

When working with plants, it is especially important not to get too relaxed and stare enough to see a false aura. Remember: if you're looking at a green plant and see a red aura, you might be seeing the reverse color due to retinal burn out. Close your eyes for a few minutes and try again, softening your gaze and remembering to move your eyes. You might find that gazing at plants is so relaxing that it becomes a trance technique for you. Or, you might find it so boring that you'll move on to other forms of aura viewing.

* *Try to see a plant's aura.*

Day 157

Aura Drawings

Creating aura drawings is a fun way to record your psychic development progress as well as the changes in your own aura over time. I like to make aura drawings for others as a way for them to remember having their aura read by a psychic. It might feel a little nerve wracking if you don't consider yourself an artist, but it can also be an interesting way to develop your artistic abilities. It helps to keep in mind that you're the only person who can see auras the way you do. In a way, you have a duty to share this beauty with the world.

I like to use colored pencils, but any artistic media will do. If you feel intimidated by drawing the human form, start with a stick figure or an outline of a person. Try drawing your own aura by looking in the mirror. Instead of drawing firm lines, notice where the light falls and start drawing the things that pop out to you. Ignore the lines and forms that don't draw your eye. You don't have to spend very much time on your picture. A fleeting sketch may do if you find that concentrating on drawing makes it harder to see the aura. You may find that your vision of an aura doesn't conform to the classical halo art that others have depicted, and that's okay. When I draw auras, they often look more like fiery flames, bubbles, flowing vestments, or even a coffin. Let your creativity take flight.

* *Try drawing your own aura.*

Day 158

Mental Health and the Psychic

Modern Western culture does not take kindly to people who "see things," so by this stage in your psychic development, where seeing things is a goal, you may be having some doubts. Some powerful psychic visions can be downright scary, or at least spooky at night, like dealing with ghosts. It's okay to start wondering now where the line between mental health and mental illness is, as you stretch and stress your mental abilities.

Seeing things in a spiritual and psychic context does not make you mentally ill. However, losing control and letting scary or otherwise disturbing visions take over your life activities is a problem. If you ever feel completely unable to ground and to control your clairvoyance, it is time to get help. It's a good idea to be aware of local resources such as a physician, a therapist, and a crisis hotline. In fact, later when you get to learn more about reading for others, you'll need to know that information so that you can refer clients to them. Take time today to evaluate the role that psychic visions play in your life.

  * *In your psychic log, record local resources, such as the numbers for a crisis hotline and a local physician and therapist, in case you or a client should ever have need for one.*

DAY 159
....

Out-of-Body Experience

We laid the foundations for an out-of-body experience back in part 1, when I asked you to study the room in which you were sitting. You've also tried ethereal travel in dreams by flying out of your body. Now, you can start concentrating more on this discipline. Start by traveling short distances out of your body. Look for small details you can verify. Over time, you may be able to move on to advanced feats of remote viewing.

Begin with the familiar practice of sitting and observing the room in which you shall meditate. Then close your eyes and try to rebuild the entire room in your memory with as much accuracy as possible. If you forget some details, don't open your eyes, just fill in the blanks through visualization. Then, visualize yourself leaving your body and walking out of the room in which you are seated. Some people like to visualize a cord connecting the spirit self to the body, belly button to belly button, that cannot be severed. As you walk away from your own body, look for interesting details. What time does the clock say in the other room? If you have one, what is your pet up to? What does the weather look like outside? Record your experience.

* *Practice having an out-of-body experience.*

DAY 160
....

Remote Viewing

Remote viewing is an out-of-body experience that results in the ability to clairvoyantly see information. To develop this skill well, I suggest performing this activity with a partner. Ideally, you will get somebody to verify some things as you travel outside your body for longer distances so you can check your accuracy. You can start in your own home with your friend drawing a playing card in another room. Try to use out-of-body travel to discover the card. If the other person is looking at the card, you may find that you are actually sensing your friend's perceived images.

For a more challenging experiment, try having your friend stay at home and not focus on anything in particular. With your friend's consent, try remote viewing your friend's room by allowing your psychic self to float out of your body and travel there. After your meditation, call your friend and see if you can verify some of the details of what you saw, including objects in your friend's house, what he or she was doing at the time, and anything else in particular that you saw. Record your friend's confirmations as well as any mistakes or confusion.

* *Try remote viewing with a friend.*

Seeing Ghosts

Seeing ghosts in dreams is one thing, as we've already relegated the world of the strange to dreams and feel safe with it there. Seeing ghosts in your waking life with clairvoyance, however, may be jarring for some people. Before you progress with your clairvoyance, be honest with yourself about whether or not you would like to see ghosts with your waking eyes. If you do want to see ghosts, in what context would they be welcome to you?

Would you be overjoyed to see a dead loved one randomly in your home while you cuddle up in your easy chair one winter night? Or would you rather that spirits only made an appearance when you are properly prepared and asking for their presence during a scrying session or while you meditate in a trance? Would you like to save your ghost sightings for special occasions like Halloween and visits to graveyards, or do you want to invite your ancestors to be more of a part of your everyday life? Make a choice, and then openly inform the spirits that may care about you, such as your ancestors, about your choice.

* *Put out an offering plate for your ancestors before you go to bed. Let them know whether you would like to see them, and in what context they are welcome in your life. Assure them about what they can do to make contact with you without scaring you.*

A Vision Board

Visualization doesn't have to only exist in your mind. In fact, it can enhance your own visualization abilities as well as your ability to create your own destiny to find ways to externally manifest your desires. Making a vision board is the practice of creating a collage, pin board, or other composite of visual imagery surrounding a goal of yours. This practice uses the magical law of attraction, which states that like energies attract like things. Therefore, if you focus on seeing certain images with all your psychic abilities, you will bring those circumstances about.

Think about a goal that you want to achieve. Your goal can be a house that you want to buy, a fitness ideal you'd like to achieve, or even a love you want to draw into your life. Find images to add to your vision board that align with your goals. For example, when I created a fitness vision board for myself, I cut out pictures that showed the silhouette of a woman running in a field with her children, and I drew musical notes to inspire me to dance. I have a friend who made a very detailed vision board of a house before she went house hunting, even finding all the furniture she wanted to buy and put in the house. Have fun imagining yourself already having what you want.

* *Create a vision board for a long-term goals.*

DAY 163

. . . .

Chakras

A chakra is an energy center or vortex inside the body. According to Hindu tantric, and yogic teachings, seven main chakras can be identified. There are many lesser chakras, perhaps even too many to count. Learning about your chakras can help you understand how your psychic energy flows within your body, aiding in your grounding and your readings of others. Different belief systems use different chakra systems. So, if you feel like you have other energy centers than the ones you read about in books, it's okay. In fact, since I'm reluctant to give anyone a specific energy pattern, especially while they are developing psychic skills, I'd like you to use this time to explore your own chakras without labelling them or fitting them into a preexisting structure.

This will be a time for quiet, receptive meditation. Your attention will be turned inward, to your body. Make sure you ground first very well. Sit up straight, feeling the energy coming up from the earth into your body. Pay attention to where you feel that energy in your body. Some feel the energy centers as a tingling sensation or just a source of excitement or butterflies. Note whether you feel energy in your body along your spine, in your face, or in your feet or hands, as these chakras may be most noticeable to beginners. When you are done, ground again, as this activity of noticing your chakras may excite your energy and make you feel jumpy or jittery unless you ground.

* *Explore your own personal energy pattern.*

DAY 164

Psychometry of Places

You've already done some psychometry, trying out your psychic abilities while touching an object. This skill can sometimes blend into clairvoyance if you tend to get visions of the object as it was used in the past. If not, you can try psychometry of places, which can tend to stimulate clairvoyant abilities more easily. Psychometry of places means that you can sense what happened in a particular location. This can be a fun field trip if you go to visit a historical place, especially a place where something notable occurred.

If you can't afford to take a field trip to a haunted castle or a battlefield, any location with a bit of history will do. Find a place where you can meditate without drawing too much attention to yourself. Make physical contact with the building, structure, or piece of land that makes the site important. Close your eyes and recreate the space in your mind's eye. Wait and allow the scenery to change or populate itself with people or events from the past. If you want, you can focus on a specific time frame.

* *Try psychometry of places by taking a little field trip.*

DAY 165

Seeing Scary Things

The downside to being a clairvoyant is that some of the truths you see might be scary or alarming. Even if you're not the anxious type, seeing ghosts when they are not expected can be startling, and seeing a murder or some other violent event that has taken place can be downright disturbing. I'd like to go over some techniques that you can use if your clairvoyance seems to be going too far and you become frightened, saddened, or angered.

If you find yourself becoming overly emotional during a psychic session for whatever reason, end the session. If there are others with you, tell them you aren't feeling well and excuse yourself. Ground yourself immediately and take time with your grounding, as if you were first practicing the method you use. Take socks and shoes off and touch the floor with your feet and hands if possible. You can hold a stone and put a pinch of salt on your tongue. As soon as you are feeling able, get up and go eat a meal to settle your stomach and ground yourself further. Write down any triggers that made this experience different from others so you can avoid an extreme reaction in the future.

* Prepare yourself a little psychic first aid kit that contains a stone and some salt for grounding, and a small snack to settle your stomach.

Day 166
. . . .

Astral Projection

Astral projection is travel in the astral realm rather than in the real world. Traveling in dreams is a form of astral travel, as is guided meditation and spirit journeying. You can also do a more freeform astral travel, where you set a destination on the astral realm and go exploring. Your destination could be heaven, the Akashic library filled with records of everything that has been or will be, the fairy realm, or the home of your totem or spirit guide.

After selecting your destination, close your eyes and build yourself a home base on the astral plane. This home base is your happy place, and building it can be fun. Make sure you include paths or doorways leading from it. These exits go in various directions so you can travel to your destination. Leave your home base and journey to your destination, paying attention to the landscapes and characters you see along the way. Just as in life, sometimes the journey matters more.

* Practice your astral projection to travel to a destination on the astral plane. What destination on the astral plane do you wish to visit and why?

DAY 167

Your Beliefs—What's a Ghost?

As you continue on the psychic path, it's wise to explore and revisit your beliefs. Seeing is believing, and soon your most fundamental beliefs may begin to change as you experience new things. Now is a good time to write about this in your psychic journal. Create a snapshot of your working hypothesis about the spirit world. In a year, you might have things to add or even things to subtract as you begin to interact with the spirit world more. Here are some writing prompts that may help you to explore your beliefs as they stand right now.

Where do ghosts come from? Where do they go?

What material makes up the body of a ghost?

Is there a way to help a ghost? Is there a way to harm a ghost?

* Write out some of your beliefs about ghosts as they stand right now. Think up some questions and techniques you can use to explore your beliefs further.

Day 168

What Does a Ghost Look Like?

Different clairvoyants see ghosts in different ways, and you might see ghosts in varied forms throughout your experiences. Think about the ghost forms in art and literature. Some cultures believe ghosts are just a mist, while others see them as corporeal as you or me. Some ghosts may appear as skeletons or gruesome creatures, while others might seem to be beautiful, translucent, glowing beings. You can request that spirits appear to you in a form you find pleasing, but what you see may largely be defined by the culture in which you were raised.

Because the manner in which spirits appear to you may also change over time, it is worthwhile to sketch what sort of ghosts you see in your psychic's log. Even if you only see ghosts in dreams, draw what you see. Again, it's okay if your drawing doesn't appear very artistic or accurate. As long as you can tell whether it looks like a banshee tearing at her hair or a classic ghost rattling chains, it will hopefully jog your memory in the future.

* How do you see ghosts or how would you like to see ghosts?

Day 169

If You Don't Want to See Ghosts

If you don't want to see scary things, you know to end the session and ground immediately. However, ghosts are a special circumstance, since they have minds of their own. In the case of ghosts, it's good to start out with grounding, because that dampens your psychic abilities enough to make you less sensitive to the appearance and activities of the ghost. This makes you better able to confront an entity, which is really the next step, if you want the ghost to stop its behavior.

The easiest way to stop your ghost visions after grounding is to tell the ghost, out loud, to go away and not come back. Be explicit that you don't want to see the ghost anymore. If the ghost comes back anyway, you can exclude it from a place using a sage smudge and saltwater. You can hang mirrors and smear garlic on windows and mirrors. In general, most ghosts don't need all of these precautions. But, just like humans, ghosts can sometimes be jerks.

* *Gather a sage smudge and a lighter, some salt, and a vessel you can fill with water as a ghost busting kit, just in case.*

DAY 170

Your Greatest Hopes and Dreams as a Clairvoyant

Setting smart goals is the way to advance your practice. If you've already been able to achieve psychic visions, you've already achieved something amazing with your psychic development and should push yourself to do more. If you have not yet been able to see a vision, that is a good place to start. Today, psych yourself up to push yourself further. A smart goal is one that is specific, measurable, attainable, and has a time frame.

Think about what sorts of things you'd like to achieve with your clairvoyance long term. Would you like to help others? Would you like to see a deceased loved one? Would you like to start your own clairvoyant business?

Think about what skills you will need to develop to achieve those goals. Pick no more than three and write them down, and don't forget to give yourself a time frame. You're less than half way through a year of psychic development, so six months out might be a useful deadline.

* *Write down some goals, no more than three, for your psychic development over the next three to six months.*

DAY 171
....

Barriers to Your Clairvoyant Practice?

If life was perfect, we'd all be able to run away to the woods to be psychics and yogis whenever we want. As a busy mother of two small children, I can't tell you how often I fantasize about a solitary spiritual retreat in the woods. In reality, though, I admire you if you've been able to be faithful to these short daily exercises. It is perfectly okay if you've strayed and have to drag out the program longer than originally planned.

Take a good, hard look at the barriers to your psychic development right now. It doesn't matter whether the barriers are valid or just excuses. Write down your barriers without censoring yourself. You may have some obvious challenges, like balancing a job and a family. You might have some more subtle issues; personal discomfort is certainly a valid personal issue. Brainstorm some solutions to your problems. Some solutions may be as easy as a lifestyle change like getting up earlier to meditate, but other challenges may require altering the timeline of your goals.

* *Write down the barriers to your clairvoyant practice and brainstorm some solutions.*

Day 172
·············

Photo Reading of a Person

Connecting with a person's photo doesn't feel quite the same as psychometry. Sure, you're holding and concentrating on an object, but it could be that the subject of the photo never physically held the photograph you are using for your clairvoyant reading. Thus, you're not really tuning in to the feel of energy on the paper of the photograph or on your computer screen, but with the identity of the person pictured.

Try practicing with a photograph of a person you don't particularly know very well given to you by a friend. You can also try looking up a picture of a celebrity you don't know very much about, since some details about the person can usually be verified afterward. Start out your meditative session by concentrating on the photograph. Then, close your eyes. At this stage, different clairvoyants may use different techniques. You could try remote viewing to travel to the person in the photo, or you could try asking simply asking the person or a spirit guide questions in your mind. You could even try meeting with the person on the astral plane.

* *Try a photo reading of a person you don't know very well.*

Day 173
·············

Photo Reading of a Place

Sometimes psychometry is inconvenient, especially when you want to investigate the history of a faraway place with your psychic abilities. I love traveling to try to see ghosts in sacred spaces, but it's not always possible to visit every site I'd like to explore psychically. I use this technique sometimes when clients contact me and want a haunted house explored but don't want to pay to fly me to another state to check it out in person. It may be more challenging to get details this way than going in person, but photo reading is always a good way to stretch your clairvoyant abilities and get some visualization practice.

Try meditating on a photograph of a place that you have never visited. Close your eyes and rebuild the scenery in your mind as if you were there. Try to "see" with your clairvoyant vision some of the sights that were not visible in the frame of the photograph. After your meditation, if you had any clairvoyant visions, you might be able to ask someone or look up the information about the landscape beyond the photograph to verify if what you saw was true.

* Try performing a photo reading on a place that you have never visited.

DAY 174
....

Combining Psychic Senses and Clairvoyance

Clairvoyance is a skill that combines very well with other psychic methods and techniques. The reason I wrote about the other clear senses at the beginning of this section is that clairvoyance is often naturally combined. When you see a vision, it won't necessarily be like watching a movie screen. It might be a picture of a rose in your head combined with the scent of a rose on the breeze. You might feel the rumble of a car driving on the freeway and hear a horn honk as you wake up from a dream of a car.

The next time you meditate or enter a trance state with the intention of having a clairvoyant vision, try to pay attention to your other senses as well. Ask your psychic self to give you a full experience of the psychic senses you need. Since people are such visual creatures, those extra senses might have been occurring already but unnoticed. Go through the list in your mind of the five senses: Sight, hearing, smell, touch, and taste. If you are able to observe or to induce another sense to become active, make sure you record your experience in your psychic log and revisit that sense again first next time.

* Try to experience as many of the five senses at once during a
  psychic session.

DAY 175

Combining Divination Tools and Clairvoyance

You can also combine divination techniques with your clairvoyance to enhance them. This is a good time to bring out your tarot cards and start using them with your clairvoyant practice. Try meditating and concentrating on the cards, even using them in the same way you might perform a reading on a picture of a place. You may begin to have visions or dreams that incorporate the tarot symbols, giving you a rich understanding of your clairvoyance. You might also get clairvoyant flashes when touching or reading your tarot cards, allowing you to fill in the details on a tarot reading that might otherwise go unspoken.

Try combining clairvoyance with divination tools that are not as visually based as the tarot cards. For example, when pendulum dowsing, using your body as a pendulum, or casting bones, a clairvoyant flash can add depth and richness to a session that might otherwise be a puzzle of *yes* or *no* questions. Tea leaf reading pairs well with clairvoyance too, as it has a visual component and a meditative component—drinking the tea, during which time you can induce a trance for a clairvoyant vision.

> * Combine a divination tool with your clairvoyant practice.

DAY 176

Seeing Fairies

Are fairies real? That question may elicit a quick answer from you based upon your belief system. However, fairies as representatives of forces of nature and the universe have existed in many cultures in countless forms. Knowing that your psychic abilities allow you to see symbols of truths as they exist in the world, seeing fairies can be entirely within the realm of your experience. Think of fairies as symbols or your real friends. Either way, you can see them in a psychic way.

This exercise is best performed in nature, even though fairies can also be found in human homes. If you can, visit a garden or a wooded path. Especially good times to see fairies are at dawn or at twilight. Fairies take many forms, not just cartoonish small people with wings. You might see them as lights, as mists, or even as shadows or monsters. Calling out to the fairies or acknowledging their existence might cause them to flee from you, so walk or sit in silence. Be sure to leave an offering of something sweet for the fairy folk, as a token of thanks for giving you the fairy sight.

> * Have fun going on a garden or nature walk and leave a gift
> for the fairies to ask them to grant you psychic fairy sight.

Day 177

Unwanted Clairvoyant Visions

Repeated clairvoyant visions that are disturbing or annoying can be a pain. You already know to ground yourself quickly and if it involves a ghost to tell it to go away. That will solve the problem for the time being. But if the problem is ongoing, you'll need to investigate what about *you* is causing this issue to occur. Is there an underlying medical problem causing you to have visions? Are you getting enough sleep? Are you eating enough?

Once physical or mental issues have been ruled out, you should investigate how grounded you are on a daily basis. Set an alarm to practice grounding throughout the day, every two or three hours. At first this may be distracting, but view it as taking your medicine to inoculate against psychic problems. Practice shielding yourself in the morning when you wake up and at night before you go to sleep. Consider going barefoot more often and carrying a piece of hematite with you for grounding. Smudge your home with sage to drive out any negativity you may be sensing. If you pray, a simple protective prayer can be the most effective means of warding off spiritual troubles.

* *Evaluate how grounded you are on an everyday basis. Could you be more grounded? Work grounding back into your everyday practice if you've let it slide, and boost the frequency of your grounding if you've experienced any troubles as a psychic.*

DAY 178
....

Clairvoyant Vision Sketching and Communication Tips

If you've kept up your sketching in your psychic journal, you're either an artist or a trooper. If, like me, you find that drawing takes much longer than writing, you may have opted for more written descriptions than sketches. That's okay for the most part, but you may be missing the components of journaling that could jog your memory when you come across repeated symbols. For example, a quick sketch of the shape of a unique doorway will be more compelling for your memory than the descriptor "doorway."

Make it a point to leave better notes for yourself. Practice your communication skills for reading for others, use a combined approach. Diagram the basic shape and nature of the symbols in your visions and then fill in the details with words. For example, since my memory is often in black and white when I recall things long term, I like to sketch out a drawing and then add labels for colors that stood out to me in my mind. I also use these word labels to enhance my drawings when I find myself limited by my artistic ability. If I can't quite capture the glory of a sparkling campfire or a snowstorm on a mountain top, I'll sketch out the basic layout of the scene I saw and then add those compelling details as little word labels.

* *Renew your sketching practice with dedication. Try adding drawings to your words and words to your drawings.*

Day 179

·············

Taking Clairvoyant Visions into Your Dreams

Just as you can use your dreams to puzzle out a question, you can also use your dreams to ruminate on a psychic vision that does not quite make sense. If you see a collection of symbols in a clairvoyant vision that seems like an impossible riddle to solve, meditate upon those symbols before you sleep. You will have all your psychic self to mull them over all night long. You can even give one of each of the symbols that you are thinking about to your worry dolls, and then see if they help do the trick.

I often see people in clairvoyant visions I do not recognize. These people puzzle me for a while, because I'm not sure if I am mistaken about the person's identity, if the person is just a symbolic representation, or if the person is a real person I've yet to meet. By making a sketch of the person's identifying features and studying that sketch before I go to bed, I can have a dream about that person. I recreate the clairvoyant vision I had as it happened in my mind, and replay it over and over again as I'm falling asleep. I may catch more of a glimpse of the person in my dreams, or my subconscious may reveal the person's identity.

> * *Find a record in your psychic journal of a clairvoyant experience you had with an earlier exercise. Rehash that experience before you go to sleep, so you may enhance or extend it in your dreams.*

Day 180

....

Expand Your Symbolic Repertoire

Have you been studying your tarot cards? Each of those seventy-eight cards contains a myriad of symbols that can be added to your knowledge bank, along with the interpretations well known in tarot studies. You can add even more symbols to your brain by learning more about symbolism. Find dream interpretation books, several of which may be available in your local library. The dreams symbols may carry over into scrying and other clairvoyant visions.

Learning what symbols mean in your subconscious is almost like learning another language. The more symbols you learn to interpret, the more letters you add to your alphabet. So stay hungry for symbols. Study astrological symbols and what they mean. Look up on the Internet the symbolic meanings for any animals you see in visions or dreams. Pick a subset of symbols to start investigating at this stage. It's okay if you don't agree with their interpretation. Write down in your psychic log how you interpret that symbol and why you don't agree with the common ideas about it.

* *Pick a set of psychic symbols to investigate so that you can learn to interpret them on sight from memory. This can be as mundane as being able to recognize national flags, or it could be the study of an occult alphabet.*

....

Spirit Guides

Spirit guides are entities that aid psychics by delivering messages, often clairaudiently or clairsentiently. Members of the Spiritualist movement first came up with the idea of spirit guides in America. Spirit guides were often once living people, who chose to help psychics after their deaths. A person might have many spirit guides, some of whom step forward to help when their expertise is particularly appropriate. Psychics who choose to work with spirit guides often wish to learn the appearance and name of their spirit guides so that they can call upon them as they work.

I suggest that you meet a spirit guide on the astral plane. It may be easier to meet him or her in a dream, but if you use a lucid journey to the astral plane you may be more easily able to access that spirit guide at will, if only by going back to the astral plane in a quick meditation. Start out in your home base and travel out of it to a meeting place or to the home of a spirit guide. Be alert for your spirit guide to take any form, including any that are nonhuman. Ask your spirit guide's name as well as a sign for when his or her presence is near you. Ask where he or she likes to stand near you. For example, if you feel a presence behind your left shoulder, that might be a particular spirit guide. You may wish to ask about the guide's history. Don't forget to thank your spirit guide before ending your session.

  * *Meet a spirit guide through astral travel.*

DAY 182

....

Take Your Dreams to Clairvoyance

You can bring your clairvoyant visions to your dreams, and you can also bring your dream visions out of your dreams to work with them during your clairvoyant sessions. I find this practice helpful if lucid dreaming starts to feel like hard work. It can take me days of dreaming to puzzle out a particular dream, whereas it might take me only an hour to find out what I need to know by meditation. Also, you have more control during waking meditation, no matter how skilled a dreamer you are. This can be an asset to you when dealing with topics that sadden or frighten you.

You'll have to start by being diligent with your dream journal. Write out your dream and include sketches to jog your memory. Then, when you sit down to meditate, read through the pertinent dream entries aloud, and concentrate on the sketches you've made. Close your eyes and walk yourself through the dream as you remember it, beginning to end. Focus only on the replay of your dream. If it begins to extend itself in your mind, allow the change to flow naturally into a clairvoyant vision in your mind's eye. Add anything you discover to the margins in your dream journal.

* Choose to meditate on a particularly compelling dream that you've
  had before.

DAY 183

....

Taking Visualizations Further

You're more than halfway through your year of psychic development. If you've been struggling with this section on clairvoyance, get serious about inducing your visions by combining some of the tips you've learned. For example, wait for a full moon and try fasting for a day before your clairvoyant session. Lengthen the time you spend meditating and induce a deep trance before getting started. Use a scrying divination tool such as a crystal ball to simulate your visions. And of course, always record what you see or don't see.

If you've been successful thus far, go ahead and push yourself as long as you continue to feel safe. You can set up more tests for yourself with a partner. Write down any mistakes that you make, as well as your successes, and look for patterns in your techniques or timing that produce the results you see. Review the goals that you've recently set and consider whether you want to make any of them bigger and better in light of your subsequent development. Think about how your psychic ability might be able to help others. Use that as motivation to build your endurance for meditation and to continue on with your clairvoyant studies.

* *Think of ways and reasons to push yourself further with your psychic development, and write down the sources of your motivation and encouragement.*

Day 184
....

Obstacles with Visualizations

The practice of banishing your obstacles with visualizations is sort of the opposite of creating a vision board. You don't want a constant reminder of your challenges in life staring you in the face. Instead, you'll need to find a way to destroy or transform them. Think of using the four elements: burning by fire, burying in earth, being carried gently away by the wind, or sinking, floating away or washing away in water.

If appropriate, you certainly can make a vision board of your barriers in life and then burn that vision board. Conversely, why not use simple meditation? Sink into a meditative state, visualize those obstacles, and then visualize their destruction, transformation, or harmless removal from your life. When you are done, be sure to ground the energy into the earth so the banishing energy does not affect anyone negatively. Focus on harmless ways you can banish obstacles. For example, if an annoying co-worker died, that would be sad because he's still a human being just like you, but if he found a better job somewhere else where he couldn't annoy you any more, everybody wins.

* *Practice visualizing your obstacles and then removing them through destruction or transformation.*

Producing Psychic Visions Under Pressure

Psychic sessions can be languid and luxurious, a relaxing escape from daily obligations. However, the more you add onto your practice, the harder it will feel to fit this psychic development into the hustle and bustle of your daily life. When you begin to read for others, you will feel social pressure to hurry up and receive your psychic messages. Even a very good friend will not want to sit through an hour of meditation just to get a psychic reading. It's okay to feel the external pressures encouraging you to hurry up and produce results. Like other activities, psychic activities can be stretched out long or clipped short as needed. After all, on a day off you might go fishing, but if you have less recreation time, you might settle for an outdoor jog.

In order to master the art of the quick "light trance" needed for many psychic activities, remember the following: look to the rituals you've already established when undertaking a longer psychic session. Maybe you seat yourself and cross your legs a certain way. Maybe you choose a particular incense. These patterns you naturally follow are the stuff of ritual. If you can bring those moments into your more brief psychic readings, they provide the key to opening the same headspace. If you don't notice any natural patterns occurring, make some up. Perhaps say a certain prayer or move your hands into a certain position each time you undertake your regular practice. You can draw on these keys in times of pressure.

* *Notice the rituals you go through before a psychic reading. If you don't have any, create some.*

Part Six

Intuition
and Empathy

Day 186
....

When are Your Emotions Your Own?

There's a particular problem in life unique to empaths. When you are an empath, you naturally pick up on the emotions of others. If this happens to you without consciously trying, then the experience might feel like you are having those emotions yourself. If this doesn't sound like you, think back to when you were a teenager or small child, as they are more likely to be natural empaths. When a small child's parents are fighting, for example, it doesn't matter if they aren't arguing about her. All she knows is that the room is filled with palpable anger, and that it is oppressive and confusing. Sometimes that child will turn to anger, not understanding that it wasn't her own but had been transferred to her. In my early twenties, I didn't know when my emotions were my own in relationships. I constantly wanted to know what my significant other was feeling or thinking. If he was unhappy, I was instantly unhappy. Needless to say, this made for a pretty miserable relationship for both of us.

When you feel emotions today, take stock of those around you. Are you having your emotions, or are others projecting them? Retire to privacy if you need to crosscheck. Ground yourself once in privacy and see if you feel differently. If so, you may be a slightly out-of-control empath.

* Be aware of the source of your emotions. Practice grounding to test the source of your emotions.

Grounding, Shielding, and Empathy

Grounding is an awesome skill, and I've been promoting it rather frequently. But for some psychics, new and old alike, grounding is a real downer. Grounding properly and thoroughly might completely destroy the energy buzz needed to perform a psychic reading. But how can you use empathy appropriately when you feel overwhelmed? Luckily, you can avoid the problem of killing your reading completely or being completely flooded with emotions that aren't yours by using techniques in the right order.

The main trick is to ground before and after a reading, not during. If you ground during a reading, you're wasting all the energy you made an effort to accumulate. Try to read even when you shield yourself well: imagine you're using a permeable shield. Your main task today will be to experiment with timing your grounding. Try to anticipate your psychic abilities and ground before things get emotionally uncomfortable.

* *Push yourself a bit today. Do something that usually emotionally overwhelms you such as taking a busy bus, giving a talk in public, meeting a new friend, or shopping at a huge department store sale. Experiment with timing your grounding and shielding.*

DAY 188

Third-party Readings

Third party readings can be a valid ethical concern in the psychic community. A third party reading occurs when a person comes to you asking for a psychic reading on someone who is not in the room with you and thus included in your reader/subject privacy agreement. The most common of these requests in my experience is when a client asks me about a significant other or ex. It can feel wrong or voyeuristic, but the flip side of the coin is that the information is out there and available to all of us.

What helps me is conceptualizing psychic reading as drawing from the universe at large rather than sucking information directly from another person. Your psychic abilities are readily available to you whether you're separated from your subject by an energetic shield or miles of concrete walls. You don't have to affect your subject's energy in any way to perform a psychic reading. Just as you we share air particulates that might once have been breathed by dinosaurs, we all share this world, and we can all read the signs that mother earth has provided.

* *Decide whether you are comfortable providing third party readings or not. It is okay if you are uncomfortable providing them, but it is better to be prepared with an explanation before turning somebody down.*

DAY 189
....

Volunteering

If you need to develop your empathy, volunteering with others is the best way to do so, plain and simple. It may seem too mundane or cliché to be true, but it is an essential truth of our species. If you cannot connect to human suffering in a concrete way, you will never be able to access it in a spiritual way. The best way to confront suffering is with solace or assistance. There may be many opportunities in your community for you to connect with and help people who are in an emotional state of transition.

Investigate volunteer opportunities near you. It's okay for you to choose a particular cause that speaks to you. If you love children, consider becoming a foster parent or leading after-school activities. If you feel comfortable around the elderly, volunteer at a nursing home. If you have a heart for people suffering from psychiatric problems, visit some in your local hospital. If you've suffered poverty yourself, reconnect with the poor by helping to feed them. You don't have to push yourself outside of your comfort zone. Just allow yourself to soak in some perspective and to find healthy boundaries as an empathic psychic.

* *Choose a volunteer opportunity near you that will help you build empathy.*

Day 190

Bells and Chimes

It is an eerie constant through many cultures—Eastern and Western, to the north and south—that bells and chimes are used to frighten away evil spirits or to cleanse and clear an area. There is something about the sound of a bell or chime that also clears the slate for a psychic. Thus, it can be helpful to procure a bell or chime of your own. You don't need to shell out a lot of money for Tibetan singing bowls or real silver bells. In fact, one of my favorite bells is a tiny little thing I found on the ground that must have fallen off a bike, a little bell used by motorcyclists to scare off gremlins.

The best way to improve your psychic development with a bell or chime is to just start using the thing. Try ringing it before and after each psychic session. Ideally, the bell will become part of the basic ritual you use before entering a trance and performing a psychic reading. Just as Pavlov's dogs were conditioned to salivate at the sound of a bell ringing, you too can become conditioned to enter a trance and to perform a psychic reading the instant you hear the unique chime of your bell.

* *Procure a bell or chime, even if it means lightly tapping the side of a drinking glass, and use that sound to begin and end your psychic meditation sessions.*

Day 191

....

Enlightenment and Psychic Development

The Hindu and Buddhist concept of enlightenment may add to your understanding of psychic abilities. Enlightenment represents a blissful state where one is free from desire. Some teachers or gurus are said to have achieved enlightenment in just one lifetime, although this is rare. In the eyes of those who believe in reincarnation, these special people have escaped the wheel of death and rebirth. Obviously, such perspective might allow people to develop psychic abilities without guile or bias. Thus, even were they to be sensitive to them, they would be unattached to the earthly problems picked up in psychic readings.

Today's exercise is a journaling one about your beliefs, since we will be exploring more of your faith later in part 10. Do you believe in reincarnation? Do you believe your psychic abilities might be able to pick up past lives or the effects of past lives on a current one? Do you believe that one goal of psychic reading might be to understand how to achieve enlightenment based on current or past life influences? Like it or not, your deepest beliefs will influence how you steer a psychic reading for yourself or others, so you'll need to be aware of them now.

* *Write out your understanding of how past lives and enlightenment might affect the goal or outcome of your psychic readings, if at all.*

Day 192
....

Tomorrow is Another Day:
Failure and Being Overwhelmed

As a psychic, I feel incredibly responsible when I fail at a psychic reading. After all, it is not within the cultural norm for me to be performing psychic readings at all. It would be perfectly acceptable to many people if I stopped my psychic practice entirely. Sometimes, when I sit down on my own and try to look at my life using my psychic skills, I am genuinely at a loss. This is because I am too close to my own life and problems at that moment to be able to deal with whatever situation I'm in.

It's okay to take a step back if you are feeling too close to a situation to effectively read for yourself or for somebody else. The solution to a problem may be as simple as rephrasing the question so it is not as intense. However, you may have to take a break before coming back to the question. You may need to buy or trade a reading with another psychic to distance yourself from the subject at hand. At any rate, the important next step is to get back into psychic practice as soon as possible. Avoid the mistakes you've made in the past and keep going.

* *If you've suffered failure along the way, what steps can you take to avoid feeling that sense of disappointment in the future?*

DAY 193

Only When in Balance

As an empathic psychic reader, your headspace, emotional state of being, and stress level will affect every psychic reading you do. There is no way around being human, despite exquisite grounding and a flawless execution of a shielding technique. Choose to perform psychic readings especially for others, when you are in balance with your emotions, mental status and level of stress. Today is your time to think about that option and how it fits in with your psychic life.

A period of abstinence to regain balance may work well for a lot of people, when pressure affects their psychic effectiveness. In fact, the biggest challenge for such people may be to get back into the game after the break. For others, psychic abilities may not be so easily "turned off," or they may be such a vital part of spiritual or personal practice that refraining from reading may not be an option. It's best to decide now, before you need a break, how you feel about abstaining from psychic readings when you are personally not at your best.

> * Under what circumstances would you not want to perform a psychic reading on any topic? How would you know when you are once again ready to return to your psychic development?

Letting Go

In psychic readings, many of the problems clients encounter have one simple solution: just let go. After all, letting go is an essential part of human life. It appears in the Hero's Journey. It is a story that plays out in each of our lives again and again. For empathic psychics, letting go can be an especially difficult thing to do. When your energy intermingles easily with those around you, letting go of relationships or letting go of things can feel like tearing off a part of yourself. As a developing psychic, you must cultivate in yourself the healthy ability to let go of things, people, and outcomes. If you never develop this skill, how will you ever be able to advise others to do the same when it comes up as a solution in one of your psychic readings?

Think of the areas in your life that could use some pruning or letting go. Sometimes it helps to begin with the physical. Perhaps your home needs some spring cleaning. Perhaps for the sake of your health, you need to eliminate some unhealthy habits. Then there is the mental and emotional clutter. What relationships no longer serve you or others well? Finally, look toward the spiritual. Clear out any negative energy so you can make room for new and better things in your life. Pick one of these things to do today to move forward with the cycle of letting go that makes up life.

* *What do you need to release in your life? Take steps today to let go.*

DAY 195

Electronic Interference

I have a few friends who save their psychic activities for rooms that don't have any electronic equipment. In fact, we have gone to spiritual retreats together, far away from any televisions or computers, to a place with no cellular phone reception. It's not that these electronic devices inherently interfere with psychic energy, but by their very nature, we are subject to our devices' beck and call. They inhibit our concentration simply by being an active link to the material world.

When I am meditating, the siren song of my computer's social networks or my cell phone's applications call to me. It's more fun to be surfing through the Internet than to battle through the initial stages of concentration to achieve a trance or deep meditation. Consequently, I like to place my devices out of sight as much as possible. Sometimes I even remove my watch, out of respect for sacred space, where time does not apply. Ironically, removing your watch may drive you to use a timer, but that is still better than glancing at your wrist or the wall every few minutes.

* *Minimize electronic distractions in your psychic workspace. Treat your meditation place as sacred space.*

Day 196
....

Ego

Let's have some real talk about ego. As a developing psychic, your ego may be in flux. You might struggle with feelings of low self esteem if you're unable to complete an exercise. On the other hand, you may feel focused on your own ego so acutely that you become a bit set in your ways. If you feel unwilling to try something that sounds different or challenging, or if you find yourself becoming a bit insensitive when you read for others, your own ego may be taking control.

Personally speaking, performing psychic readings is sometimes more about my ego than about finding a spiritual or helpful purpose. I want to see good things for myself. I want to see reflected glory. I love to hear praise from other people when I read for them, and it makes me feel important to be able to give somebody advice. If I feel too much of that ego rising, I have to evaluate my purpose and shrink my ego down a bit. I need to reflect on my weaknesses and how I can improve upon them. I must acknowledge the dark sides of my nature. I must help others get what messages they need, even if it means keeping my mouth shut when I have unwanted advice to give. Think today about how you can quell your ego if it rises up like a monster.

* *What are some ways you can humble yourself in your
  psychic practice?*

DAY 197
· · · · · · · · · · · · · ·

Psychic Sickness

In other cultures, psychic sickness or spiritual illness is often a real deal. In Haiti and some areas of West Africa, sensing spirits or being sensitive to the emotions of another might strike someone with a malady that acts like a physical illness. In the Middle East, psychically detected entities can cause somebody to become listless until they are driven out by the beat of a drum and the dancing of the victim. In the Western world, we have evidence-based medicine, which is an incredible blessing, and not to be ignored. That said, spiritual care departments have popped up in our hospitals, acknowledging the fact that we can benefit from spiritual healing as well.

When you become ill, please continue going to your doctor and taking your medicine. Don't let it stop you, though, from considering some psychic first aid as well. Try grounding more frequently when sick. Though meditation can be hard, it might be the best medicine. Try cleansing your living space with frankincense or sage incense when you are feeling off. Your faith and skill, combined with your immune system and traditional medicine, may bring you back to wellness more quickly and smoothly.

* *Write a note to yourself in your medicine cabinet or your first aid kit to try grounding and cleansing after treating your illness or injury.*

DAY 198

. . . .

Getting a Second Opinion

When you don't get the answer you like from a psychic reading, your first natural impulse will be to try again. You'll want a second opinion, even from yourself. For example, when you are reading from the tarot cards, it can be easy to assume that the card that felt wrong was a dropped card or a mistake. You want to shuffle the cards and start again. In extreme cases, you might want to go to another psychic for a second opinion. Then another for a third. This is not crazy or out of the ordinary; some of my intelligent and stable clients have done this, all in efforts to hedge their bets.

If you get an answer you don't like or you think is plain wrong, try to step back and take a look at the situation as an outsider. Is there some very real personal bias in your reading that might render it invalid? Are there any choice and decision points ahead that could change the outcome? Rather than repeated readings and duplicate answers, it may be more helpful to change your approach. You may need to abandon the psychic approach entirely. If not, is there another psychic you can trust? Can you make a choice before visiting that psychic to change the course of your destiny first?

* *Find another potential psychic you can trust in case you ever need a second opinion. You don't have to use that other psychic today. In fact, you shouldn't if you can take life-changing action before then, but it is good to have a resource.*

DAY 199

Emotions Around a Place

You've already attempted to have some clairvoyant visions in a specific place. I asked you to do this first because when in a historical place, I believe it is easier to experience empathic emotions than clairvoyant visions. Keep in mind that if you suddenly have fearful or angry emotions when in a new place, you have every right to leave before receiving any more psychic information. Also, if you are still having problems with your emotions overwhelming your other psychic senses, it is okay to review the section on grounding and part 5 (on clairvoyance) before proceeding.

If, on the other hand, you are ready to confront your emotions, choose to visit an emotionally charged place today. The classic example field trip would be to a local graveyard. Do not necessarily look for visions or any other sensory perceptions, although it's okay if they do occur. The goal is to allow yourself to be open to emotional change. If you feel peaceful, mournful, frightened, or confused, note your emotional sensation when it happens. As you move throughout the site, your feelings may change multiple times.

* *Visit a graveyard or another emotionally evocative site for you as a psychic.*

Day 200

· · · · · · · · · · · · · ·

Criticizing Your Intuition Constructively

Now that you have acknowledged your ego and know how to deflate it if necessary, the next step is to find a positive way to confront failure. Otherwise, your only option may be to quit or, worse, accept a job poorly done. I've developed the acronym AUM (which also happens to be the universal mantra for meditation) to help you remember the three steps to get over any problem with your psychic development: Avoidance, Understanding, and Meditation.

What does "avoidance" mean? Think about how could you have avoided past problems. Could you have delayed the reading or changed the question in any way? Could you have referred your client to another reader? If you were reading for yourself, could you have waited for another time? Next is understanding. What, exactly, caused the problem with your reading? What were your expectations and how were they not met? Finally, meditate and reflect upon improving your reading skills. Be very precise with your next attempt so you won't run into the same problems as last time.

* *Choose your least productive psychic reading to date and use AUM to analyze how you could have done it better, and how you can do it better in the future.*

Anxiety

Anxiety one of the largest problems a developing psychic reader will face. Essentially fear, anxiety can present as physical symptoms. Anxiety can be the quickening of your breathing, the increased pace of your heartbeat and the prickling of your skin. Each of these symptoms is reason enough to stop your psychic reading, if only for purely spiritual reasons. After all, how can you achieve a meditation or trance at a frantic pace? How can you pay attention to minute details about your surroundings if your body and mind are screaming for attention?

Anxiety is often the symptom of a deeper issue. It may be that you have clinical problems with anxiety that need to be treated through professional health care. If so, you can still continue your psychic practice, but you must do so with a little help from your doctor or therapist. In other cases, it could be that your anxiety is triggered by specific aspects of your psychic practice. If so, you'll need to journal your psychic activity in complete detail, and eliminate any practices that might cause anxiety one at a time. Add them in afterwards to verify that they were what was really causing the anxiety, and not just confirmation bias.

* *Examine your life for causes of anxiety. Begin a process of elimination to try to get rid of those causes. Experiment with reading possible causes in afterwards, in case you were mistaken.*

Grief

Grief is the number one reason I refuse to perform psychic readings for some clients. It is all-encompassing and devastating, and when a person is in a state of grieving, there may be no logical way to offer advice. Even if you were to say the most intelligent and proper thing in the world, it could still harm a person who just needs to focus on eating and sleeping and surviving until his or her brain is ready to process the issue. For that reason, I am inclined to delay readings that focus on the spirits of loved ones who have recently passed.

There is no reason to fear the delay of a reading after death; the person will still be dead after a month, a year, two years, and so on! The only thing that may feel improper is the social idea that we should all do what we can for the grieving. Unless asked, please don't offer your psychic resources for the grieving right away. Instead, offer something practical, like a hug or a home-cooked meal.

* *Come up with a game plan for what to do if somebody you love loses someone important. Have a comfort food recipe set aside that includes ingredients you have on hand and have a condolence card at the ready. Remember, don't offer too much too soon.*

Anger

Anger is a pretty frightening experience to have as an empath, especially if you happen to be female. As women, we are trained our entire lives that anger is an inappropriate emotion to show, especially if it becomes violent. We are encouraged to show compassion, tolerance, and forgiveness. Some of these virtues are good, indeed. They help people of either gender to avoid serious misunderstandings that could ruin friendships or other relationships forever. But in other cases, anger can be a welcome emotion, helping us defend ourselves against unwanted assaults. It can be the first step toward transforming emotions about something that can benefit us in the long haul.

So the next time you feel angry, try first to discern the source of the anger. Is this anger truly yours, or is it coming from someone else? Try to empower yourself by using your psychic abilities to sense the anger in different ways. When I am in the same room with an angry person, I tend to visualize a taut sheet with a stone or something else weighting it down where the angry person is located. It seems as if everything in the room is pointed at that person. In this way, you can sense the presence of an angry person with your eyes closed. This skill is used by karate practitioners in combat situations, and it can be useful for you, too.

> * *Find a way to visualize or sense the emotion of anger so*
> *you can determine its source when you feel anger affecting you.*

Day 204
....

Sadness

I have special disclaimers about persistent sadness; many developing psychics who struggle with this have contacted me about it. Sadness that turns to hopelessness that is long lasting may be a sign of clinical depression. Dealing with feeling empathic sadness on top of depression can be devastating to the developing psychic. If you struggle with depression, it is important to manage your illness with a doctor and have support in your life from professionals, family, and friends before experimenting with your empathy. Those who have any emotional illness will need a support system in place, should empathy development go awry.

Sensing sadness can be difficult for a psychic, because a common reaction is to withdraw into oneself. This social withdrawal is not conducive to sensing the message the sadness may be delivering or even discovering its source. For example, if you sense sadness in a location associated with the spirit of a person who died there, your first response might be to go home and lay in bed. It's much easier to curl up and eat ice cream than try to reach out and communicate with a spirit. And yes, it's hard to ask the reason for its sadness and offer your help. Your task today will be to make a commitment to delay self-soothing behaviors (when safe) to seek the true meaning of sadness through meditation next time you feel inexplicably or empathically sad.

* *If you struggle with depression, make sure you have your therapist's and medication provider's numbers on hand in your psychic log for quick reference in an emergency. Otherwise, spend the day sensitive to feelings of sadness you receive from external sources, and meditate upon them.*

DAY 205
....

Insensitivity

The flip side of empathy is insensitivity. This is a common automatic and subconscious defense the developing psychic might use. Everyone has the capacity to be insensitive to others, and this social response is pervasive because of its protective value. How do you know whether you are acting insensitively to others due to your developing empathic abilities? The same way that insensitivity often manifests—you may receive frequent feedback, especially from significant others, about apparent aloofness, bluntness, or even rudeness. You may find it difficult to make or keep friends, especially friends who are more emotional.

Fixing insensitivity is very challenging, because you must open yourself up psychically and allow yourself to become emotionally vulnerable. Rather than faking an apology and moving forward, you'll need to reach out and allow the emotions of others to wash over you and then harmlessly ground. In this way, you can get a taste of how others are feeling without feeling emotionally overwhelmed yourself. Once you have grounded the energy and stabilized, consider carefully how to respond. The old chestnut of treating others how you would like to be treated may come into play. If you do need to distance yourself, you can now do so with closure and compassion rather than with insensitivity.

* *Practice opening yourself up to the emotions of others briefly, and then grounding the energy and reacting sensitively to any problems you may be able to solve.*

Day 206

....

Tolerance

The next level of banishing insensitivity is developing tolerance. I'd like to share a personal story of a time when I found this especially hard. Years ago, I was in a spiritual worship group with a friend I dearly loved. She was experiencing a domestic abuse situation at home. Due to my level of empathy, especially in a spiritual context, I felt unable to tolerate the abuse she received. I desperately tried offering help, giving advice. I simply could not tolerate her willingness to put up with her abuser. Finally, I delivered an ultimatum to her, which was actually the last thing she needed. As a result of my concern, she was now being victimized by yet another controlling person, ironically. In the end, she refused my terms and as a result, I chose to leave the worship group. I had let intolerance get the better of me.

Other people may have treated the situation differently than I did. There is no one right answer to such a painful situation. Perhaps approaching my friend with tolerance would have provided her with the support she desperately needed in life. Even if you consider yourself a tolerant person, there may be situations like this that could blindside you. Think about the types of behaviors in others you do not tolerate for whatever reason. Even if you can't invite those people into your home, think about a way you can tolerate them in your heart.

* *What kind of people or behavior do you find hard to tolerate? How can you safely build more tolerance while keeping your boundaries?*

Day 207

Transparency and Engagement

Interacting with others as a psychic, whether reading for them or not, depends on your openness, as we have discussed. Even in everyday interactions when you're not wearing your "psychic" hat or calling yourself by that title, your psychic abilities will cause you to be perceived in different ways depending on your actions. We've already discussed transforming insensitivity into tolerance, and the next step is to add some more pleasant qualities to your daily interactions. As a bonus, these qualities will help you when you read for others.

Being transparent in psychic terms means being willing to answer questions about what you can and cannot do and sense. It may be tempting to keep an air of mystery around your psychic ability, especially if you are afraid of being mocked or rejected, but your openness will help the perception of psychics at large, and encourage others to be more relaxed around you. This relaxation will prevent hostile emotions that require your defense or neutralization tactics. Being engaged with others means consciously giving and receiving from the flow of energy between people during conversation. As a psychic, you may be carefully sampling and experiencing those energies, but it is important to not put up too much of a wall between you, and it is just as vital to offer as much of yourself as you receive from others.

* *Notice the flow of information and energy in your conversations today. Are you giving as much as you are receiving? Seek balance when appropriate.*

DAY 208
....

Loneliness and the Psychic

Loneliness has a particular effect on a psychic, especially when experienced long term, and especially when a psychic is developing his or her empathy. For someone sensitive to the emotions and energy of others, being alone can feel just as debilitating as losing one's sense of sight or hearing. Like a fish out of water, the developing psychic may feel unable to reach full potential and uncomfortable in his or her own skin. This doesn't mean that every psychic must have marriage and a family. I know several accomplished psychics who live happily alone. However, it does mean that the empathic psychic would not be at his or her best living an entirely solitary life as the yogi hermit on a mountaintop.

Now may be the time to begin looking for more friends who are open to the idea of your psychic development. Later, in part 10, you will have prompts to make new friends of other psychics or through a book club. For now, consider reaching out to your existing friends to see who is friendly and amenable to the idea of psychic development. Some of your potential best new friends may be members of your extended family, and they may share your innate abilities and skills.

  * Consider broaching the subject of your psychic development with friends and family that have not yet talked about such things with you.

DAY 209

....

Geomancy and Feng Shui

When I was a child, I visited Hong Kong and saw a building with a giant hole right through the middle of it. My mother told me that they had built the hole so dragons could fly through it without stopping. The dragons, of course, were actually energy, or *qi*. The energy in your environment flows similarly, unless blocked by impediments. Years later, when my husband and I bought our first home, I made him move pots and pans that were blocking a large pass-through hole in the wall between the kitchen and the living room. "You're blocking the dragons!" I said. To me, the clutter in the pass-through broke up the free flowing energy between the two rooms that I sensed should be there.

Feng shui has so many principles that it is difficult to get a feel for it in a day. In part 1, I asked you to observe your environment and how it affects you. Today, return to those initial observations in your journal, especially about grounding methods and the visualization lesson on Day 13. Repeat the exercise indoors. This time, determine how much of those energetic feelings you receive are from the flow of energy in that environment. When your surroundings are affecting you, perform an experiment to see if your feeling shifts over the next few days. For example, just clearing off a coffee table can make the space feel more expansive, and reorienting a bed can change your waking and sleeping experience.

* *Observe the energy flow in your environment. Experiment with changing your surroundings to help the energy flow through the space more smoothly.*

DAY 210
....

Encouragement for Your Psychic Self

You've gone through some serious goal setting and have stretched yourself in your development so far. Right now, you should take stock of what you are already doing now. Everyone has natural strengths and weaknesses. Now that you know that psychic development is not just a single skill but a complicated skill set, you'll notice that you excel in some techniques and struggle with others. It's great to challenge yourself and set new goals or go back over things you thought were tough. However, don't forget to celebrate your accomplishments. Noticing your natural strengths will let you go further in some areas of development. Best of all, writing down some positive things about yourself will help encourage and motivate you to further study as you move through the rest of the year.

Write down three of your greatest strengths as a developing psychic. Try to make the strengths as diverse as possible so you can see the range of your skills laid out before you. They don't all have to deal with psychic aptitude, since being a keen observer and following through on your daily lessons with dedication are also worthy pursuits. If you're like me and have a hard time complimenting yourself, go through your psychic journal for reminders of some of the things you've been able to accomplish. When you are done, circle one of your strengths about which you feel the most pride. Remember to choose that strength to highlight it in an upcoming psychic session.

* *Write down your three greatest strengths as a developing psychic.*

DAY 211
....

Being Impulsive and Spontaneous

Being psychic is only useful if you can act upon your psychic flashes quickly without second-guessing them too much. If you beat down your intuition and consistently let your head make decisions instead of your heart, you're actually suppressing your training. How do you train yourself to trust your psychic flashes? Easy—without taking big risks, learn to latch on to your first impulses and go with the flow, following wherever your psychic senses lead you. If this sounds a lot like impulsiveness, that's because it is!

Today's exercise is to do something on a whim. The easiest form of this exercise may be to simply go for a walk in a city or town you know well. Don't have a destination in mind. Every time you get to a crossroads, be conscious about that decision point in the road and in your life. Go with the first impulse that crosses your mind. If you find a spontaneous desire to stop inside a shop or to go to visit a friend, follow that whim as well. Afterwards, journal about your experience. Did you discover anything surprising? Did your spontaneity feel natural or forced? Was it difficult for you to hold on to your first impulse without letting it go and following a different thought instead?

* *Do something on a whim today.*

DAY 212

....

Leaving Your Comfort Zone

We all get set in our ways. When I teach apprentices, I am able to follow closely and view their strengths and weaknesses so I can get them to build all their skills, no matter which one is easier than the other. In turn, I have been challenged by my spiritual mentors to cover every base, even though I would much rather have skipped some of them. If you are studying alone, your job will be a little harder. From here, there's no way for me to assess which skills are the wobbly point in your repertoire and simply need practice to feel more natural.

Write down and re-evaluate some of your psychic development goals that have been challenging you. Brainstorm to find out why those goals are particularly hard for you, noting some of the barriers you've already observed (not enough time, et cetera). Some of those barriers are simply not going to be removed. Take special note of some of the challenges that could be overcome through practice, like beginner's anxiety or even boredom. Make a note to practice those skills in short duration, but with greater frequency.

* *What are some ways you can leave your comfort zone with your psychic practice in small but manageable increments?*

Day 213

Mentors

Finding a mentor near you is one terrific way to develop your psychic abilities to their fullest. I had several psychic mentors who helped me get to where I am today, and I know I can still call them if I want to develop further or times when I fall into a rut. I highly recommend an in-person mentor, as opposed to a long-distance telephone, email, or online mentor. Somebody you can meet with face-to-face on a regular basis will get to know you in a well-rounded way. They can keep track of your life's ups and downs and can learn to sense your energies directly. An established mentor who can commit to meeting with you in person is also less likely to simply disappear in a few months or a year, effectively scrapping your mentorship investment.

Start out by seeing if you can find a peer mentor. A friend of yours who is also interested in psychic development may be just the ticket. Or you could explore local groups that meet up and discuss psychic development. Professional teachers can be paid for apprenticeships if a working relationship is more your style. If you happen to have a faith tradition sympathetic toward psychic development, you may be able to find a resource in the leaders of your spiritual community as well.

* *Find a mentor or peer mentorship opportunity near you. This may take time and some creative thinking, depending on your region, so get started today.*

Day 214

·············

Reliving an Emotional Memory

Having an emotion hit you out of the blue can be a very uncomfortable experience, especially if the emotion is negative. As an empathic psychic, you will be developing your ability to draw upon and experience intense emotions. The resulting emotions may cause you to relive memories of points in your life when you experienced a similar emotion and intensity of feeling. This can be troublesome and require grounding for those who have had traumatic life experiences. Practice in experiencing these emotional impacts will make you less likely to recoil from a psychic experience too quickly, thus losing the message that would have come through despite, or because of, the emotions.

Start inoculating yourself to your emotions with an overwhelmingly happy one. Try a meditation in which you relive some point in your life that was so happy you were nearly brought to tears. Next, relive a slightly less happy one, such as an argument with a loved one. This is usually pretty safe, since we naturally relive these moments emotionally when processing such scuffles. Finally, tackle an angry or fearful situation, because those are two that may come up in psychic visions, especially if you are empathically experiencing a spirit's emotions. Let the feelings flow through you without panicking you, and then ground them thoroughly.

* *Practice some meditations in which you relive intense emotions.*

Cleansing Your Body

Cleansing is a big part of psychic practice in cultures across the world. Ablution, or spiritual cleansing, is done before prayers in Islam. Ritual cleansing is practiced in Haitian and Wiccan magic. The reason it arises spontaneously in so many cultures is because washing with water is naturally grounding and symbolically prepares the practitioner for psychic work with a clean slate. You don't have to take a ritual bath before every psychic session, but I do so on especially important or spiritual psychic readings. The bath is not part of your psychic work, so leave yourself enough time to practice some meditation after your bath is complete.

Take a bath or shower in which you strongly visualize the cleansing taking place on all levels. Visualize distracting thoughts being washed away. Dutifully scrub your body, doing your best job to make yourself as squeaky clean as possible. You may add salt and herbs to your bath if you like, but any bath or shower can do. This ritual can even be reduced to a simple prayer for cleansing whispered while washing your face in the sink. Pay special care to your feet and hands, as those are often used as conduits for energy in your practice.

* *Take time for a ritual cleansing bath before your psychic
meditation today. See how this affects your practice.*

Day 216
....

Slowing Down

As a professional psychic who does her work day in and day out, I'm guilty of rushing my psychic sessions. I'm to the point where some of the basic techniques are so ingrained into my psyche that they come automatically. That part is great. However, in my daily meditation practice, I work to slow down the psychic information as it comes to me. Jumping from one symbol or feeling to the next may feel exciting, like solving a puzzle, but you might miss the whole point of the message if you rush. In fact, any additional psychic senses you get may be your psychic self just repeating the message in different ways until you get it.

Today, choose a psychic technique and practice holding the results in your mind as your receive them. For example, if you are scrying and you see a heart shape, close your eyes and envision that heart shape as clearly as you can. Impress the vision in your mind and meditate upon it, driving all other thoughts from your mind. Let yourself focus on just your initial perception for the entire session instead of moving on to other perceptions or other questions.

* *Practice slowing down your psychic reading so you can focus on one thing at a time.*

Transcending Emotion and
Letting It Pass Through You

Transcending emotion feels much different than experiencing it, but it is needed for some psychic circumstances. For example, imagine you are performing a psychic reading on a house haunted by a serial killer. The serial killer's spirit is full of murderous rage. There's no reason for you to be filled with that sort of anger, even in the safe context of a psychic reading. You don't need to worry about being insensitive toward a dead person who is a bad guy anyway. Thus, you don't have to force yourself to become immersed in those emotions. However, if you shut yourself off completely, you may not receive any psychic messages at all. A delicate balance must be struck.

To practice reading on some emotions you do not wish to experience, start by continuing to make shielding a part of your psychic practice. If you do sense an emotion you don't want coming through a shield you've purposely left semi-permeable for the purposes of doing a psychic reading, let the emotion pass you by the same way you release thoughts that arise during your meditation. You can observe the emotion clearly without letting it settle in you. You can practice this by reading for an emotional friend or family member, or by simply using the same techniques when reliving your own emotional memory. When you are done with the reading, ground the energies well and check in with yourself to make sure you are properly grounded.

* *Practice being unaffected by emotions during a psychic reading today.*

Day 218
....

Getting Solitary Rest and Sleep

When I asked you to go on a short spiritual retreat, it could have been a week out camping or a few hours in the bathtub alone. Again today, solitary rest should be on your agenda. If you can, practice sleeping alone this time. It may be a tall order for you to fill if you feel like you cannot sleep without your partner in bed with you. Or perhaps your family or housing situation does not allow for a day away from sharing a bed. If it's possible, though, try it. If this is a rare experience for you, be sure to note how it affects your dreams.

If you normally sleep alone, take some special time out for solitary rest and relaxation today. This includes a little break from electronic communication as well. Practice not being at the beck and call of others for a little bit. Focus instead on rejuvenating yourself. What should you do during this time? Practice your grounding and shielding. These two skills feel different when you are not around other people, and they may be more effective for you during a solitary and restful day. It's okay to take a break from performing a psychic reading afterwards today, if you like.

 * *Rest on your own today, and focus on how different your energy
   feels when you are solitary.*

DAY 219

. . . .

Opening and Closing a Session

Since psychic reading may be a daily practice for you, too many rituals or bells and whistles to open and close your psychic reading sessions may constrict your time. However, having a set opening and closing to your psychic readings can help you to set that time apart in the day. Opening and closing your psychic sessions formally can also help you when you are reading for others, giving social cues to your subject about when the reading is beginning and ending. You've also learned that some ritual keys can help snap your brain into the right frame of mind. Incorporate those keys into your opening.

Your opening can begin with some of your psychic keys, be they incenses burned, the removal of shoes, or sitting a certain way. You can say a quick opening prayer, asking for clarity, if you like. Your closing should be equally symbolic, if not more so. Consider incorporating a physical movement that cues you to ground yourself, like bowing or touching hands to the floor. You may choose to say a prayer of thanks to the universe, your deities, or to your higher self.

* *Design a short and sweet opening and closing for your psychic sessions, and write down any words or motions in your psychic log.*

....

Words and Promises

One basic law of magic that applies to psychics is that thoughts are things. As you visualize your destiny during a psychic reading, you also bring it about in your real life through hard work, luck, and other circumstances. The words you speak are also very important things. All psychic practitioners and magicians are affected most extremely by the words they speak, especially when acting as psychics. You've seen what a difference the phrasing of a question for your psychic readings can make. So too can words and promises that you make in everyday life affect how good a psychic you can be.

Consider the following: You make a New Year's resolution to join a gym and work out three times a week. You tell everybody that you know about your resolution. After the first month, you get bored and quit going to the gym. How likely are those friends you told going to believe your psychic readings if you didn't follow through with your words about going to the gym? More pointedly, how is your own subconscious going to cooperate with you in a psychic session? How will you believe yourself? Consider your words carefully today.

* *Work toward honest words and promises today.*

Release What Holds You Back; Reevaluate Limits

You've explored your barriers and you've explored your challenges. Now it's time to confront your excuses. Some excuses for avoiding psychic development (or anything else in life) are good enough. It's okay to avoid some psychic work, for example, when you are still grieving someone's passing. Or you might not have time right now because of career demands. Today's job is to realize that many of your limitations are, in fact, self-imposed. Take a look at the previous examples; they're certainly good and valid excuses, yet they are self-limited. The person affected by grief could choose to take a risk. The person with no time could portion out free time more meaningfully. If those options aren't really good ones, the self-limitations are valid.

However, self-limitations can be insidious. Even when they stop being valid, they can still feel valid. Or you may think your partner or your parents have placed them on you, when in fact they haven't. Think about some limits you have placed on yourself. Review the barriers and challenges to your psychic practice you've written down before. Underline some of those that appear to be self-imposed, even if for good reasons. Meditate on your limits and whether or not it is appropriate to remove them.

* *Meditate on your self-imposed limits without judgement or censorship.*

Day 222

. . . .

Fear in Intuition and Empathy

Fear comes from two sides of the developing psychic. So far, we've worked with what you should do when fear arises from your environment, a spirit, or from somebody for whom you are performing a psychic reading. You've learned how to rise up and defend yourself while still performing a psychic reading. You've also learned a little bit about how to deal with your anxieties related to performing readings. When these two types of fear come together, however, they can be especially confusing for the empathic psychic, as one can feed into the other.

Today's exercise is going to be another combination of familiar skills. Get ready to have another session of reliving an emotional memory, this time one of fear. Before the session, though, you will do a preliminary exercise designed to prevent one fear feeding into another. Get out your psychic journal and write down some of your worst fears about being a developing psychic. Some of them may be ones you have dealt with before, like the possibility of seeing a really scary clairvoyant vision. Others may seem silly when you write them down, but do it anyway. You might say, for example, "I'm afraid that other psychics may make fun of me." As you write down each fear, ground your energy. When you are done with the preparation, you should be grounded very well and ready to practice letting the fear wash through you.

* *Practicing meditating on the emotion of fear.*

Part Seven

Symbols

Day 223

....

1

Throughout part 7, we will go over common individual symbols. I didn't give you these earlier because I wanted you to come up with your own meanings for symbols. This part will remain limited as well, as your own personal symbol dictionary grows as a result of your work. However, it is useful to see some common meanings for symbols, since some meanings arise independently in many people, or are shared across cultures. In this chapter, I will be sharing some of my personal meanings, which in turn come from my culture as well as from the common human experience and from common teachings.

First, consider the number one. This number represents independence, assertiveness, and aggression. The number one is the first forward and the winner of every race. Yes, the number one can be lonely. However, the number one can also merely be at the top of many. Notice today how many times you see the number one appear, whether it be on a clock, on an address, or in an oddly shaped puddle on a sidewalk. Think about how the number one relates to your personality, your life, and what it might symbolize.

* Meditate on the number one.

Day 224

....

2

Two represents the joining of two singular people, ideas, or concepts. Imagine the number two as representing two lovers entwined, or two people, meeting for the first time, engaged excitedly in talk. Two is symbolically two number ones and all it represents. So, when two aggressive and assertive people come together, you know that the union will not necessarily be relaxing. Still, the coupling that comes with the number two can be exciting. It can create change. The number two represents the union of two things that ensure life will never be the same again, symbolizing a new beginning.

Again, today, explore your world searching for the number two. Notice what people and things are around you whenever you see the number two. Are you drawn to a heart-to-heart talk with somebody else? Are you forging a bond? Are you meeting somebody new? The number two may herald new doors opening in your life. Journal your experiences with this number. Think about points in your life where you embodied the number two, either because of the coming together of great minds on the same wavelength, or because of a new opportunity presented by networking or collaborating with another.

* *Meditate on the number two.*

Day 225
....

3

The number three is the concept of birth. When those two individual number ones that come together unite, they produce a baby, and the result is this number. This nuclear family represents a family unit as well as creativity, fertility, and abundance. Think about the triangle. The triangle is a very stable structure, so much so that it is used in bridge architecture. Even though a triangle may have pointy edges and look awkward (especially if you are trying to roll it like a sphere), it represents stability and growth, two blessings that are hard to achieve individually.

Be alert today for the number three, and think about how it appears in your life. When you notice the number three, are you feeling secure, sedentary, or in a situation where you feel stable? Conversely, are you feeling like you could stretch, reach up, and find an opportunity for growth in your surroundings when you see the number three appear for you? What creative projects might the number three represent for you right now? What do you consider your "baby"?

* *Meditate on the number three.*

Day 226

....

4

The number four is a very stable number; it is the number of legs on a table and the number associated with a house's foundation. Some of these foundations may run so deep that they contain secrets. The number four is a positive and lucky number, because strong foundations are a good thing. If you're wanting to build up to higher achievements in life, you'll certainly want to see some high numbers in your bank account and advancement elsewhere, but you may have to start out lower. Four is this starting point, the stable base from where you can build onward and upward.

When you see the number four today, pay particular attention to your environment. After all, four walls encase a room. Are you enclosed in the four walls of your home? Are you in a cubicle? What sort of little cubbies or prisons do you lock yourself in for safety and security during the day? How do you use these home base places to interact with your world? The number four represents closing yourself off from the outside when you need it.

* *Meditate on the number four.*

DAY 227
. . . .

5

Remember when I said that the triangle has pointy edges, but is still a stable structure? Well, the number five has pointy edges, but it doesn't have the stability associated with it in the same way as the number three. Instead, the number five is all about dynamic instability and change. Five is the tension between five people seated at a boardroom table, each arguing loud enough to be heard. The number five is the sight of five athletes in a sports game, each one grappling with another even as they work as a unit. This number can represent trouble and strife, but it can also represent positive changes and hope that comes after such changes.

As you search for the number five today, notice whether things are busier in your life when you spot that number jumping out at you. What sorts of energy interplay is going on around you? Are you engaged in a battle of some sort with others, or with your computer system, or with yourself? Notice whether the situation feels transient when you see the number five. Chances are, these phases of imbalance will pass, and with them, a new level of stability will be found.

* *Meditate on the number five.*

Day 228
· · · · · · · · · · · · · · ·

6

You've journeyed a long way through the single digit numbers, and the number six is sometimes related to looking back at the past or even your roots like your nationality or ancestral origins. The number six is that new level of stability you have reached after the tension and battle of number five. You get a chance to take a breath and look around you, recognizing the wisdom and abundance in life you have achieved from your struggles and triumphs.

When you notice the number six today, it may be a sign of the little successes on the way toward bigger successes. Who do you have to thank for the success you feel in the moment? What sorts of challenges have you overcome to be where you are today and at this time and place? You've come a long way, and you still have quite some way to go. You can do it if you keep on following this pattern of even and odd numbers, this pattern of stability and instability in life.

* *Meditate on the number six.*

Day 229
· · · · · · · · · · · · · · ·

7

The number seven is the number of mystery and the unknown. Sometimes the number seven represents the good kind of mystery, like not knowing what is going to happen at the end of a novel or exploring a new magical spell that will bring good luck. The number seven can also represent the bad kind of mystery too, like a loved one lying to you or not knowing all the information you need before choosing a new job. As seven is an odd number, you know it is a number of instability. This time, you've climbed the numbers enough to have experience and a foundation beneath your feet, but the number seven says that you don't know everything quite yet and will have to trust your instincts.

Keep watch for the number seven today. Mysterious number that it is, this number may appear to you in a sneaky, subtle, or fleeting manner. What is hidden to your eye when you see the number seven? What are some unknowns in the equation? What are some hidden mysteries you would love to explore? The number seven beckons you to explore the secrets scientists and magicians have yet to reveal. Perhaps some mysteries cannot be spoken.

* *Meditate on the number seven.*

DAY 230
....

8

At last, we've come to one of the peaks of stability, the number eight. The number eight represents an achievement that has taken quite some time to attain. This is the number of financial success—not merely a windfall, it is painstakingly built through hard work and much consideration. This is the number that represents diligent study and the pursuit of academic degrees. Despite the stability here, this is also the number that represents long journeys and travel that is carefully planned and undertaken over a long period of time.

If you see the number eight appear today, it is a good sign that you have journeyed long on your path. Think about what small steps you have made to pave your path. Do you have more study to undertake before achieving your highest goals? Do you have a long journey you have always wanted to make? Is there a next step you must take to improve your career, one that has been a long time in the making? The number eight is all about taking what you already do well and perfecting on it.

* *Meditate on the number eight.*

Day 231

....

9

The number nine is the pinnacle of numerology. Rather than moving onward to ten and eleven and further, we'll stop here. Numbers with more than one digit are mere combinations of these first nine, and each digit can be added together again and again until being reduced to a single digit number for analysis. Thus, you can think of the number nine as the ultimate success; winning the game of life. Nine is by far the luckiest number in Chinese numerology, and with its success connotations, it doesn't do so poorly in Western numerology either!

As you watch today for the lucky number nine, give yourself a pat on the back when you see it. The number nine is a sign that you have cause for celebration. It represents the many resources you already have, and the many more that are out there for you to attain. This is the number for parties and meeting with friends old and new. This is the number of financial joys and the richness of family life. You've succeeded in exploring all of the number symbols. Tomorrow, we'll move on to colors.

* *Meditate on the number nine.*

Day 232

Red

The meaning of colors can vary widely. They don't hang together as a system the way that numbers do. Also, who is to say that the color red that I see is the same as the color red that you see? Take these color sections with a grain of salt; write out your own feelings as you go, even if you disagree with mine. Today, consider the color red, the color with the shortest visible frequency, which is why lasers are most commonly red. This color is one of dynamic energy and passion, and is associated, of course, with fire and heat.

Pay attention to the color red as it appears today, and perhaps choose to wear something red to see how it affects you. Notice when people around you are wearing red. Does it suit their usual disposition or mood today? Look hard and see if you can find anyone with a red aura or red anywhere in the aura. What does this red seem to indicate about the person's intentions or demeanor? What sorts of everyday things do you see with red in them, and why was the color chosen? Meditate, for example, on the reason stoplights are red to get people's attention. Don't meditate too long, of course, because you'll have to move along soon.

* *Meditate on the color red.*

Day 233
. . . .

Orange

Orange is a masculine and happy color. Think of the brilliant orange sunlight streaming through a window and warming a bed on a weekend morning. Think of the joy of a child's laughter. These are the happy thoughts of the color orange. Wearing the color orange today, even if just a little bit, might offer a bit of a pick-me-up. Seeing others with the color orange on their clothing or in the aura may indicate a smile or a joke is coming your way. Orange represents the positivity that makes us destined for success.

When you see the color orange today, consider it a sign of harmonious growth and of success. That said, orange doesn't necessarily mean a lottery win. Think about it as the subtle glow of a grow lamp in a greenhouse, or a small child learning the alphabet by building with alphabet blocks. As you look for orange in your life, look for the joys that come with it, and notice how they spread warmly over other areas of your life. Orange reminds us that small acts of kindness and moments of bliss can buffer us from the life's cruelties.

* *Meditate on the color orange.*

Day 234
. . . .

Yellow

We're still in the bright and sunny side of the color spectrum. Yellow can represent all of the success, sunshine, and joy of orange, but it has additional meanings as well. Yellow also represents the intellectual and the intangible. Yellow may be the color to wear while you study for a test, or the color your aura shows while you wax philosophical about your favorite geeky subject. Therefore, yellow is both a positive color and one that is associated with things not yet substantial or manifested.

Today, look for the color yellow. Notice the personality types who choose to integrate this bright color into daily wear. When you see the color yellow, what thoughts are racing through your mind? It may be a cue to catch those first impulses of intuition and hold them for a moment in thought. Spying the color yellow may be a cue that you need to take a particular subject into further study to bring about greater success and happiness in your life.

* *Meditate on the color yellow.*

Day 235

Green

Your day with the color green should be fun for you. Green represents growth and abundance of all kinds. Think of the new green growth in springtime. "Going green" means thinking about things in an ecologically responsible way. Think of green cash. Green can even represent the fertility and abundance only indirectly associated with the green of springtime. It can also refer to new babies, for instance. Think of green as relating to anything that can grow itself seemingly due to chance or under its own power. If you have a goal and need energy to get yourself there, this is the color that can help.

As you look for green today, notice the energy flow around where you see the color. Green evokes drive and forward flow. You are invited to invest your own energy, time, and money in your future. Notice anyone wearing the color green. Pay attention to which signs and logos include the color green, and what activities they invite. How do you feel when you meditate on green? You may find it challenging to hold still while picturing a vivid green, or relaxing while visualizing a forest green.

* *Meditate on the color green.*

DAY 236
....

Blue

When you see the color blue, you might think of "the blues," that is, feelings of depression or sadness. However, the color blue has many different associations. Of course this color doesn't always mean sadness; otherwise people would naturally shy away from wearing it. They wouldn't paint it on cars, logos, or houses either. I prefer to think of the color blue as representing deep emotions of any kind. Blue, of course, represents water and the sea. It also represents healing. I like to light a blue candle when saying healing prayers for friends and family.

Look out for the color blue today, in human-made things and in nature. How do you feel when you see this color? When others are around the color blue or wearing it, what emotions are they displaying? This cool color has soothing qualities. Do you see more of the color blue during times of relaxation, or when day turns to night and time begins creeping toward bedtime? Allow yourself a long and relaxing meditation on blue, especially if you need healing. Do some tones of the color blue feel different than others energetically? For example, does a pastel blue feel different from navy?

* *Meditate on the color blue.*

DAY 237
....
Purple

Once a rare dye in some regions, purple came to be associated with wealth and royalty. As such, purple is now still associated with the divine. When you think of purple, think about the divinity within you—perhaps its your higher self, a god or goddess consciousness, or simply a greater sense of connection with the world around you. Purple is the color of the psychic. Some choose to visualize purple light at the third eye (the point between the eyebrows) as a representation of psychic understanding. In our culture, purple is often considered a feminine color, and thus more associated with goddesses than gods.

As a psychic, you can use purple to enhance your psychic abilities. If you're uncomfortable wearing purple, this can be as unobtrusive as pulling a piece of purple gemstone like an amethyst out of your pocket. If you enjoy wearing this color, drape yourself in it, imagining that you are wrapping yourself with psychic abilities. When you look around today for people are wearing purple, consider whether the people you see are naturally intuitive, or have some aspects of the divine feminine.

* *Meditate on the color purple.*

Day 238
....

White

White can be considered the combination of all colors or the absence of all colors. When you combine all the colors in a prism of light, you get white light. And yet white paint is generally considered as lacking pigment. White is considered to be a color of blessings. It is also the color of new beginnings. The color white is associated with purity, hence the white of wedding dresses. You can burn a white candle before your psychic readings to invite cleansing energy to clear away any negative or obfuscating energies.

Today, look at all shades of white around you. Notice the color in nature, and as the backdrop we choose for much of our décor. Where do you see white being used as a symbol of purity? White is used on walls to present an image of cleanliness. Used in the dresses of fairytale princesses, it symbolizes virtue and virginity. In reality, the walls aren't any more germ-free, nor are the women any more virginal when they're covered in white. The color is used to impress upon others its symbolic message.

* *Meditate on the color white.*

Day 239
....

Black

Like white, black can be thought of as all colors or no color. No light in any spectrum, of course, is the pitch black of darkness. Yet many paint colors mixed together can create a matte black. Black is the color of mystery, coldness, and things that go bump in the night. Black is the color of magic. Black candles can be burned for protection, especially against black magic. Think of a black cloak wrapping around you in the dark of night, concealing you from any who may harm you. While you wait in the shadows, you can observe everything going on around you while remaining unobserved. This is the secret of the color black.

Black is a difficult color to notice every day, since it is the default for so much around us. Still, you may be able to notice an overabundance of black, for example, if someone around you has dyed their hair black or dressed in black from head to toe. Consider how such people may be employing black's protective qualities. When you meditate, try to find a place where you can meditate with your eyes open but in pitch black darkness. This works for me if I stuff a towel under a bathroom door to block the light. Strange things go on in the mind when your eyes are open but see nothing. You can jumpstart clairvoyant visions using this method.

* *Meditate on the color black.*

DAY 240
....

Silver

Silver is another Goddess color. Think of the silvery light of the moon, cast down over the earth, coating everything in eerie muted shades of gray. Thus the color silver is one of magic, power, and great value. Silver is feminine, and it represents strong but muted beauty. There is something about precious metals and how they have continued to captivate human attention long after printed paper became the default currency. Silver also conducts electricity, and that power is a metaphor for its ability to act as a conduit for spiritual energy.

Notice those around you who wear silver jewelry today. Do you think it is done for beauty, the comfort of the energy, or its power? When you meditate on the color silver, preferably you will be able to do so with a bit of silver in hand. Perhaps you have a silver coin or a silver ring (sterling silver is just fine for this exercise). Hold it in your hands. Feel the way it conducts the warmth of your fingers. Close your eyes and visualize this object as having more than its properties of chemical and conductive power. Consider the magic in its beauty.

* *Meditate on the color silver.*

DAY 241
....
Gold

Gold has amazing properties. It is highly conductive, much more so than silver, and malleable, allowing it to be formed into almost any shape imaginable. Most interesting of all, gold has captured the interest and desire of humans around the planet since it was first discovered as nuggets in riverbeds. Wars have been fought over this metal, and people have died for it. In many cultures in ages past, unless you were royalty, wearing gold was a crime. Gold is a masculine color, and it represents the radiating energy of the sun. Gold is a symbol of success, joy, wealth, and ultimate power. A person wearing gold is basking in the light of the noon day sun no matter what the time of day or cloud cover.

Notice today who is wearing gold. Is it a sign of power, wealth, or privilege? Or does the person wear the gold for the comfort and joy it brings? Ideally, you will be able to meditate while holding a piece of gold (gold-plated jewelry is just fine for this exercise). Clasp the gold and feel the way it warms quickly in your hand, conducting the radiant energy. Close your eyes and be aware of the people who have struggled to earn or steal gold throughout civilization—people who would covet the power that you now are privileged enough to hold, if even for a moment.

* *Meditate on the color gold.*

DAY 242

....

The Fool

Next, we'll take a journey through the symbolism revealed in the tarot's major arcana. Hopefully you've procured a tarot deck by now. If it is not close at hand, you can meditate on the card as you picture it in your mind's eye, or you can look up an image on the Internet. I will keep my descriptions general in case your deck features different images. Keep in mind that you still may not see some of the things I describe here if you have a deck not based on the popular Rider-Waite-Smith version. That's okay; just pay attention to what your own eyes and intuition tell you. What you read here are just guidelines.

The Fool is the very start of our journey. Here is pictured a man foolishly gallivanting along a path. He wears rags and carries only a bundle on a stick. Either he is overconfident, or he has no idea how far he will go. A dog nips at his heels, as if to warn that he is about to take a tumble off a cliff. This cliff is the leap of faith, and it is just the beginning of his adventure. Indeed, the fool is not supposed to take heed of the dog, or else he would miss out on all the fun! Meditate on the times in your life when you have "played the fool."

* *Meditate on the Fool tarot card.*

DAY 243

The Magician

The Magician card shows a character in a completely different light. Is this the same fool or somebody new? Now we see a man dressed not in rags but a magnificent robe. He has an altar on which tools are set out, and he brandishes a wand. He seems powerful and ready to do something spectacular. It is the magician's job to share a message. The magician is a communicator, for truly any form of communication really is magic. The magic of getting the right message to the right people at the right time is challenging indeed.

When you meditate on the Magician, think of yourself as a person in power. You already have all the tools in front of you. Perhaps you have had them all along. What is the grand message you would like to share with the world? Does the world need to take notice of you or of one of your passions? When you communicate, are you manifesting your full potential? How is your message being accepted? Are your communication attempts falling on deaf ears?

* *Meditate on the Magician tarot card.*

DAY 244

The High Priestess and the Hierophant

The High Priestess and the Hierophant are two different cards, but I'll present them here together so you can see the male and female duality that repeats itself in human symbolism. The High Priestess is a woman of mystery. Her cauldron is the cauldron of rebirth. Death happens on our planet, magic happens in the womb of a woman, and new life follows. This mystery is as everyday as it is ancient and miraculous.

The Hierophant, however, represents rules and tradition. If the Hierophant were to go out with a girl on a blind date, he would definitely bring chocolates and flowers, even though they are cliché and a bit trite. He would be downright angry if the girl asked him before he asked her. The Hierophant's rules can be constrictive, but they represent power and the well-trodden path. As you meditate on each of these cards, think to yourself about times in your life where you have chosen mystery over the predicable and vice versa.

* *Meditate on the High Priestess and the Hierophant tarot cards.*

DAY 245

The Empress and the Emperor

The Empress and the Emperor are also two separate cards, although they may not be as far apart in nature as the High Priestess and the Hierophant. Both are in positions of power, bossy and unyielding. Their power comes from different sources, however. For the Empress, her power comes from her symbolic fertility. In some tarot decks, the Empress is even represented as very pregnant. She may also hold other symbols of fertility, for example, sheaves of grain or a cornucopia. She represents a project that is coming to completion.

The Emperor, of course, does not have the same creative power. Instead, his power comes from his stature, his wealth, and his composure. Both the Empress and the Emperor have the commanding sort of power. When they appear in a psychic reading, it often means a person in authority is coming down hard on the subject of the reading. Either that, or that the subject of the reading needs to rise up and claim power as the bossy one for a while. Think about your own life. Do you need to take charge of something or control a situation?

* Meditate on the Empress and the Emperor tarot cards.

DAY 246
....

The Lovers

The Lovers are a very attractive card to receive if you've got any love questions in your reading. In many decks the figures are reaching out to each other. In some decks they are embracing or becoming even more intimate. The union seems blessed, but sometimes the people don't seem entirely relaxed; a serpent threatens their peace. The serpent, the symbol of life, often throws challenges our way. To me, the Lovers card represents passion that can sometimes be driven to obsession.

As you meditate on the Lovers card, there may be several hidden meanings for you. If you are involved with a passionate romantic relationship, the symbolism for your love may be readily apparent. If you are not currently driven to find passionate romantic love, you might see the same passion directed toward your work, raising small children, or a pet project. To what do you tether yourself? What passions do you feel could drive you to insanity? Do you have any loves so deep that you would not wish to release your bondage to them, no matter what sense of freedom would result?

* *Meditate on the Lovers tarot card.*

DAY 247
....

The Chariot

The Chariot features a horse-drawn chariot charging forward. The two horses are not matched, however. In many decks, one horse is black and the other is white. Some decks even show that the horses are each drawing the chariot in opposite directions, preventing easy travel. To me, the Chariot represents somebody whose project is getting derailed in a similar way. If the card appears in a reading, perhaps the subject is good at getting things started but somewhat less successful at continuing things for the long haul.

As you meditate on the Chariot card today, think about the major projects in life. What loads would you set carefully in your chariot? What sorts of forces might be pulling your chariot apart from within? Are you better at starting projects or following through? This is one of those essential questions about whether you are a leader or a follower. Perhaps the Chariot card truly represents the follower who is taking a chance at becoming a leader.

* *Meditate on the Chariot tarot card.*

DAY 248
....

Strength

The strength card often represents a classic fairy tale. In the strength card, you often see a hero or heroine pulling a thorn from the paw of a lion. In all his strength and glory, the lion is humbled by a simple girl's assistance after being crippled by the smallest of thorns. The girl must show all her strength in pulling the thorn from the lion's paw. At the moment, he may be helpless, but what is to cause him from turning upon her once his full strength is restored? Strength is a funny thing, as it can be an internal characteristic and also a physical one based on chance and circumstance.

When I see the Strength card in a tarot reading, I know I am reading for a strong person—physically, mentally, or both. However, that strength may need careful cultivating and directing in order to do any good in the person's life. It doesn't matter how strong the lion may be if the thorn impedes his path of travel. In the same way, it doesn't matter how strong a person you are inside if you have nowhere to direct your strength. Today, meditate upon your true values and how you are using your strength to support those values.

* *Meditate on the Strength tarot card.*

The Hermit

The Hermit card sounds like a lonely thing, but the hermit often looks pretty satisfied in his solitude. He may be standing in beautiful scenery. Usually, he carries a lantern that shines outward. Consider whether he is using the lantern to light his path, or whether he is trying to signal to someone else far away. Perhaps he doesn't even know or care who sees his lantern light. When I see the Hermit card, it is sometimes a downer if I'm reading for somebody who wants to be in a relationship, because this is a card that centers on the self and time best spent alone. But it also shows hope and a desire to reach outward.

Today when you meditate upon the hermit card, think about a phase in your life that may have been hermit-like. If you ever do feel like a hermit, what are some ways you can communicate or touch others you haven't yet tried? You may have to think outside of the box here. If you decided to live a life of spiritual hermitage, what would be the force that drives you into the mountaintops alone? What would you seek, and how would you know that it was time to leave a life of solitude, if ever?

* *Meditate on the Hermit tarot card.*

. . . .

The Wheel of Fortune

The Wheel of Fortune card represents fate, randomness, and destiny. Sometimes symbols or objects are shown at various points along a wheel, as if it were some sort of spinning game, the results of which must be interpreted. In other tarot decks, the wheel may take different forms, as perhaps a creative force or a protective shield. The wheel shape is a boundary between the time before and after a chance is taken. When the wheel of fortune is drawn, a choice comes up that can change your life forever. One must decide whether the leap of faith is worth the risk.

As you meditate on the Wheel of Fortune today, think about what sort of gambles you are willing to make in life. Some of these gambles may seem rather small. You take a chance every time you get out of bed. If you drive a car to work or school, you're taking quite a bit of risk. What is the payout you can receive for playing these games? Are there larger risks you have been avoiding? When you do so, is it because the reward is not great enough, because you have too much to lose, or some combination of the two?

* *Meditate on the Wheel of Fortune tarot card.*

Day 251

. . . .

Justice

The Justice tarot card represents balance. In almost all tarot decks, there is a clear representation of balance, often shown by scales, or with hands that seem to be judging the weight of two objects. Often a sword is shown, because justice can be cruel or cutting indeed. Take note whether there a person depicted in your Justice card. Is this the person determining whether true justice is being meted out, or is this the person delivering the blow of justice?

When I see the Justice card in a reading, I know somebody has to focus on getting their life into balance. What in your own life is out of balance? Who is the one creating this imbalance and what will eventually be the force that balances? Another good thing to consider with the Justice card are the aspects of life that tend to be ignored completely while you go through a phase, like things that must eventually be revisited. For example, perhaps you have been neglecting a proper diet or a proper amount of sleep each night due to a demanding career.

* *Meditate on the Justice tarot card.*

DAY 252
....

The Hanged Man

The Hanged Man typically shows a man hanging upside-down from a tree. He's not hanging from his neck, and he's not dead. Actually, he usually looks rather at peace. Sometimes one leg is bent, as if he were shaping the number 4. Why would somebody look so relaxed when dangling from a tree? How did he get there, anyway? Who tied him there? How will he get down, if ever? Imagine how you would feel if you were hanging there upside-down, blood rushing to your head. What thoughts might go through your mind? Would they only be thoughts of escape? What thoughts might distract you from your predicament?

Getting the Hanged Man in a reading might be disappointing at first, because obviously he isn't going anywhere soon. Usually, when performing a psychic reading, you're trying to progress toward a particular goal. However, consider the man's enigmatic face. How can you also find joy or relaxation in the present? What is the best way to spend your time if you are strung up on the tree of life?

* *Meditate on the Hanged Man tarot card.*

DAY 253
....

Death

Don't freak out if you get the Death card in a tarot reading. The Death tarot card rarely means literal death. If it did, getting through a tarot reading alive would probably have worse odds than diving with sharks. Instead, Death in the tarot represents the destruction of the old in order to make way for the new. In nature, death is part of the cycle of life. The decaying plants break down to make the soil rich and ready for fresh sprouts in the warmth of the sun. The life of a rat is sacrificed to feed a hawk. When I see this card in a reading, the "death" in question is usually more symbolic. The clearing of the old can be as simple as spring cleaning, or as complex as cutting ties with an ex-spouse.

As you meditate on the Death card, look for the signs of life in the art. Think about the circle of life and death in nature, and the times in your life when you have been able to notice death as a peaceful influence. Think of some things in your life which may need to be drastically reduced or cleared. There may be some connections that need to be severed. If you have trouble thinking about this, try thinking backwards—have any of your goals stalled? For example, if your career isn't moving forward because you're stuck in a dead-end job, your job needs to go.

 * *Meditate on the Death tarot card.*

DAY 254
....

Temperance

The Temperance card usually shows someone pouring water from one vessel into another. It is almost like this person is a chemist or engineer, taking great care to get the right results. We all embody Temperance when we undergo self-improvement. The fact that you have picked up this book means that you are likely to get the Temperance tarot card in a reading. When it comes up in a reading, I usually recommend being kinder during self-improvement. It can be easy to beat yourself up or criticize too harshly, and both sabotage the process. As you can see, the temperance card is usually quite serene, and any upset to the flow would tarnish the results.

When studying the Temperance card, take time to ponder the true nature of self-improvement as a gradual and careful process. Guiding yourself takes time. If you overcorrect, you may ruin what you are doing. Certainly you have a decision point, beyond which your lifestyle may change for the better. However, careful steering and reevaluation must happen along the way. This gentle approach requires an even gentler attitude toward the self.

 * *Meditate on the Temperance tarot card.*

Day 255

The Devil

The Devil card appears very different in different tarot decks. Sometimes a pair of people who look like the Lovers are shown chained and seemingly held captive by a demonic looking beast. However, if you look closely, their bonds are loose enough that they could easily be removed. The figures seem complicit in their own beastly captivity. What does this represent? Passions are getting away from the person so much that the person is powerless to stop it, even if the key to freedom is right there. The answer to the devil card is surrender.

When I see the Devil card in a reading, often I know that the subject of my reading is his or her own worst enemy. This is sort of the extreme of the message of the temperance card, in which you must really look at ways you could be sabotaging yourself through harsh opinions. Moving forward, relaxing, and giving the self over to the flow of things is the only solution to the Devil card. This sort of surrender may feel intolerable to some.

* *Meditate on the Devil tarot card.*

Day 256

The Tower

The Tower is a scarier card than Death; the scene is always of destruction. Often a lightning-struck tower is surrounded by stormy seas and jagged rocks. People leap out the windows of the burning building, certainly to their demise. There is little cause for hope. Is there any way the people can survive by perhaps falling into water? Is there any way the tower can survive the storm? Could the tower be rebuilt? A more important question may be to ask whether the tower should be rebuilt in this location.

When I see this card in a reading, I know there are some unstable foundations in the person's life. If castles in the sky remain as they are, it's likely they'll come crashing down. As you meditate on the Tower, think about the foundations in your life and how you can strengthen them. For example, the foundation of your good marriage might be friendship, kindness, and each partner going above and beyond for the other.

* *Meditate on the Tower tarot card.*

Day 257
....

The Star, Moon, and Sun

There are three celestial cards in a tarot deck. In order, they are the Star, the Moon, and the Sun. The Star represents hopes and dreams. Think of the first star you see in the evening and the wish you could make. The Moon card represent cycles of hopes and fears. Do you ever feel like you keep seeing the same pattern happening over and over again in your life? That's this cycle at work. The Sun represents growth, success, joy, and harmony. Think of the plants rejoicing under the light of the sun, soaking up nourishment from its rays.

As you contemplate these three celestial cards today, notice how different the scenes in them are so that you don't get them mixed up and confuse their meanings during a reading. The sun's scene looks jolly and the moon's scene looks spooky. The star should seem fairly neutral, but generally positive. Think about how these celestial bodies represent the goals in your life and how you approach them. Do you walk forward with hopes, fear, confidence, or some combination of the three?

* *Meditate upon the Star, Moon, and Sun tarot cards.*

DAY 258
....

Judgment

The Judgment tarot card is not to be confused with the Justice tarot card. Justice is an ongoing process in which balance or fairness is sought. Judgment is an earth-shattering process, in which the game is called and the results are sorted out. In general, Judgment is a good thing when things turn out the way they are supposed to be. If you're not living in line with your own true values, however, Judgment can be a startling and painful process. No matter what happens, though, you know for sure that plans are going to be interrupted and forcefully changed.

When I see the Judgment card, I know that someone's world is about to be rocked, much like in the Tower, but it isn't always a result of destruction. As you contemplate the Judgment card, consider what you cling to when your world is falling apart. Do you have a strong family or a trusting friend? Do you lean on your god, or on your own sense of logic and morals? On what systems and institutions would you be willing to bet your life? The Judgment card shows you who and what you can really trust in your time of need.

* *Meditate on the Judgment tarot card.*

Day 259

....

The World

The World card is the last card in the major arcana. In a sense, this is the end of the story of the Hero's Journey, and what a happy ending it is. The same Fool we saw at the beginning of the story is now dancing with joy, perfectly well balanced and flush with success. Even if the Fool has only a few more possessions than at the start of the journey (or even fewer possessions if the figure is depicted nude), the adventure is complete, and achievements have been won. The World represents having all you need, even if you had it all along.

When I see the World card in a reading, I consider it a very happy sign. As you contemplate the World, think about your station in life and your achievements thus far. Of all of your dreams for the future, what drives them? Is there a chance you have already succeeded in a sense, in some small way? Just as a tiny acorn can grow into a mighty oak, your success thus far may look very different than your ultimate goal.

* *Meditate on the World tarot card.*

Part Eight

Reading
for Purposes

Day 260
. . . .

Planetary Basics

Interpreting astrology can be one way that you can use a psychic divination skill for purposes. Grab an astrological calendar. Imagine that the planets are all characters acting on a stage and that their aspects are the script. You may have to use the key to your astrological calendar to read the stage directions here. In other words, the calendar key will tell you how the planets interact on any given day. I'm going to just go over the classical planets for basics.

Sun: A hearty male character, the sun represents ego, life force, success, and financial power.

Moon: An emotional female character, the moon represents memories, moods, magic, and mystery.

Mercury: A trickster male, Mercury has to do with communications, electronics, and business deals.

Venus: This lovely lady represents love.

Mars: This gentleman is a solider of war.

Jupiter: This male character is a boss in a position of authority and has a goal-driven mind.

Saturn: This male character (usually older) embodies a sense of duty and the powers of destruction.

Now, notice how each planet's aspect interacts with the others on any given day. A conjunction represents stress. A sextile or trine represents a happy interaction, while an opposition or a square represents a negative interaction.

* *Look up a planet on your astrological calendar this month, one that has to do with a topic of concern in your life. Is that planet in a "fight" with any other planets, or are they generally getting along?*

DAY 261
....

Days of the Week

Knowing the energies of the different days of the week can help you decide which day to do a particular psychic reading for best results. Each day of the week is particularly suited to certain topics. Here's a key to the best times to do your psychic readings during the week:

Monday *("Moon Day")* **is best for readings on:** Cycles, feminine issues, magic, mystery, motherhood.

Tuesday *("Tiw's Day")* **is best for readings on:** Conflict, surgery, matters of anger.

Wednesday *("Woden's Day")* **is best for readings on:** Business, wisdom, studies, contracts, and lies.

Thursday *("Thor's Day")* **is best for readings on:** Leadership, authority figures, fatherhood, ambition.

Friday *("Freya's Day")* **is best for readings on:** Love, passion, sex, beauty, pleasure.

Saturday (*"Saturn's Day"*) **is best for readings on:** Destruction, duty, ridding one's self of something.

Sunday (*"Sun Day"*) **is best for readings on:** Financial gain, goals, good health, development, growth.

* *What topic should you read about today, based on the day of the week and your interests?*

Day 262
....

Planetary Hours

Planetary hours are a way to narrow down to the very best time of day for a reading on a particular topic. Planetary hours start at sunrise, on the day of the week associated with that planet. Then, each hour cycles through the planets in the ancient Chaldean order shown below. The planet order is repeated over and over again until they reset at the next day's sunrise. So, Saturday would start with the planetary hour of Saturn at sunrise. Here are the planetary sunrise hours for each day of the week. Review the weekday associations from yesterday to choose a topic of interest. Then you can determine which planetary hour is best.

Saturn (*Saturday*)

Jupiter (*Thursday*)

Mars (*Tuesday*)

Sun (*Sunday*)

Venus *(Friday)*

Mercury *(Wednesday)*

Moon *(Monday)*

* *Which day and hour would be best for a particular topic of your interest? (Hint: sunrise on the right day of the week would be an easy pick.)*

Day 263
....

Your "No" List

Sometimes, it's just not the right time for a reading. We've gone over how a reading too soon in the grief process may be overwhelming. We've learned that a reading on a question that is too similar to the last one or poorly phrased is a bad idea. Maybe your *"yes"* and *"no"* stone divination system simply says *no* to the idea of a reading. Now it's time to take an inventory of what sorts of topics you won't touch at all. This way, you won't have to hem and haw if somebody asks you to read on it. In addition, when an urgent situation comes up and you're feeling tempted to read for yourself on a topic, you'll know it's a bad idea.

It's already obvious that we shouldn't read for ourselves or someone else when emotional or physical harm might result, either from the message we might receive or from the course of action we might follow as a result. But there are other topics you should put on your *"no"* list. For example, domestic violence and rape may not be topics you'd like to experience through a psychic reading, especially if you yourself have been victimized in the past. Some people choose never to read for children or for adults who may not grasp the true nature of a reading. It's all up to you.

* *What are some topics that would be off-limits for you personally?*

DAY 264
. . . .

North

There are several reasons to learn the compass directions that correspond to various topics. Firstly, facing in the direction appropriate to your topic can help fix your mind on the psychic activity at hand as well as help align your energies to the task. Secondly, the directions and their associated symbols can help add to the symbol dictionary in your mind. You will have some navigational beacons on your psychic map when answering questions.

North is associated with the feminine and the element of earth. North can give a feeling of cooling and relaxation, granting stability to a psychic who feels adrift. North is sometimes given the color green to represent foliage of the earth, or the color black to represent the dark of a forest at midnight or a cave. Think about what these things may mean to you and what imagery comes to mind when you think of the earth. Some people use salt or dirt as a focus point when meditating on the north.

* *Meditate while facing north.*

DAY 265

·············

South

The southerly direction is associated with the masculine. It also represents fiery passion and love. Think of the heat of the South. When you feel energy from the south, it is more dynamic than northern energy and perhaps even chaotic. The passions of the south can just as easily turn from love to rage. Think of the color of the south as red or another fiery color. Some think of the color white to represent the blinding light of the sun at noon. Some people use a sharp knife as a focal point while meditating on the south. I like to think of the association as the prick of the knife feeling much like the burn of the fire.

What other free associations can you make from these correspondences? Depending on where you are located, your thoughts may be influenced by the topography of the land. As you meditate while facing south today, consider thinking of a topic that makes your blood boil or at least run a little hot. The energy of the south will help you process those feelings into dynamic action.

* *Meditate while facing south.*

DAY 266

·············

East

East represents new beginnings. Think about how the sun rises in the east, and you'll remember that association. Some people even give east the color red, for the rising sun. Others give east the color yellow for that dawn light, or as a stand-in for the invisible element of air. Since east is often associated with the element of air, it is associated with other invisible things like the intellect, creativity, inspiration, and other mental aspects. Some people use a wand as a focal point for the east. I like to think of a conductor waving his baton in the air to conduct beautiful music to make this association complete.

When you face east, think about what new beginnings you would like to invite into your life. Think about any intellectual or study goals you might have at this time. If you want to learn a new language or to get a college degree, east may be the direction to give your extra special attention. The experience of an east-facing meditation may be a series of flighty thoughts.

* *Meditate while facing east.*

Day 267

West

West represents endings because it is where the sun sets. Some choose the color gray to represent the west, as it is the color of twilight. Others choose blue, because west is also a direction associated with the element of water. My home is in the Pacific Northwest, where the Pacific ocean is to the west, so it makes sense to me. In fact, I even have a creek running outside the western windows of my home. Where you live, you might feel tempted to switch directions when contemplating water. Just be aware that the people for whom you perform psychic readings may associate water with the west.

As you face west, ponder the true nature of endings. You can think about death or faster cycles such as the end of day and the beginning of night. Consider how age has played a role in gaining wisdom in your life. When associated with water, west is also strongly associated with emotions. Thus, meditations while facing west may have a strong emotional component to them.

* Meditate while facing west.

Day 268

Topic Morphing

Some questions need reformulation not because you're asking the question incorrectly, but because you are asking the wrong question entirely. I saved this form of rephrasing for now because it takes advanced skill to realize that you are chasing down the wrong topic. Sometimes, the questions you're asking need to be more general. For example, if you're wanting to know how to gain the love of a specific person, you might want to instead ask how you could be happy and satisfied with your life in general, regardless of relationship status. Other times, the category needs to get shifted. For example, if you're asking yourself for a psychic reading on which job is best for you and all the specific steps needed to get from interview to working at your new job, simplify it by asking how you can have financial stability. The topic shifts and becomes slightly more simple.

Today, take a look at some of your frequent topics of interest, and think about the specific situations in your life that bring those topics to the forefront. How might the topics be simplified, shifted, or refocused in order to improve perspective? Sometimes, just shifting your topic to a new angle will yield new insights.

* *Notice how some topics blend together, or are two sides of a similar coin. Consider any topics that you may have been focused on that are not necessarily the true topic of focus.*

DAY 269
....
Halloween

Certain times of year are better for psychic readings than others, for energetic or social reasons, or both. I'd like to go through a few ideas for psychic readings on some of these days so you can consider including them on your calendar. Halloween and its corresponding other point on the wheel of the year, Beltane (on the eve before the first of May), are both days when Wiccans believe the veil between our world and the world of the dead is especially thin. For this reason, these dates are ideal for seeing ghosts, or going on a psychic journey to another realm.

On Halloween, I make time for a dumb supper and try to speak with my ancestors. I sometimes get together with fellow psychics, and we have a curious combination of a solemn and celebratory occasion. We laugh and chat and remember, and we share our experiences interacting with ancestral and other spirits through our psychic abilities. Make sure to add a psychic session to your calendar on both Beltane and Halloween, and think about what spirits you'd like to contact.

* *Mark your calendar for a Halloween psychic event.*

Day 270

New Year's Day

There's nothing esoterically special about the first of January. However, it has taken on a very real and meaningful psychological significance in our own minds. We make resolutions. We start writing a new year in our calendars. Perhaps at work or school, sweeping changes come about in our schedules based on this point in the calendar year. Collectively at this point in time, we start thinking about the upcoming year, what we'd like to change, and how things will be different.

This time is also perfect for performing a New Year psychic reading. Choose a psychic technique and do a reading about what potentials lie ahead in the new year. Be sure to record extensively. You might even want to choose automatic writing. If you do a clairvoyant reading, sketch and note any details—especially verifiable ones—even if they are seemingly insignificant, like gas prices for example. Next year, make a note to go over your recorded reading and see how much of it was correct. You can use this to track your progress with your psychic development.

* *Make a note in your calendar to do a New Year reading.*

Day 271

Valentine's Day

There's also nothing particularly energetically special about Valentine's Day, except that the Romans would use this time of year to banish evil spirits and participate in a fertility festival. In our present culture, thoughts turn to love and romance. If you're in a relationship, you might choose to do a reading with your partner at this time. I suggest performing a tarot or tea leaf reading, or some other form of divination you can both view together. Ask some positive questions of the tools such as, "What are some ways we show we love each other? What are some ways we could love each other even more?"

If you are alone, you might choose to do a reading on relationship potentials, or what you need to do before finding a relationship. It's okay if you have no desire to have a romantic relationship or are otherwise not particularly needy in this area. If you like, you can throw a psychic Valentine's Day party and offer your services. Or offer to share divination tools with your friends so they can try reading for themselves. It can be a fun and flirty affair.

* If you like, make a note on your calendar for a love reading on Valentine's Day.

Day 272

Birthdays

There is something special about your birthday. Imagine a snapshot taken of the night's sky the moment you were born. This is what your astrological natal chart depicts. The patterns in the sky above reflect the patterns in the earth below and can tell you information about your personality and potential. Drawing up astrological charts is an advanced skill, and astrological software can be expensive, but you can search for a free natal chart on the Internet or visit an astrologer near you, if you're interested.

Your birthday is a good time for making wishes and performing a psychic reading. This can be much like the New Year reading, in that you look at how this year of your life will be different. However, the focus may be more on your personal life than in the general changes in the world around you over the next year. Consider especially any self-improvement you wish to make.

* Make a note in your calendar for a reading on your birthday. Consider adding a note a week or so ahead of time to schedule an appointment to have an astrologer draw up your natal chart.

DAY 273
....

Moon Phases, Signs, and Topics

If you take a look at an astrological calendar, you'll notice that the moon enters each sign just like the sun does. Though the sun sign definitely affects your readings, psychics often choose to primarily observe the sign the moon enters because the moon's phase has such a dramatic effect on psychic readings. Following is a list of which topics are best in which moon signs.

Moon in Aries: Anger, ambition, conflicts.

Moon in Taurus: Beauty, pleasure, stability.

Moon in Gemini: Communication, intellectual topics.

Moon in Cancer: Belongings, mood swings.

Moon in Leo: Matters of pride, performance arts.

Moon in Virgo: Peace, knowledge, analysis.

Moon in Libra: Justice, diplomacy, devil's advocacy.

Moon in Scorpio: Protection, endings, overcoming adversity.

Moon in Sagittarius: Long-term goals, freedom, travel.

Moon in Capricorn: Organization, career, duties.

Moon in Aquarius: Arguments, gathering facts, academics.

Moon in Pisces: Friendship, politics, creativity.

* *Look at your astrological calendar. Which sign is the moon currently in? Based on this, choose a topic you should read on today.*

DAY 274

....

Houses and Apartments

Oftentimes, we want to read on an ideal new living situation. This can be tricky with some forms of psychic readings, since your ideal house is not likely to be printed on a tarot card. What I recommend is a multi-pronged approach you'll see several times in the topics that follow. It's great to start out with a tarot reading to see what things you need to consider before moving. Then, a crystal ball reading or other form of scrying can be used to look for letters in city names or topographical clues to the best location for you. At this point, you may even see an image of your new home. Finally, you can use a pendulum dowsing over a map of potential areas to see which one is calling to you.

Go ahead and try out this multi-pronged approach to practice seeing where you might like to live next. It's okay if your move isn't until retirement or is otherwise delayed. You can also practice by helping a friend or family member who may be contemplating a move. Don't forget to write everything down if you seem to get more than one answer. The choice may be left up to personal preference.

* *Try a reading on a new home.*

DAY 275
....

Lost Objects

Finding lost objects with your psychic abilities is an awesome practical tool. It can feel like exciting confirmation, even if it is just your subconscious mind communicating with your conscious mind. This is an excellent opportunity for you to break out your dowsing rods and try searching around your home for the point at which they seem to want to cross. If somebody far away is asking you about a lost object, you can sketch a map for a pendulum dowsing. For example, suppose your sister lost a ring somewhere in her house. You could sketch the basic floor plan and use a pendulum to try to find the lost ring.

Has something been missing for a while? Try using your dowsing rods or a pendulum dowsing to find it. If not, you can ask a housemate to hide an object for you. Or you can always wait until the next time you misplace your cell phone. Before calling the phone, test out one of your psychic methods. Remember, this process isn't perfect. If it was, everything ever lost would always be found.

* *Try finding a lost object with your psychic abilities.*

Day 276
....

Events

Typically, we want important events to happen at the right time in life. You can use some of the timing tools you've used already to make that happen. For example, when planning a wedding, it could be when the moon is in Taurus for stability and pleasure, and on a Friday in the hour of Venus. If signing a contract to buy a house, you could try for when the moon is in Gemini and on a Wednesday in the hour of Mercury. Otherwise, you can use a pendulum to narrow down the best year, month, and even day.

Try thinking about an important event in your life. You may have to work within real life barriers. If you're signing on a house, you might only have a one- or two-day window and should rely on planetary hours or even yes/no stones to know if the time is right. If you have something more distant in your future like a wedding you are planning, you have the rare luxury of picking the right moment. You may even have the time to have dreams on the subject.

* Plan the best date for an event in your future based on your
   psychic abilities.

Day 277
....

Business Ventures

When reading on a business venture, there are several things that you should consider. First of all, the timing may at first seem obvious. Maybe you'd like to choose the time when the moon is full in Gemini for making deals where a lot of money is involved. Perhaps you'd like to sign contracts on the day and hour of Mercury. However, you also have to consider the nature of the business. If the business has to do with defense, perhaps you should look to the hour of Mars and to Tuesday, for instance.

The same thing applies for timing your readings. So whether you've ever dreamed of opening your own business or helping a friend, think about the best time for doing a psychic reading for that business venture. You can read on the best actions to take. Meanwhile, you can use your knowledge of correspondences to choose the most auspicious time, or you can divine the best time.

* *Do a reading on the topic of business ventures.*

Day 278
....
Places

We've already read on finding the best location for a home and on finding a lost object. Let's delve a little deeper on the topic of reading places. Sometimes reading places can be a bit tricky. After all, the pendulum isn't an instrument with an expansive repertoire of communication unless you're using a complicated pendulum diagram you've managed to guess is the right one. You may need a lot more narrowing down on a place before you even bright out the map and pendulum, and you may need a lot more refinement even when looking at the map.

When trying to zoom in on places, it's good to focus a little bit more on your scrying or other clairvoyant methods. If you're more comfortable dreaming, spend a few nights focusing on the place you're trying to locate or learn more about. If you're a fan of crystal ball reading or some other scrying method, by all means use it. Make note of the symbols you see, so you can meditate upon them further. This may be a riddle for you. Once you narrow down beyond the map phase, don't be afraid to go to the place in person, if possible, to feel the energies of the place.

* *Try doing another place reading, focusing on either scrying or clairvoyance or on visiting the place in person to verify.*

Day 279

Sex

Reading on sex is a little different than reading on just love. Some of the correspondences will be the same; you may use the day and hour of Venus, for example. However, the focus will be more on pleasure, communication, passion, and dynamic connection. These can all occur together, of course, but if you are narrowing your topic, you will need to narrow your focus. Reading on a sexual relationship may involve a lot more literal questions than figurative, so you may have to choose a scrying or dreaming technique rather than other forms of divination.

If you need to read about a sex relationship, you might start with some dreaming techniques and take those into a scrying session. Meditation can also be helpful for seeking the answers you need. Be prepared for symbolic representations of power exchanges, communication, and other interplay in the relationship. Try to phrase questions in a way that won't lead to psychically spying on other people.

* *Attempt a psychic reading on a sexual topic.*

Day 280
....

Education

Questions about education fall into several categories. If choosing which college you'd like to attend, you can use the same techniques you've used for finding a home's location. However, divining a course of study can be trickier. If you're already set on a specific course of study, it may be easiest to simply verify whether you are on the correct path or if you should search for some other one. If your current path is confirmed, there is no need to worry about further investigation. If your psychic investigation reveals that you do need to reconsider, you can narrow subjects down with the tarot and then try some scrying to search for specific relevant symbols.

Even if you're not a college student, education is always relevant. Think about the next great intellectual pursuit in your life. Try performing a psychic reading to try to narrow down the nature of your studies. Chances are, there are several components to your learning, and they will all show up in your psychic reading.

* *Try a psychic reading on education.*

DAY 281

....

Coworkers

Reading on coworkers? Isn't that strange and unethical? It depends—refer back to your own thoughts about third-party readings and whether or not you are able to read on others without their consent. That said, if you do choose to observe your colleagues using your psychic senses, it is important to use unobtrusive observations. One of the best ways to do this is to try to observe any auras your coworkers project at the office. People can withdraw and protect their auras when they want to making them tricky to see, but other times they may be displayed like a peacock's feathers. You may also notice observations related to palmistry, such as jewelry on unusual fingers like the pointer finger to show leadership or the pinkie finger to show business acumen.

Continue reaching out with all your senses while observing the people you work with. Besides auras or palmistry-related signs, you may receive clairvoyant flashes or receive symbols later in dreams. If you know of any fellow employees who are particularly open to friendly psychic readings, offer a reading.

* Do a psychic reading on your coworkers, if you feel comfortable.
  Try offering a reading to a friendly workmate.

....

Problems

Specific problems can be puzzled apart by looking at each component. For example, a common tarot spread can be used to look at each part of the problem. Following is a classic spread called the Sword. Try this reading for a problem you have right now.

The first card you set down is the very heart of the matter, even if it's not the obvious presentation. Set a card to the left of this one to represent the beginning of the problem. A card below the first card is your foundation. A card above the first card is a helpful chance for success. The next three cards will be the point of the sword, extending to the right. The first, closest to the hilt, will be the problem that is being solved, the second is your needs, and the third is your outcome or the new revelation to be had from this reading.

* *Try problem-solving with a tarot reading.*

DAY 283

....

Goals

So far, I've coached you to read with your goals in mind rather than reading and hoping that what you see happens to align with your goals. By now, you should be able to design a psychic reading session with goal-setting as well as achievement in mind. Try first using your psychic abilities to divine some of the best goals for you at this time. This may require a tarot reading or some dreaming to narrow things down. You can then verify whether this is the right time to achieve your goals with a pendulum dowsing or by simply using your yes/no stones. Finally, you can perform some meditations and reading techniques of your choice to decide how best to go about achieving your goals.

Today, try to work with your psychic abilities on one goal. Try to move through the process completely, from goal setting to visualizing its completion. Throughout the process, you should be able to use your psychic abilities both as an exploratory technique and a way to trust what you already know.

* Use your psychic abilities to set one new goal and discover the route to its completion.

Day 284
....

Messages from the Recently Deceased

If you ever have occasion to contact a recently deceased spirit, be aware that the experience may be strange for both you *and* the ghost! Even if it is a spirit you don't feel a special emotional connection with, you might receive messages that seem garbled and confused. Some believe that recently deceased spirits may not know that they are dead. Others believe that it may take a span of at least three days before any messages can come through to a psychic at all. As a result, it may help you to use calibrating techniques like you did with your pendulum. Ask the spirit to show you what yes and no look like no matter what tool you use, and build from there.

Today, try to contact a recently deceased spirit. If you're feeling particularly ambitious, look in the newspaper and try to help out the spirit of somebody who has recently died a mysterious death and may have a message to pass on. Just remember that if you do receive helpful information, contact the authorities using a nonemergency line. Do *not* contact the family.

* *Practice the techniques used for contacting a recently deceased spirit.*

DAY 285

Spirituality and the Soul

Anyone of any spirituality has the potential to develop psychic abilities, since psychic ability exists independent of creed. Having personal spirituality or belief in the soul, however, may make some aspects of psychic development easier to understand. After all, you would have to believe in the persistence of the soul after death to even bother contacting spirits with your psychic abilities. Having a spiritual connection with your psychic practice can also give you more questions to ask in your readings. You can discover your spiritual path, confirm what beliefs are true for you, and empower yourself with advice on growing spiritually.

Today, take some time to think about how your spirituality over your lifetime affects your psychic development. Was the spiritual environment you were raised in friendly and open-minded about psychic development? What do you believe happens to the soul after death? What are your spiritual goals in this lifetime, and how do you intend to reach them? If a spiritual question arises during your thoughts, perform a psychic reading to answer it.

* *Read on the topic of spirituality.*

Day 286

················

Personalities

Reading on personality characteristics are a big part of psychic readings in general. It may seem pointless to do on yourself, but it can be fun. Additionally, confirming the good and bad bits of your personality can be the first step toward truly accepting who you are and choosing courses of action that highlight your strengths and downplay your weaknesses. Knowing yourself is integral to choosing a relationship partner, a career, and a course of study. If there are negative aspects of your personality, you can mitigate those or even change them over time if you acknowledge them first.

So, how do you do a personality reading? Choose any psychic method you want, and there are a few that are particularly suited to personality readings. For example, you can use numerology to figure out your expression number. Line up the letters in your name with the alphabet, starting with A at 1 and restarting at 1 when you get to the letter I, and so on. Add them together, reduce them, and look at the number meaning. If you had a natal chart drawn, astrology can be very helpful as well. Or you might read a palmistry book to explore the link between personality and the lines in your hands.

* *Do a psychic reading using a technique of your choice, inquiring about your personality traits.*

Dying

A lot of people are afraid to get a psychic reading because it is thought that a psychic will reveal sudden death or grave misfortune. By now, you've been reading long enough to know that the revelation of death in a psychic reading is not a death sentence! That said, consider now what you will say if someone requests a reading about death so you won't be completely caught off guard. Will you refuse to do it? Will you take the time to explain how malleable the future is? It is tempting to flat-out reject such a reading without explanation, but it can make the client nervous, perhaps even suspicious that you already see something bad. Decide what you are going to say.

Some people want to know a specific time of death. If you are one of those people, think about why you are asking that question. Is it simply because you don't want an early death to throw you a curveball? If so, it's time to rephrase the question. Ask instead, "What can I do to increase the likelihood of a long life and to prolong my good health?" Try using palmistry, lucid dreaming, or meditation to find the answer. If it is because you already know that you have a terminal illness and want to get your ducks in a row as you approach death, you might ask, "What should I be thinking about to approach the end of my life with peace and joy?"

* *If you're comfortable doing a death reading, try one on yourself. If you are not comfortable doing such a reading, think of what you would say if somebody asks you, and practice saying it in the mirror, kindly and confidently.*

Day 288

....

Past Lives

If you believe in reincarnation, reading on past lives can be fun and fulfilling. Even if you don't believe in reincarnation, it can be a topic of interest for other people, so you can practice the techniques to help be prepared to answer their questions. A tarot reading is one simple way to address this very complex topic. The following past life reading is a common one you can try if you don't want to get wrapped up in a dream or a vision about a past life.

In front of your left hand, lay out three cards vertically. Starting out from the bottom, these are the physical, mental, and spiritual realms of one of your past lives. Lay out three cards in the same way in front of your right hand. These represent your present life. Lay out one card between the two columns of cards. This card is a link between the two lives—for example, a karmic lesson that needs to be learned.

* *Try doing a reading on a past life.*

Day 289

....

Family Planning

If I had a nickel every time a client asked me to perform a reading to determine whether a pregnancy existed, I'd be quite rich! Of course, I point out that a pregnancy test from the drugstore is more appropriate—and cheaper, to boot. Generally, you should shy away from performing pregnancy readings because you're not qualified to diagnose anything with your psychic abilities. However, there are other family planning questions you can address.

If a pregnant woman wants to know whether she's having a boy or a girl, for example, you can use a pendulum dowsing to discover the gender. If they've picked a name, you can use numerology to find the expression number for the child. If a couple is hoping for children in a few years, take a look at the active (or dominant) hand for each of them. On the percussive edge of the hand, just under the pinkie finger, are parallel lines coming in from the edge of the hand that represent significant relationships. Smaller lines perpendicular to these may represent potential children. Lines pointing up may be boys, while lines pointing down may be girls.

 * *Perform a reading for somebody hoping to start or grow a family.*

Day 290

. . . .

Pets

Readings on pets can be fun. Here is a pet tarot spread called the Black Cat. It isn't as common or well-known as the other spreads I've given thus far, but it's my own creation and has worked well for myself and others. When laid out, the second and third cards angle away from the first card like ears and the first card is turned sideways like a face. The four cards at the bottom are paws. The order they are laid out draws a number "2" on the reading surface and the final layout should be shaped somewhat like a cat, if you use your imagination.

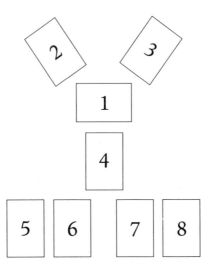

1. **Significator (the pet):** Its mission.

2. **The Owner:** The pet's bond to its owner. Why the pet is in this owner's life and what can be learned.

3. **Others:** The people around the pet. The pet's bond to other people.

4. **Emotional:** To whom or what the pet's heart belongs. The pet's state of mind.

5. **Physical:** The pet's health, location and surroundings.

6. **Past:** A look at the pet's history.

7. **Present:** The pet's situation.

8. **Future:** An overall look at the pet's destiny.

   * *Try performing this reading for a pet.*

Day 291

Friendship

When reading on matters of friendship, make an effort to bring your friend in on the reading. In fact, a psychic reading can sort of act as a peer mediation session. This is a chance for both of you to scan the tea leaves or tarot cards, and see what sort of decisions you can reach together. If you're in conflict, try thinking up solutions to the problem you can try for a limited time, like a week. If your friend isn't willing to meet with you in person, invite him or her to dream with you.

If your friend absolutely refuses to speak with you on the matter, you might try a third party reading. But suppose you think a third party reading, especially on a friend, is a bad idea? Instead of reading on your friend directly, focus on your own actions. Consider asking yourself whether or not it is worth renewing the friendship or what you can do to best repair the problem at hand.

* *Try doing a friendship reading.*

Day 292

Health

I have a lot of caveats about health readings, and for good reason. No matter how good they may be, psychic abilities alone do not qualify anyone to diagnose or treat any disease. A psychic reading should never delay treatment, even if a person is low on money and wanting to check with a psychic reading before risking an expensive doctor visit. The stakes are just too high if you make a medical error. That said, psychic readings can be a parallel spiritual service that can complement regular medical care.

For example, a tarot reading might reveal what aspects of life besides health should receive attention at this time. Remember that the tarot's suit of Cups can represent health, especially emotional. Pentacles can also represent physical health and nutrition. A scrying tool really comes in handy with health-related readings, because you might see symbols of the issue at hand. Examining a person directly using a pendulum dowsing or by viewing the aura can show problem areas on the body as well.

* Perform a simple health reading on yourself, making sure you're up to date with your regular health checkups first.

DAY 293
....
Family

Psychic readings on family matters are common client requests. Usually there's either a family conflict or a family member who may be in trouble in some way. If you have any way to bring the troubled family member in on the reading, do so. It may be the oddest family counseling session you've ever had, but it could be worth your trouble. Tarot cards can be useful here, especially paying attention to the court cards, who may represent family members. You might even wish to do a tarot reading using only the court cards, drawing one at a time to see who needs the most support and who may be an ally or a peacemaker. Another tip is to look at the palm of your hand, and notice if a red, blue, gray, or black dot appears on your palm when a family member is in trouble. Here are some locations in the palm of the hand that represent family members. Consult a palmistry chart to help locate the planetary mounts.

Mom: A red or pink line on the lunar mount on the percussive side of your hand.

Dad: A line or branch from your destiny line on your mount of Saturn under your ring finger.

Kids: On your Mercury mount, underneath your pinkie finger, rising or descending perpendicular to relationship lines that lie horizontally from the percussive edge of your palm.

Sister: Markings found on the mount of Pluto at the base of your palm on the inside of the lunar mount (found on the lower percussive edge of your palm). Your sisters, or spiritual sisters, can be shown as any lines or dots.

Brother: Markings found on the mount of Pluto at the base of your palm on the inside of your mount of Venus (found at the base of your thumb).

Grandma: Markings found within the lunar mount at the lower percussive edge of your palm.

Grandpa: Markings found at the lower end of your destiny line (rising line to your middle finger), or it can also appear as a branch on your mount of Saturn from that same line.

Cousin: Markings found above your lunar mount at the lower percussive edge of your palm.

  * *Try a reading on the topic of your family.*

Day 294

....

Careers

Career is another popular subject. Most clients want to know if they're on the right path with their career. In that case, a pendulum dowsing can be used. Some clients want to know about a complicated problem in the office. For that I like tarot cards, because the suits can show which issues have to do with making money and which ones have to do with office politics. Some clients want to know what sort of career is best for them. This is a good time to try out a scrying method and look for symbols having to do with a potential job match.

If you have any questions about your own career, take a look at what category they fall into. Are you having difficulty getting along with bosses or coworkers? Do you need to create a better work-life balance? Maybe your question is more straightforward. Perhaps you just want confirmation that things are going to continue progressing smoothly. Choose a tool accordingly and try a reading.

* *Try a reading on your career.*

Day 295

....

Money

A reading on money may be very different from a reading on career. A reading on money implies that you're not concerned about where the money comes from, as long as it comes legitimately and possibly quickly. Now, a psychic can't necessarily divine the winning lottery numbers. If that was the case, I'd be too busy rolling in my winnings to bother writing. However, you can investigate your money issues with a psychic reading. As with health, the caveat is that your psychic abilities do not make you a qualified financial planner.

Beware, because money readings tend to have us asking the wrong questions, like "When will my first pay check arrive?" or "Will there be enough money for college?" Steer yourself away from these powerless questions. Instead, empower yourself. Say, "What can I do to increase my chances of having enough money?" If you need specific numbers, you can try a spirit board or divination with tea leaves or a crystal ball. Remember that these numbers may be mixed up.

* *Try a reading on the topic of money.*

Day 296

Love

Finally, we've reached the number one topic of clients who want a psychic reading: Love. If you're in a relationship, bring your significant other in on this reading and try poring over tarot cards or teacups together. If you're alone, be alert to choose the right question from the myriad questions that may not be very practical or empowering. Think about your love goals, be it marriage, starting a family, companionship, or passion.

If you're single and looking, the best question may be to ask how you can draw the ideal relationship into your life. If you're pining over someone in particular, it may be hard to ask that question, but it still may be the best question to ask. Open yourself up to seeing other options. Try scrying and dreaming on the issue and look for faces that may appear. Don't be surprised at all if you have more than one love potential—that's good news!

  * *Try a reading on the topic of love.*

Part Nine

—————— ✳ ——————

Reading
for Others

Day 297

......

Seeing Auras

You were shown how to feel the auras of other people. You've worked on seeing and drawing your own aura and those of animals and even plants. However, reading the auras of human beings has its advantages. Chief among them is that people can help boost their auras, to make them larger and vibrant enough to see. You may remember this from Day 37 about feeling an aura.

Grab a partner who would like an aura reading. Now is a good time to practice your aura drawing so your partner can leave with a memento of the occasion. Ask your partner to close their eyes and imagine they are on stage giving a speech on a topic about which they are passionate. This should cause the aura to grow and brighten.

* *Try creating an aura drawing for someone else.*

Day 298

......

Séances

A séance is a meeting conducted with at least one psychic medium (that would be you) and a gathering of like-minded friends or family members for the purposes of contacting a spirit. Think of a séance as a sort of psychic ghost party of sorts. A séance is a good way for you to practice your psychic readings while having fun with friends in a group setting. Before performing the séance, make sure to brief everyone on the practices of grounding and shielding, and get everyone to agree on the questions to ask the spirit before you begin.

Traditionally, séances were done with channelling, often aided by a crystal and a bowl of water with oil. You can certainly try channelling in this way with a crystal ball. If you'd like a little more divinatory assistance during your first séance, try a spirit board. Spirit boards have worked even in children's slumber parties, so they can certainly work for your séance.

* *Consider inviting some friends over for a séance.*

Day 299
....

What Might Not Be Ours to Know

Some people shy away from psychic readings because they don't want another person spying on them, privy to their deepest hopes and fears. It is important that you respect peoples' boundaries. Always talk over with people what sorts of questions you are going to ask your psychic self before you delve into a reading. If you change the question of the other person, because his or her question wouldn't work out right, be sure to explain why you made the change and get the other person to agree to try your version.

Some topics may feel off-limits to you because they reveal too much information or you may find them too invasive. It's important to think about which topics those are now so you can be ready and confident to turn them down. For example, you might not want to read about other peoples' sex lives. That's perfectly okay. Just be ready with an explanation.

* *List any topics that you wouldn't want to read on for somebody else because you feel that a reading would be too invasive.*

Day 300

Minding Your Own Business

A client of mine was walking down the street with her daughter one day when she was accosted by a strange man. "You have strong intuitive energy," he said, "and I see a boon of money coming your way in the future." Smiling, he handed her a business card for his psychic business. She hurried away and told me about it later that day. Even though she was a regular psychic reading client, she found the man's approach incredibly rude and mentioned that it frightened her daughter, whom she was keeping ignorant about psychic readings as a condition her ex-husband gave during their divorce.

To some people, an unsolicited reading (even if it was a positive one) may feel like a violation. As a budding psychic, you may be overflowing with joyous information, eager to share it with the world. But before you compliment somebody on her beautiful aura, stop yourself. It's not your place to engage this person with a psychic reading before asking permission.

* *Imagine a scenario in which you would like to give somebody a psychic reading because you pick up on something about him or her. What would you say to bring up the subject and ask permission?*

Day 301

Seeing Bad Things

Minding your own business as a psychic can feel devastating if you pick up on something bad. However, if somebody doesn't want to have a psychic reading, it is still a violation to even give that person a warning. What's a psychic to do? Before you even ask permission, make sure you can give the warning in the form of positive advice on how to avoid problems. Then you can introduce yourself as a psychic and ask if you can share your psychic impressions.

If the person says no, accept the refusal gracefully and walk away. There is a chance that you were wrong, after all. That person is in charge of his or her own destiny, and it could be that he or she is destined to confront the challenges ahead in the best way possible. Take a moment to reflect today on the worst news you've heard yet in a psychic reading. Put that bad news in perspective and think about what would have happened if you or the person for whom you were reading didn't want to follow the advice of the reading.

* *Do tragedy and adversity play a positive role in life?*
  Meditate upon your beliefs on this matter.

Day 302

Banishing Negativity

There are a lot of people out there who want you to sugarcoat a reading and put a positive spin on everything you see. Some psychics are repulsed by the idea, as it smacks of dishonesty. However, consider the context. If you're not willing to bite your tongue when there is bad news, you may not want to read for a bride at a bachelorette party or for a child at a birthday party. These and situations like these may be readings you should cross off your list.

If you are okay with giving a negative reading at a client's special request, here are some ways to do it. Firstly, ask your psychic self for some good news. Even if the question at hand has a negative answer, ask for the silver lining, or for a good result that can come after the problem runs its course. If you do see some bad news, think about some empowering ways of phrasing the delivery. And finally, if the client firmly asks you not to share any bad news, know when to keep your mouth shut and end the reading.

> * *Think of some bad news you've received from a reading. What were some positive things that resulted from that life situation, and how could you have shared that with yourself at the time of the reading?*

Day 303
....

Compassion and Kindness

Being kind and compassionate to the people you read for should be your number one priority. As a developing psychic, you may have gotten used to receiving surprising or unsettling news. If you're delivering that sort of news to another person, do so with kindness, and give time for the words to settle in. Make sure your reading's subject is doing all right.

If you notice that the person is experiencing emotional upset, pause the reading and engage with him or her on an interpersonal level. Ask if he or she would prefer to end the reading. Offer a tissue. If the reading was bad news, let the subject know you feel genuinely sorry that the reading was not more positive. I like to pray before I read that I will only speak words that are true, necessary, and kind.

> * *All day today, practice speaking words only if they are true, necessary, and kind.*

DAY 304

Avoid Projection

Projection is a psychological phenomenon where you are likely to see your own problems in others, even if those problems are not truly there. This psychological issue is common to all people, including psychics. For example, if you've recently been hurt by a cheating lover, you might have trouble doing readings about relationships because you are likely to suspect dishonesty is at play. I have a psychic friend who always thinks her clients have gluten intolerance, probably because she has a gluten intolerance herself.

Take a look at the issues close to your heart right now. It may feel like everyone has a problem similar to yours, but that may simply be because the issue is too raw for you. Emotional issues of your own may be especially easy to project on the people you read. The only cure may be to jump on those issues yourself. You can also take a break from reading on that particular topic.

* *Which emotional issues might affect a reading for someone else? Work on that issue today by yourself.*

DAY 305

Telephone Readings

Telephone readings have surprising similarities to—and differences from—readings in person. One similarity that might surprise you is that the information still flows freely. Remember, you're not sucking information out of a person through the phone lines but drawing upon your own psychic ability and your tools. One big difference is that in phone readings, you will feel more forced to hurry. Gaps in the phone conversation where you get your psychic bearing will feel like an eternity. It always feels awkward to have an open phone line, and you dread the moment when the other person might ask if you're still there.

Today, grab a friend who is willing to have a telephone reading. Try doing a reading over the phone and then ask for feedback about the reading. Did the reading seem to lag in parts? If so, which ones? Were you ever speaking too quickly during the phone reading? Did you leave a natural pause at the beginning and end of the call for questions?

* *Try giving a psychic reading over the phone.*

Day 306

Email Readings

Email readings can be a boon and a bane for the developing psychic. The good news about an email reading is that you can take your time composing your answers. There's no need to worry about how long your meditation is taking, and you can rewrite your email until everything reads pretty clearly. The bad news about an email reading is that it forces you to give the reading in one big chunk, so if your subject has related questions as they arise, they will all hit you at once after the reading, which can feel overwhelming.

Today, get a partner who is willing to have an email reading or a written reading given to him or her. Ask for all the questions up front, and make sure you address each one in turn in the reading. After the reading, ask for some feedback. What about the reading wasn't very clear? What were some follow-up questions that perhaps could have been anticipated?

* *Try doing an email reading.*

Day 307
....

Setting Limits for Yourself and Others

Once you open yourself up as a psychic who does readings for others, you may find that you get a stampede of people coming to your door. In some cases, this can become overwhelming, and it might feel like certain people are taking advantage of your student psychic status. Rather than get burned out, it's time to set some limits you can apply to everyone.

Consider the following: Do you want to set specific hours for your hobby? Do you want people calling you at dinnertime or the middle of the night for a psychic reading? Do you want to set limits to the amount of time spent on one reading, or can somebody keep asking you follow up questions and stretch the reading out as long as they want? Can people keep asking you the same question over and over again until they receive the desired answer?

* *Come up with some limits and ground rules for your psychic service.*

Day 308
....

Referrals

By now, you probably have a number of situations on which you'll refuse to read. It's time to write down some referral numbers in your psychic journal, so that in times when you turn people away, you can send them to others who may be qualified and comfortable with the topic. Be sure to write down the number of a local suicide hotline and crisis line for people in need. You may also wish to have the number of a local counselor, therapist, doctor, lawyer, and financial planner for those sorts of topics when they come up.

Finally, get the number of a trusted and reputable local professional psychic. There may be a situation that makes you uncomfortable due to a projection issue or the limits you've set, but it might be fine for another psychic. In this case, you can set up another good psychic with some referrals.

* *Write out a list of referral numbers in your psychic log.*

Day 309

New Places to Perform Readings

At this point, the best way to make progress with your psychic development is to practice. If you want to read for strangers, how do you get a steady influx of interested strangers? If your area has a psychic fair, this can be a good way to start out. Check out your local metaphysical bookstore, too, as they may allow guest readers to volunteer for a regular time shift at the shop. If your region has neither resource, try asking around at local coffee shops to see if they would be willing to let you have a corner table and a sign to offer readings. You can also search online for local psychic meet-up groups or offer your readings directly through the Internet.

Think about how you'd like to get involved with the public. If you want regular practice, committing to a shift at a shop may be your best bet. If, on the other hand, you just want to get your feet wet first, try a psychic fair. If you get overwhelmed, don't forget to bust out your referral list.

* *Try giving a psychic reading to a stranger.*

Day 310

Regular Reading Subjects

Is the woman you gave a reading to at a local coffee shop now calling you every couple of weeks to set up another psychic reading? Congratulations, you've got your first regular! A regular is a person who visits on a repeated and predictable basis, be it once a year or twice a week. Regulars are a blessing because they already know your disclaimers and you already know their style.

When you get a few regulars, don't forget to keep committed to your limits and boundaries. Just because they're your acquaintances now doesn't mean you should let them walk all over you. Remember that the more regulars you get, the more stressed you'll be if you've let them all get away with murder. For the time being, start thinking of a communication system to keep your regulars apprised of any schedule changes or new additions to your reading techniques. Consider starting a website, email list, or social networking page to help keep track of all the people volunteering for your readings.

* *Consider how you will manage regulars if and when you develop them.*

Day 311

Accepting Gifts

Some people you give readings to will be so grateful that they will want to shower you with gifts. One of my aunts likes to give me jewelry and dresses for helping her out. It's a nice gesture, but performing psychic readings for gifts or money is a game-changer. The extra pressure and responsibility that comes with this exchange may feel daunting.

It's okay to accept gifts, even if you're a beginner. In fact, performing psychic readings can be a great fundraising activity for a charity or cause you support. When I was a young college student, I accepted donations to a student group at a fundraiser for an event of theirs. Later, I worked with another organization to raise money for a medical condition.

* *Decide your own personal comfort level with accepting gifts or donations before it happens, and write it down to remind yourself.*

Day 312

Reading for Children

Performing readings for children can be fun. You can play the classic role of the fortuneteller and know that the child you are reading for is going to cherish the memory. There are a few cautions to consider before reading for kids, however. And remember that it is always perfectly acceptable to not read for kids if the idea makes you uncomfortable.

Always get a parent's permission before you read for a child. Even if you are at a public fair giving out readings, kids will cheerfully turn around and run to find a parent if you demand permission first. Secondly, be careful with your tarot cards. Some tarot cards feature nudity or violent scenes. Set aside a special deck for kids that doesn't have those elements in it or use playing cards instead. Finally, check your attitude to make sure it's not too scary or negative for kids. Children don't really understand abstract concepts, so if you say five good things that are sort of unclear and one bad thing, the bad thing will be all they remember.

> * If you're comfortable reading for kids, find a willing kiddo and
>   offer a reading.

Day 313

What Power Do You Have?

Even the most humble psychic in the world is in a position of power when he or she begins a psychic reading for another. If you have been asked for a psychic reading, by requesting the reading your subject has already placed himself in a position of owing you attention and perhaps respect. If you are the more knowledgeable person on the subject of psychic readings, you hold the power of that information and the ability to hold that mystery over a person's head or to shed light upon it.

Think about the power you've had in psychic readings, even when you performed them for yourself. In what ways did your psychic readings empower you in the past? Did you ever feel a sense of powerlessness when you received an answer to one of your psychic readings? Consider how you can control the feeling of empowerment or powerlessness in others.

* *Meditate on the power of a psychic reader.*

Day 314

Your Responsibilities

In society, you probably have several different roles. For example, I'm a wife, mother, daughter, sister, friend, and professional fortuneteller, among others. Each of these roles comes with certain responsibilities. Some of these responsibilities are passive or prohibitive. For example, we have the responsibility not to cause undue harm to others. Some of these responsibilities are proactive. For example, I believe I have the responsibility to be honest and clear with my words whenever possible.

Consider your responsibilities as a psychic. Start by thinking of your responsibilities in other roles you play in your life. Some of these responsibilities may carry over easily to people you serve as a psychic reader. Think of the active and passive responsibilities that require your mindfulness.

* *Meditate on the responsibilities of a psychic.*

Others' Beliefs

As a psychic, you will be exposed to many belief systems. Psychics tend to attract spiritual people of all stripes. It may be either easy or difficult to tolerate other belief systems, depending on your personality. It can always be hard to respect beliefs that seem silly. Now is the time to decide how you will deal with beliefs that are different from your own. If you don't believe in angels, would you be willing to search for an angel in a crystal ball for someone? What if that person believes in a spirit guide that takes the shape of a pink bunny? What if a person thinks a psychic reading is evil?

There are two ways to respect beliefs that are different from your own. The first is to be tolerant of the belief, respecting the person in question's wishes and trying to work from that point of view. The second and equally viable option is to politely decline the reading because you just can't wrap your head around the view.

   * *Are there any belief systems that rub you the wrong way?*
     Consider how you would kindly and compassionately confront
     that issue if faced by somebody from that belief system.

Day 316

Managing Expectations

When somebody accepts your offer for his or her first psychic reading, there may be some wild expectations in mind. He or she might expect that you can read minds, predict winning lottery numbers, see his or her death and basically have omniscience. If you jump into a reading right away, such a person will be confused or disappointed. There's no sense in scaring your friends and coworkers who want to try a reading. Before you get started, make an effort to find out what the person's expectations are coming into a reading.

It's okay to ask if a person has ever had a reading before. If not, you might want to explain what a "psychic" does and give a brief overview of any tools you plan to use during your reading. You can even ask directly what answers the person expects from the reading. If you sense some unreasonable expectations, slow down and patiently clear up any misconceptions before starting.

* Try offering a reading today to somebody who has never had one before.

Day 317

Questions Before a Reading

Before a reading, there may be a flurry of questions back and forth between the psychic and the person receiving a psychic reading, even if the person is a friend who knows you very well. You may get the majority of the questions, but it is okay to fire some back yourself. If the person feels uncomfortable answering any of your questions, however, you can back off and allow the other person to share only what he or she feels compelled to share.

A good first question is to simply ask if the person has had a reading before. The next good question to ask is whether the person has a topic of focus or a question that he or she would like answered by the reading. If the person asks a question that isn't phrased quite right, ask why he or she asks that question in preparation to rephrase the question. Make sure to ask whether your rephrasing is correct. Finally, you can ask for any other details you need for your reading technique, for example a birth date if you are doing a numerology life path number.

* *Perform a reading for another person, focusing on asking more curious questions before the reading so you can start on the right foot.*

DAY 318

Readings and Ongoing Feedback

During your psychic reading, practice not asking the person receiving the reading too many questions. You're trying to develop your psychic skills, not your art of deduction or cold reading skills. Cold reading is a process by which a mentalist can pretend to know more information than he or she actually does, simply by reacting to cues from the person getting the reading. As a developing psychic, you may even accidentally perform some cold reading techniques if you ask questions and base the direction your reading goes on the answers to those questions.

How do you avoid tricking your psychic sense with regular ones? Keep questions to a minimum. Even asking "is that clear?" or "is this making sense to you?" will prompt a yes or no answer that could swerve your reading away from the course you wanted. Instead, push through your reading as if you had to talk uninterrupted. It's okay to be polite and clarify if the person doesn't know the definition of a word you used, but encourage people to keep most questions to the end of the reading. After you're finished, you can welcome questions.

* Count how many times you solicit feedback during a reading for another person, either by asking questions or pausing and waiting for a nonverbal response.

DAY 319
....

After a Reading

The time after your reading is perfect for clearing up any potential questions. Don't leave your friend hanging! Ask "Is there anything else I can do to help you today?" Then you can start asking some questions of your own. After a reading is a good time for a developing psychic to solicit feedback. The person who received your reading might be shy about criticizing you unless you let him or her know it's okay.

Ask the person whether there was anything that was surprising about the reading. Ask if there was anything you could do better. If you already have a personal concern, like your level of detail or pacing, you can ask specifically about that. Remember that if you're giving someone close like your mom a reading, she might be more likely to tell you that you're perfect and wonderful, even if that's not necessarily true.

* *Come up with a list of survey questions to solicit feedback after a reading.*

Day 320
....

Life Coaching

Some psychics use the title "life coach" instead of "psychic" or add "life coaching" to their list of services they offer to other people. Life coaching differs from the standard psychic reading in a few ways. A life coach can be more like a cheerleader than an advisor, helping people with goal-setting and encouragement but without emphasis on warnings and advice.

Decide whether you want to have a life coaching focus when you read for others. You can try a session with somebody where you try to focus on being a coach rather than an advisor. Coaching takes some of the focus away from the classical psychic reading aspect of searching in the past and the future, but it can bring out some of the personality characteristic readings well. It is also valid to choose not to identify as a life coach, as that can confuse your purpose and function as a psychic reader. It may even make it seem like you are avoiding affiliation with the psychic community.

* *Consider life coaching as a psychic style.*

Day 321

·············

Confidentiality

In my experience, most clients of professional psychics assume that the content of their readings will be confidential, which is odd because we are not typically pledged to confidentiality like clergy members or medical professionals. In fact, some of us may be mandated by our day jobs as teachers, counselors, or otherwise to report cases of abuse, neglect, intent to harm, or suicidal behavior. Be aware that many people who come to you will assume that you will hold their session in the strictest confidence.

If you want to write out a personal confidentiality policy for yourself, be clear: what does confidentiality mean to you? Will you protect the names of people who come to you, and will you also never speak of the content of the sessions, not even to your spouse? Are you keeping records like emails and phone numbers secure? Under what circumstances would you break confidentiality? Would you do so if a person admitted to you that he or she was in danger?

* *Write a first draft of a confidentiality policy.*

Day 322

·············

Conflicts of Interest

A conflict of interest means a situation has come about that may confuse your motivations as a psychic. Usually, your motivations are pretty clear; you'd like the person who comes to you to get an honest, clear, precise, and accurate reading from you. However, certain circumstances can arise that make things a bit more complicated.

Suppose your best friend asks for a reading on her loser husband who you wish she'd divorce already. You have a conflict of interest, since you want the two of them to break up so she can have a better life, at least in your estimation. What if a person comes to you for a reading on someone else you've already read? In such a case, it might be tempting to give insider information. For the most part, readings containing a conflict of interest should be referred to another psychic. You may find that in some cases, the question can be rephrased, changing the focus so there is no longer a conflict of interest.

* *Brainstorm some situations that might be a conflict of interest for you.*

Day 323
....

Bias

Personal bias often happens when you want a specific reading outcome or when you think a particular outcome is overwhelmingly likely before you even start reading. Everyone has natural biases in life. It will be impossible to entirely eliminate bias from your readings. The best you can do to combat bias is to recognize when bias is present and take steps to mitigate it.

For example, I often do readings for myself, but if I want a particular outcome really badly—such as a happy outcome for my kids and husband—I will look hard for signs that this will be the case and tend to ignore signs of trouble. Steps I can take to mitigate my bias is to consciously look for both positive and negative signs, and possibly ask another psychic to do the reading if I feel my bias is too great.

* *What is a topic on which you would be extremely biased?*

Day 324

Reading for a Lover

Performing a reading for a lover can be an intimate experience that can bring the two of you closer. When you do a reading for a lover, you may notice the power imbalance that places you in a position of power, if the power roles are reversed. For example, if your lover is usually the more dominant or powerful one in the relationship, or if the two of you are usually equals, he or she may be nervous or hesitant to receive a reading since that would place you in a position of power.

When first reading for a lover, try to have fun together. Avoid biases by not reading on any specific relationship problems. Instead, read on a topic where you have a lower vested interest, such as some of his or her friendship issues or problems at work. To balance the power, you might invite your partner to do some of the reading. Instead of giving advice, for example, show some of the symbols on the card or tea leaves and ask, "What advice do you think this gives you?"

* *Try a psychic reading on a lover or somebody with whom you feel an intimate emotional connection.*

Day 325

Reading for a Family Member

Readings for a family member have a few special considerations. You may feel under pressure to perform, as it is natural to feel you are representing and needing the approval of your interest in psychic phenomena. You might be more likely to disrespect a family member's differing beliefs because you know you can get away with it. Your family member is more likely to push his or her comfort zone because they feel safe with you. Therefore, you have an extra responsibility to be cautious.

Assure your family member that you are not involved with anything dangerous. Try demonstrating and teaching your grounding and shielding techniques if the person is willing to learn. Try talking through your psychic experience, letting your family member know what you're feeling as you go along.

* *Try performing a reading for a family member.*

Day 326

When Someone is Determined to Have a Miserable Experience

It is rare, but at some point you might run into a person who is determined to make things difficult for you. The person may be an immature bully who wants to test and taunt you for entertainment. More likely, however, you'll run into somebody who is just so angry and sad about other things in their life that the anger and sadness will be directed at you during the reading. Some people seek out a psychic instead of a therapist because they feel you're the only person in the world they can trust.

Regardless of how much the person may insist on a reading, as soon as you begin to sense that things are not going well, ground yourself and end the reading. You can simply say, "I'm sorry, but I can't see a way to make this reading become a positive experience for us." Be ready with your referrals.

* *Think of a time in your life when you were having such a hard time that even people who were trying to help you felt your prickliness. What kind words could people have said to keep your anger or sadness from spilling outward?*

Day 327

Honesty

Hopefully, you've already been watching your words. What you say has an effect on you and everyone around you. As a psychic, honesty affects you at the deepest psychological levels. After all, you can't trust what you see as a psychic if you haven't developed a deep instinctive honesty with yourself. Thinking and speaking honestly is important. However, honesty is not an excuse for being cruel, vulgar, or even blunt. You don't owe your client all of the information you see, especially if that information could hurt someone or violate privacy.

Nobody wants to think of themselves as a dishonest person. However, there are some cases in which you will need to think twice before revealing further information. Or you might want to reveal only part of that information. For example, if you see somebody having sex with another person, you don't really need to go into details about the act. If you see the death of a pet, ask first if the person is willing to hear some sad news that might just be symbolic.

* Consider some situations where complete honesty might not be the best policy. Think about how you can adjust the information you give out to remain truthful but kind.

DAY 328
. . . .
Reading for a Skeptic

Reading for a skeptic doesn't have to be a bad experience. In fact, you might end up having a convert on your hands. Most skeptics who want a reading aren't out to trip you up or make fun of you. Skeptics like to have fun, just like anyone else, and a psychic reading is fun because it is a story about yourself. Everyone likes hearing about themselves.

Start a reading for a skeptic with a brief orientation. These people have low expectations, but they may still have misconceptions about what it is they think you can do. Point out that you don't read minds and don't think that you're omniscient. Explain that psychic readings can be used as a psychological technique to see a situation's different angles. Invite feedback after you're done, as skeptics can notice quickly where you have room for improvement and are eager to point out factual errors.

* Offer a psychic reading to a skeptic.

Day 329

Reading for Another Psychic

As a developing psychic, reading for another psychic may seem a bit intimidating. However, it can be a positive experience for you both. Realize that even as a beginner, you can offer a wonderful service to another psychic who may be avoiding reading on a specific topic due to personal bias. You can also benefit greatly from tips from an experienced reader.

When performing a reading for another psychic, use this opportunity to evaluate your skills. You can even ask the other psychic to watch for specific problems you think you might have when reading for others. During the reading, you may notice the flow of the reading changes. For example, when reading tarot cards, you won't have to introduce and explain the meanings in the same way as you would to someone who has never seen them before. When you are finished with the reading, encourage the psychic to comment on it. Take notes, as this might be the best sort of feedback you receive. You can even ask the psychic if he or she can recommend any exercises or tips.

* *Offer another psychic a psychic reading.*

Day 330

Finding the Positives

In some readings, picking out any bits of positive information might seem difficult. Forget about sugar-coating a reading, but beware of a negative trend. If all your psychic readings are doom and gloom, people are going to stop wanting a reading from you. If you notice a negative pattern, especially on a specific topic, make sure that you're not projecting about some internal issue you need to work upon independently. Don't forget to ask your psychic self to see some of the positives. That said, even the worst things in a reading can be phrased in a way that empowers others. Try some of these sentence starters.

"Though it might look bad for a while, things will pick up in your life when…"

"This challenge is an opportunity for you to…"

"While this aspect of your life is in flux, try focusing on a more stable part of your life, like…"

"This sacrifice might eventually bring rewards, such as…"

* *Read on a topic you know may get predominantly negative answers right now, but focus on the positives.*

Day 331

Fear of Psychic Readings

Some people are afraid of psychic readings. If somebody doesn't want a psychic reading due to fear, you shouldn't push that person into trying one, even if those fears are unfounded. The fearful attitude might sour the person's experience of the psychic reading and create a bad memory they'll carry with them for the rest of their life, when you could have simply waited for that person's fears to abate. I've been overenthusiastic and convinced somebody to have a reading who didn't want one, and I didn't feel good about it afterwards.

Some people, however, may want a psychic reading in spite of their fears. In these cases, you can happily try to mitigate those fears. Manage their expectations and assure the person that a psychic doesn't normally see death or impending doom in a reading. Offer to give a reading that only focuses on the positive. If the person is afraid of some of your divination tools, offer to do a reading using playing cards instead of tarot or offer a reading with no divination tools.

* *Try offering a psychic reading to somebody who might be a little afraid of them. If you don't know anyone fearful of psychic readings, practice the fear mitigation techniques on anyone who would like a gentle reading.*

DAY 332

Ridicule of Psychic Readings

If someone tells you they think psychic readings are stupid, they will usually avoid coming to you in the first place, or if they do come in, will rarely keep their opinions to themselves. When this happens, assess the situation quickly to see if the person wants to have a positive reading experience or they just want to harass someone.

It could be that this person is a skeptic who is still willing to be at least entertained. Watch body language and tone of voice, and ask outright whether the person is willing to share a positive reading experience with you by being respectful and kind. If they are, proceed with the reading. If not, you've at least avoided a confrontation. You don't have to evangelize the virtues of psychic readings to those who don't want to hear.

* *Offer a psychic reading to a die-hard skeptic, asking first whether they're willing to have a positive reading experience.*

Day 333
....

Have Fun!

New psychics rarely take themselves too seriously, so as a beginner you're probably safe from an excess of ego at this stage. Be careful, though. Don't let your experience or personality dial the intensity up to 100 percent in every reading. A reading should generally be a fun experience unless you are addressing a particularly solemn topic. The author Doreen Valiente says that the Goddess encourages us to have both "mirth and reverence" within us. The two are not mutually exclusive!

Consider the general emotional tone of your psychic reading sessions, alone or with others. Do you usually feel excited? Jovial? Bored? Stressed? Nervous? If you don't like your typical state of mind, spend more time centering yourself before reading, especially for others. Spend some time relaxing your body during grounding. Resolve to have a good reading and to have a good time.

* *Focus on having a fun reading experience today.*

Part Ten

*

Ethics,
Theory,
and
Philosophy

Day 334

....

Choosing a Label

Reading for others means that you'll have to choose a way to explain your role. That is, you'll have to choose a label or a title for yourself. The most common term, of course, is "psychic." However you can use other terms as well. I like "fortuneteller" because I believe it invites more questions about what I do and doesn't imply that I am a mind reader. If you prefer to work with spirits, you might call yourself a medium. Still others choose different terms, such as life coach, intuitive reader, spiritual advisor, astrologer, tarot reader, and so forth.

Think about your preferred label or title. Would you be proud to list it on a business card? Would you want your name or face associated with that label? If somebody knows very little about psychic abilities, what assumptions might they make about that label?

* *Choose a label or title for yourself and stick with it for a while to see how people react to it.*

Day 335

....

Balance and Self-care

Performing psychic readings for others affects you. It affects you energetically in that you can become the energetic dumping ground for the emotions of others. It affects you physically when you have to work phone calls and appointments into your schedule. It can affect you emotionally, because you have new responsibilities on your plate and a new role to fill. You'll need to manage these stressors, or you will find yourself burnt out and deciding to quit.

First, manage your physical exhaustion or schedule limitations. Re-evaluate your limits if you find all or most of your time being tied up in readings. Set limited hours, or take a break completely. Next, take a look at your emotions. You might be reading for the wrong people, or you might put a limit on the topics you are willing to explore. Finally, take a look at how you're managing your energy during psychic readings. Consider grounding yourself more throughout the day.

* *What are some ways you can pamper yourself today? You'll be a better psychic if you take care of yourself first.*

DAY 336
. . . .

What is the Source?

From what source does your psychic energy flow? Who or what provides the conduit through which you receive psychic wisdom? The answer to this question may be a theological one. You might believe that God or one or more deities are the source of your abilities. You may believe that your psychic wisdom comes from angels or spirit guides. Or you may simply believe that the source of your wisdom is the universe or your higher self.

Today, explore your own belief system to discover the source of your psychic abilities. It may be a combination of several different things. For example, I believe that the information is freely out there in the universe for everyone to use, but I have my gods to thank for my psychic abilities as much as I thank them for the ability to walk and sing their praises.

* *Write out a statement of your beliefs about the source of psychic ability or information.*

DAY 337

. . . .

Bad Press

Every once in a while, a professional psychic out there makes a bad name for us all with some foolish choice or mistake. Of course, the media has a field day with it as they might bring to light the stereotype of the heartless lawyer or crooked car salesman. Perhaps a famous psychic made a blundering and insensitive error on national television. Maybe a small-town psychic ran some sort of awful scam.

Whenever you see a negative story about psychics in the news, your first reaction will be to distance yourself from that psychic. It would never happen to *you*, because you wouldn't choose to read in such a public way, or because you would never rip somebody off. But remember that those psychics don't think they're bad people either. Something led them down that road, and they made choices probably with the best of intentions. Think about what may have triggered those bad choices, and how you can prevent that from happening to you or to other psychics.

* * Search for a negative story about a psychic in the news, even old news stories on the Internet. Analyze the story for mistakes the psychic made that you could have made, and think about how to avoid them.*

DAY 338

. . . .

When Can Readings Cause Physical Harm?

You have amazing power as a psychic. Certainly, you can't make peoples' heads explode, but you can cause incredible blessings or real physical harm with your readings. For example, if you choose to read on a crime-related topic such as a parent who is searching for a lost child or a victim searching for a rapist or other violent criminal, you may be wasting valuable time police could be using to apprehend the bad guy. If you read for a suicidal person, you could make the problem worse. If you read for somebody who is spending her last dime on your professional help, you could actually cause her children to miss a meal.

Today, pretend that any reading you do might have far-reaching consequences. Don't let this scare you away from doing any readings at all, however! Yes, sometimes you will have to give a referral or delay a reading, but other times you may simply be able to give some disclaimers and caveats before you begin.

* *Brainstorm all of the potential consequences of a reading you do today.*

Day 339

The Right to Refuse a Reading

With any referrals you've had to or are prepared to make, you know that the right to refuse a reading can be very important. As a psychic, you may inadvertently compromise your right to refuse a reading. For example, if you sign up to work on a psychic hotline for a company or at a psychic fair, you might run into trouble with the company if you turn away a customer. The right to refuse service is why I refuse to give my service away to charity raffles, since the winner would either have to receive a reading or I'd have to pay the face value of the reading.

Today, think about how you can preserve and defend your right to refuse readings. This may be as simple as coming up with a polite phrase to turn down a reading, or it may be as complicated as placing a disclaimer of your right on your website or on a sign for your booth at a psychic fair.

* *Advertise or practice your right to refuse service.*

DAY 340

What a Psychic is Not

Psychics tend to be helper personalities; we love feeling needed! But we are no substitute for nurses, therapists, or attorneys. There are other social roles a psychic cannot fulfill. A psychic is not a substitute friend or mother. When you feel your role with a client is slipping into weird territory, set some boundaries even when a part of you wishes you could fill that role.

Think about what drives you to be a psychic, and pick any of those motivations that may not truly suit your role. For example, part of why I became a psychic is that I wish I could be everyone's best friend. I wish I could be there in the middle of the night for a client who calls me up crying about a break-up. However, the simple fact is that I can't be that for everyone, so I have to remove the role of best friend from my mind and simply be the psychic.

* *What roles do you wish you could fulfill for people that you simply cannot? How can you set some firm boundaries for yourself and others?*

DAY 341

. . . .

Recovering From a Mistake

So you've got an angry person on your hand. You really blew it during a reading. Whoops! Perhaps it was completely off-base and inaccurate, or maybe there was just a big misunderstanding. Mistakes can be a huge blow to the ego and can put you off reading entirely if you let them, so here's a process to recover. It's the same method we used on day 200 to deal with intuition failures. The mnemonic device to help you remember is the meditation sound AUM, which stands for the three steps we use before, during, and after any kind of failure, in this case with an angry client.

Avoidance: Wouldn't it be great if we could all avoid mistakes before we make them? Try to avoid mistakes by managing expectations, reframing questions, and making referrals if needed.

Understanding: During the confrontation, focus on understanding the other person. Let the person vent frustrations, even if they don't seem accurate to you. Paraphrase what the other person says to show that you are listening.

Meditation: After the confrontation, go somewhere to meditate until your heart rate is back to normal and your emotions are in check. Go over the feedback given for any kernels of truth. Resolve to implement one positive solution to any real problem in your next reading as part of the avoidance phase.

* *Practice meditating on a problem with a reading. This can even be a reading you did for yourself. Apply one of the solutions you came up with to avoid the problem in the future.*

DAY 342

Seeking Greater Accountability

Most psychics have very little accountability when they read for others. Most professional psychics, for example, are independent practitioners. They have no bosses and no coworkers to watch over what they do. When they close the door in a room with a client, they can say or do whatever they want, leaving the client as the only one to take recourse if something untoward happens. In some regions, psychics don't need a license, so there's no way to take it away or record repeated offenses.

One way you can make a better world for psychics and those who seek out psychic readings is to voluntarily seek out greater accountability for yourself. Seek out a mentor. Ask somebody to sit in on and evaluate your readings. If psychics are not required to obtain a licence in your area, see if you can apply for a business license as an advisor, or even study to be a licensed counselor. Join professional organizations and your local chamber of commerce.

* *Seek out opportunities for accountability.*

DAY 343

Trying Another Psychic

Try purchasing a reading from another professional psychic. This can be a real treat, because you'll get to see how other people do things differently, and perhaps be inspired to learn some new skills. You'll also get the benefit of being able to get a reading on a topic for which you are usually biased.

When getting a reading from another psychic, look carefully at his or her references. Be up front about the fact that you are studying psychic development and ask if he or she knows any unique divination techniques you can see first-hand. After the reading is over, compliment the psychic on anything he or she did well, and ask questions if you'd like to know more about those techniques. Don't give constructive criticism unless asked.

* *Seek out and get a reading from another psychic.*

DAY 344

Reaching Out to Other Psychics

Making friends with other psychics for educational and referral purposes is a great idea. It may seem sort of daunting as a developing psychic, but relax, it doesn't matter how good you are yet. As a professional psychic, I'm always really happy and excited to see new psychics joining our ranks in the community, even if they are competitors. There are more than enough clients to go around, and we've all got our unique talents. I couldn't serve everyone even if I tried.

See if a psychic networking group already exists in your area. Online groups are fun, but I find that I learn best from such energetic work in person. You may find a regular meet-up group in your area or a psychic fair where you can invite people out for a shared lunch. If no group presently exists, consider starting your own.

* *Reach out in friendship to other local psychics.*

Day 345

Resources for Learning More

There isn't a Hogwarts-style school for psychic development available just yet, so until formal education becomes plentiful, you'll have to be in charge of your own continuing education as a psychic. Some formal courses may well be available: You can take a sketching class at your local university to improve your aura drawings, or a psychology course to help your interpersonal communication. Psychic organizations in your area may offer workshops in specific divinations. Look around for conventions within a reasonable traveling distance for other helpful workshops and seminars.

Again, your fellow psychics may be another great resource. Ask what books they are reading on psychic development and if they'd like to chat about a book over coffee or tea once you've read it yourself. Encourage other psychics who have particular skills to start teaching classes or taking on apprentices.

* *Find some resources for continuing education.*

Day 346

Laws and the Psychic

In some areas of the world today, local laws are not very friendly toward psychics. At the time of this writing, for example, in Saudi Arabia you might be jailed or killed for performing psychic readings. Meanwhile, in the United States, being a professional psychic is actually illegal in New York. Being compensated for your work opens a different can of worms, because even if psychic readings themselves are allowed, it may be illegal to perform them without a license or insurance in some regions.

Learn about the laws in your area. Ask some of the other psychics who are openly practicing if there are any laws about which you should be knowledgeable. If you're planning on starting a psychic business, consult an attorney. If you find out about psychics being oppressed in other areas, consider writing to legislators in support of the psychic community there. Together, you and I can make this a friendlier world for psychics.

* *Research laws as they pertain to psychics.*

DAY 347

Skills Accompanying Psychic Development

If you find psychics, you'll also find a lot of parallel services. For instance, Reiki, massage, and other forms of energy healing are common. Event planning and public speaking tours are also popular. Marriage and family therapy and other counseling skills are a great pairing with psychic work. Obviously, I've chosen writing as a parallel skill so I can teach and share messages with my clients and colleagues and the world at large. Think about developing your ancillary skills—what can you do already that could aid your psychic work or be offered as a service along with a psychic reading? If you are lacking skills in one area, consider going back to school or searching for other means of learning that skill. How can your skills combine with psychic reading? How might your skills actually interfere with psychic readings?

* *Brainstorm an inventory of your skills as they might be related to psychic reading.*

DAY 348

Giving Thanks

Energetically, giving thanks has a funny way of bringing more blessings our way. Psychologically, if we give thanks even for simple and small things, we are more likely to notice other positive things going on in our lives. Life becomes a game where we look for the next thing to be grateful about. As a psychic, giving thanks for your psychic abilities is one way to develop them further. Furthermore, if you give thanks for the psychic visions you see about future events, it might increase the chances of your predictions coming to pass.

Start making "thank you" a part of your psychic session closing ritual. Thank the person for whom you are reading. Thank the powers that be for your psychic abilities. Today, you might want to give extra thanks. Thank somebody who has supported or encouraged your psychic development, or even just supported you for being quirky and different and going after your dreams.

* *Today, give thanks.*

DAY 349

The Role of Faith

Faith is a part of every human's psychological makeup. Faith usually appears in our culture in the context of religion, for example the Christian faith. However, even atheists have faith in scientific principles. More immediately, both types of people can have faith in a spouse's love or that their lungs will keep breathing in and out for them all day today. Your faith plays a role in how you believe your psychic readings will proceed. Your faith can come with its own set of biases about what sorts of messages you will and will not hear.

Today, write a little statement about your faith. You don't have to subscribe to any particular label or religion. Simply write about your faith as it pertains to psychic readings. Some questions to consider: Do you believe that humankind is basically good; that their actions result from good motivations? Or does some force need to control society in order for us to act nicely? Do you believe in true justice? Do you believe in an all-powerful deity or deities? Why do bad things happen to good people?

* *Write a statement of faith as it relates to psychic readings.*

Day 350

The Role of Prayer

If you are so inclined, prayer is a good way to open a psychic reading session. If you've never prayed before or are a little rusty, here is a sample prayer.

PERSON LISTENING
I invoke [God(s)/Goddess(es)/Spirit/Universe/my Higher Self/etc.]

RAISE PRAISE
*You who is/are the source of all good luck,
love and light deserving of my praise!*

ASK FOR HELP
*Thank you for aiding my psychic abilities,
that they may be accurate and clear.*

YOUR DEADLINE
Now

IMPERATIVES FOR SAFETY
With harm to none, and for the highest good of all. So may it be.

NOTE OF THANKS
In return, I offer you
[thirty minutes of devotional meditation, incense, etc.]

GRACIOUS ATTENTION
Blessed be.
(Meditate and then reflect on how you felt during and after.)

* Pray before meditating today.

Day 351
. . . .

Taking a Break or Retiring from Psychic Work with Others

Whether in days or in decades, there will come a time when you will want to stop offering psychic readings to others for an extended period of time or indefinitely. Over time, you can see how you might build up a large number of people who could be surprised and disappointed by such an announcement.

Of course we all anticipate a time when we can retreat from the attention of others. Business owners of all types should prepare a smooth transition for customers should their enterprise close down even temporarily. It does no one any good to simply disappear on your psychic reading acquaintances. Prepare them in advance for any extended holiday or retirement. Start looking around now for a trusted psychic who will be around for some time so you can pass on your clients and friends to them.

* *When, if ever, do you plan to retire from giving psychic readings to others? Do you have a trusted psychic referral yet?*

Day 352
. . . .

Archetypes

You know how to interpret symbols, but what exactly are these symbols you're interpreting, and why do they often share common parallels across cultures? An archetype is an overarching symbol that represents many things, often a role in life. For example, if you see a pregnant woman in a reading, it might represent a mother such as your mother, or it could represent the archetype of Mother, with all the creativity and nurturing this archetype represents. Archetypes have been analyzed in Jungian psychology, and we know they come up in dreams and other subconscious manifestations.

We have gone through some major archetypes, especially when we examined each major arcana tarot card. Today, return to the subject of archetypes and meditate on the archetypes you represent in this stage of life. Right now, I represent the Mother archetype, and thus in a way the Empress, since she embodies that archetype as well. Later on, other archetypes will be more meaningful to me.

* *Meditate on archetypes.*

DAY 353

Giving Your Energy

There is no way to avoid giving up some of your energy during a psychic reading; performing takes effort. You might even burn a few calories, so of course you are also going to use up some of your energy. Every communication with another person involves an energy exchange, so you will be giving up some of your energy during every psychic interaction with another. As you add on more psychic readings to your day and add to your list of people who want readings, the amount of energy you give up will naturally be greater. You must address this to avoid burning out.

First of all, you know I'm going to remind you to ground more often and put up semi-permeable shields that allow you to protect your energy while doing only the necessary energy exchange. How do you know whether this is working? Practice your aura sensing during your next psychic reading and turn your eyes to yourself. How is your aura acting during the reading? Is your energy coming off in waves or merely intermingling with that of the person receiving the reading? Practice controlling how much energy you share.

* *Monitor how much energy you give during an average psychic reading.*

DAY 354

Cleansing Your Energy

Perform a regular energetic cleansing. It can kickstart your grounding process if you are feeling sluggish or burned out. Taking an herbal bath can be one way to cleanse your energy, but that might not be an option in the middle of a psychic fair. Instead, you may have to use some combination of your skills in order to do a quick aura cleansing for yourself.

To perform an aura cleansing, first take the time to visualize or sense your aura. Pay special attention to parts of your aura which may seem dark, cloudy, or stagnant. Visualize those regions of stuck *chi* draining out of your body through your connection with the earth in the same way you always safely ground energy. You can even sweep your hands physically through your aura to aid the metaphorical process in your mind. Draw refreshing energy in from the earth to flush out and light up those areas of your aura.

* *Try cleansing your aura.*

DAY 355

To Know

Over the next four days, I'd like to go over with you the four powers of the mage. These four principles support my psychic practice, and I'd like to share a bit about them with you. The first power of the mage is "to know." The pursuit of knowledge is the psychic's main goal, and in your search for wisdom it will be important for you to seek inside yourself as well as outside yourself. Knowing yourself is your first and foremost goal as a psychic.

Today, ponder on what it means to truly know something. Do you know something when you can call it by its true name? Do you know something when you can explain it to another person in clear words? Do you know something once you have experienced it on a deep level? How do you know that you know something? What are some ways you can test your psychic knowledge?

* *Meditate on what it is to know.*

DAY 356
....
To Dare

The second power of the mage is to dare. Psychics must be bold and daring, because they must open up to energies and powers that may at first seem beyond control. A psychic dares to experience emotions fully through empathy. A psychic dares to travel to worlds beyond this one to bring back those kernels of knowledge we all seek.

Consider today what it means to dare. Over the past year, how have you pushed yourself emotionally as a psychic? What is the true nature of being daring? What does it mean to face your fears? In what ways are you more "open" as a psychic? Open to what? What are some other things you can do over the next year to become a more daring person?

* *Meditate on what it means to dare.*

DAY 357
....
To Will

To will means to desire with all of your heart and to manifest something as a result. A psychic not only dares to get out of bed in the morning, but she is willing to jump out of bed and actively face the unknown. When you truly will something, you can make it happen no matter what barriers stand in your way. In fact, even the most annoying or oppressive barriers will seem small and unimportant in the face of your true will.

Consider today what it means to will something to manifest. Firstly, you may have to determine the difference between wanting something and willing it to happen. To will is never passive. This power of the mage always comes from the deepest core of your being and requires effort on your behalf, even if it is controlled effort. What do you truly will in your life, as opposed to simply want?

 * *Meditate on what it means to will.*

DAY 358
....
To Be Silent

The fourth power of the mage is to be silent, and it is the most difficult one for a talkative person like myself. Silence is a powerful thing. We choose silence when we meditate receptively, to invite psychic messages without distraction. We choose silence when we preserve our honesty as psychics, because to speak lies would weaken our power but sometimes we cannot tell all. We choose silence when we don't share things that are too personal, private, or sacred, such as our deepest wishes.

When is it difficult for you to keep silent? When is it most necessary for you to be silent as a psychic? How would it impact your psychic practice if you took a vow of silence for a day? If words are powerful, how can silence be powerful? What does silence communicate when you are with another person?

 * *Meditate on what it means to be silent.*

Day 359
·············

Karma

Do you believe in karma? Karma has several meanings depending on the belief system and therefore takes many forms. It is found in Hindu, Buddhist, and New Age religions as well as in secular society. In some eastern forms, karma is what ties you to the world. Even "good" karma like lending someone a hand might be seen as a liability to the most spiritual guru, because the goal of the mystic is to escape the connection to the material world to seek nirvana, or the paradise of detachment. Karma is sometimes a communal concept in eastern thought so that nobody can advance toward nirvana until everyone is advancing toward nirvana together.

Conversely, a Western concept of karma holds that good karma received by doing good deeds rewards people in this life and the next. Bad karma then might be thought to lend bad energy to this life and the next. You can see how belief in karma might affect psychic readings, especially past life readings.

* *Do you believe in karma? Write about your understanding of karma and how it might affect a psychic reading if somebody asked you to do a reading on his or her karma.*

Day 360
·············

Thought Clearing

A thought is a very powerful thing. If you think that you won't have a positive reading experience, low and behold, you will make it so. If you don't feel you will succeed in life, this may become a self-fulfilling prophecy. My parents taught me these things as a kid. It's sort of the spiritual equivalent of "If you make that face it will stick that way."

Constantly being your own thought police is exhausting, however. If you struggle with depression or anxiety, you may need extra help clearing away negative thoughts. Otherwise, you can start by returning to the most basic meditation, clearing away all your thoughts. Once you have finished your meditation, try replacing the repeating negative ruminations in your head with positive affirmations.

* *Meditate and then think of a positive affirmation for your day.*

Day 361
....

Worry Stones

You're nearing the point of "graduating" at the end of this section, but I don't have a certificate of completion for you to sign, photocopy, and display proudly. Perhaps it is just as well; the last thing we psychics need is a sheet of paper claiming that we're finished with our psychic development. Perhaps a better gift to yourself right now would be a symbol of your continued development and devotion to self-betterment. I suggest a worry stone.

A worry stone is a small stone that you can keep in your pocket. By rubbing your thumb against this stone, you will feel its grounding benefits and soothe your mind with the repetitive motion. It may become a ritual key for beginning and ending a psychic session for you. Over time, the stone you choose may become polished or develop a divot that fits your thumb perfectly.

* *Find a worry stone that fits in the palm of your hand and is larger than the pad of your thumb.*

Day 362
....

Become a Resource for Other Developing Psychics

If you were completely new to learning about your psychic abilities at the beginning of the year, you may balk at the idea that you could now be a resource to developing psychics. However, a year of daily dedicated study may be more than many people in your community have done. Somewhere near you is a person who is just finding out that anyone can develop psychic abilities. That person might feel lost and confused and have fewer resources or resourcefulness than you.

Please consider teaching a class in your area and reaching out to new psychics. Flip through what you've read here and choose one exercise that really spoke to you over the past year. Reach out to your local metaphysical bookstore or to your library to find some space. Print out some flyers or post notices on the Internet. You can charge for your class or offer it for free. Don't forget to share your own experiences while you were learning. New psychics especially love personal stories of challenges and struggle with psychic development.

* *Find a skill you have learned that you can offer to show someone just starting out.*

Day 363
....

Start a Book Club

Starting a book club is one way you can make friends with local psychics and reach out to new developing psychics without the pressure of teaching a class.

Any bookstore or café may be open to the idea of your book club meeting there. Ask what books they are interested in exploring or suggest some of your own. Using this book as an example, I'll give you a few ways you could use it as a resource.

Jigsaw: Have each person pick a day's exercise to try. The next time you meet, have each person share his or her experience with that exercise. This way, you can all work through every exercise faster.

Partner reading: Split into pairs. Have each pair of partners try a different exercise together. Come together as a group afterwards and share your experiences.

Think-pair-share: As a group, read one exercise. Everyone should have some quiet time to think and write about the day's exercise, or to try it out if possible. Then, get together in pairs and share your experience.

* *Start a local book club.*

Day 364

Write a Code of Ethics

Morals are standards of behavior, often dictated by the heart as a personal sense of what is right and what is wrong. Ethics are a list of rules, often agreed upon by a community. I am proud to welcome you into a community of psychics. As one of us, what you do affects how society as a whole sees people like me. For that reason, I encourage every psychic to write up a code of ethics. Professional psychics should display this code proudly on their websites and in their offices. Here are some prompts that may help your writing.

It is wrong for a psychic to…

It is right for a psychic to…

As a psychic, I will always strive to…

Anyone who receives a psychic reading from me has the right to…

* *Write a code of ethics.*

DAY 365
....

Reflecting

You've come a long way, and it's been a productive year. Take time to celebrate today. Don't forget to plan for your future by following up on any resources you've found for continuing your psychic development. As you review your psychic journal, reflect on the changes you have made in your psychic abilities. Pretend that you're my apprentice, and must now show your mastery of the subject. Demonstrate to yourself what you have learned over the past year.

Have you completed any of the goals you set as a psychic? Set new goals and adjust old goals if necessary. What is one way you have improved your psychic skills over the past year? Can you prove it to yourself with evidence from your journal? What are some things that still challenge you? What lies on the horizon for your psychic abilities development? Perhaps it's time for another reading.

* *Review your psychic journal, reflect, and celebrate!*

Bibliography

Alvarez, Melissa. *365 Ways to Raise Your Frequency: Simple Tools to Increase Your Spiritual Energy for Balance, Purpose, and Joy.* Woodbury, MN: Llewellyn Publications, 2012.

Blake, Deborah. *Everyday Witch Book of Rituals: All You Need for a Magickal Year.* Woodbury, MN: Llewellyn Publications, 2012.

Campbell, Joseph. *The Hero with a Thousand Faces.* Novato, CA: New World Library, 2008.

McElroy, Mark. *Lucid Dreaming for Beginners: Simple Techniques for Creating Interactive Dreams.* Woodbury, MN: Llewellyn Publications, 2010.

Owens, Elizabeth. *Spiritualism & Clairvoyance for Beginners: Simple Techniques to Develop Your Psychic Abilities.* Woodbury, MN: Llewellyn Publications, 2005.

Pesznecker, Susan. *Crafting Magick with Pen and Ink: Learn to Write Stories, Spells, and Other Magickal Works.* Woodbury, MN: Llewellyn Publications, 2009.

Pesznecker, Susan. *The Magickal Retreat: Making Time for Solitude, Intention & Rejuvenation.* Woodbury, MN: Llewellyn Publications, 2012.

Roderick, Timothy. *Wicca: A Year and a Day: 366 Days of Spiritual Practice in the Craft of the Wise.* Woodbury, MN: Llewellyn Publications, 2005.

Tyson, Donald. *Scrying for Beginners: Use Your Unconscious Mind to See Beyond the Senses.* Woodbury, MN: Llewellyn Publications, 2011.

Webster, Richard. *Aura Reading for Beginners: Develop Your Psychic Awareness for Health & Success.* Woodbury, MN: Llewellyn Publications, 2008.